LEONARD WOOD
AND CUBAN INDEPENDENCE
1898–1902

LEONARD WOOD
AND CUBAN INDEPENDENCE
1898-1902

by

JAMES H. HITCHMAN

MARTINUS NIJHOFF / THE HAGUE / 1971

ISBN 90 247 5123 3

PRINTED IN THE NETHERLANDS

To Marie
Matt, Suzy and Dan

CONTENTS

PREFACE

This is a study of the Military Government of Cuba from 1898 to 1902. Tracing and explaining the actions of General Leonard Wood's administration during those years reveals how the United States Government resolved the questions of independence, strategic security, and economic interests in regard to Cuba. Leonard Wood, Secretary of War Elihu Root, Senator Orville H. Platt, and President William McKinley formulated and carried out policies that had a strong influence on subsequent Cuban-American relations. The broader aspects of this study, civil-military relations and American imperialism, are topics of importance to all citizens today. This is institutional and biographical history, written in the belief that a full account of the men, action, and circumstances will add to our understanding of the period when the United States emerged as a world power.

I am indebted to Professors Gerald E. Wheeler of San Jose State College and Armin Rappaport of the University of California, San Diego, who directed my research in the early stages, and to Professor Eric Bellquist of the University of California, Berkeley, for his criticism of the manuscript when it was in dissertation stage. To Professor Raymond J. Sontag I would like to pay special tribute for his guidance and inspiration through the years. The assistance of my mother, Mrs. Sue Hitchman, is deeply appreciated. My thanks go also to the staffs at the Library of the U. S. Department of State, National Archives, Library of Congress, Connecticut State Library, Colorado State Historical Society, and Libraries of the University of California, Berkeley, as well as to the Graduate Committee on Research for Travel and Grants at Berkeley. Research has been carried out in Cuban, German and American sources. The writing shows both the Cuban and American points of view, indicating a large amount of cooperation between the two groups during the years of the first occupation.

Professor Frederick M. Nunn and his wife, Diana, of Portland State University, generously assisted by editing the manuscript and checking my translation. Professors Lejeune Cummins of California State College at Hayward and Michael Onorato of California State College at Fullerton have shared their deep interest in Leonard Wood. Many persons at Willamette University, Salem, Oregon, encouraged me into academic life, among them President G. Herbert Smith, Dean Robert D. Gregg, Professors Ivan Lovell, Chester Kaiser and Howard Runkel. In various ways these friends also eased the way to completion: Mr. Harrison W. Wood of Malvern, Pennsylvania; Mr. and Mrs. John Gregory of Washington, D.C.; Mr. and Mrs. William H. Woolsey, Jr., of Berkeley, California; Mr. and Mrs. Felix Calkins of Lake Oswego, Oregon; Professors Victor Dahl, James Hart and Charles White of Portland State University; Professors William Bultmann and Manfred Vernon of Western Washington State College. The editors of *The Americas* and the *Journal of Inter-American Studies and World Affairs* have generously granted permission to use material previously printed in those journals. The support of Herbert C. Taylor, Jr., Dean of Research and Grants, and his staff, Mrs. Jane Clark, Mrs. Ann Drake and Mrs. Ruth Huffine, at Western Washington State College is gratefully acknowledged. Any mistakes in fact or interpretation are mine. Finally, I thank Dr. H. J. H. Hartgerink and Nijhoff's for publishing this book. May the reader enjoy it!

Bellingham, Washington

November, 1970

CHAPTER I

THE REASONS FOR OCCUPATION, 1898-1899

At the end of the Spanish-American War, the United States occupied Cuba with a temporary military government in order to bring stability to the island. Conditions demanded American intervention because no power existed in the island capable of rebuilding a society weakened by nearly a decade of depression and revolution. Authority to pacify Cuba was given to President McKinley by the Congressional Joint Resolution of April 20, 1898, and the Treaty of Paris of December 10, 1898.[1] These instruments indicated the intention of the United States not to annex Cuba but rather to administer the island's government until the Cuban people could govern themselves. The prerequisite for withdrawal was the establishment of an independent republic whose stability would satisfy the requirements of the United States.

The military government, which remained in Cuba until May of 1902, undertook the reform of various institutions. As administered by General Leonard Wood, it constructed the foundation for a stable, independent republic by accomplishing impressive reforms in education, the legal system, sanitation, public works, and self-government. In pursuing this course, the McKinley and Roosevelt administrations steered between evacuation and annexation. Small groups in both Cuba and the United States demanded immediate evacuation; others desired ultimate annexation. The majority in both countries, however, supported the United States policy of remaining in Cuba for a few years to establish a durable government that would render future intervention unnecessary.

The military government ceased only when it appeared that the necessary safeguards to prevent upheaval in Cuba had been obtained. These safeguards

---

[1] For the Joint Resolution and the Peace Treaty, see Appendices A and B, noting that the United States refused to accept the cession of Cuba by Spain, and with the fourth (Teller) clause of the Joint Resolution, the United States bound itself to depart from Cuba. More detail, statistics and information may be found in J. Hitchman, "Leonard Wood and the Cuban Question, 1898-1902," Ph. D. dissertation, University of California, Berkeley, 1965.

were embodied in the Platt Amendment of 1901, enacted by the United States Congress, accepted by the Cuban Constitutional Convention, and agreed upon in a treaty between the two countries. The Platt Amendment was intended to prevent Cubans and foreign nations from weakening Cuban sovereignty; it was not intended to make Cuba a protectorate of the United States. Juxtaposed with the Platt Amendment was the Reciprocity Agreement of 1903, which gave the Cubans the market they needed to revive their economy. These political and economic measures were designed to assist a neighbor state to maintain itself as a friendly republic.

This experiment in republic making eventually failed. The sad course of Cuban-American relations in the 20th century prompts the inquiry as to whether anything occurred during the intervention that might have produced such a result. The main reasons for the failure of the Cuban Republic may be found in events that came after 1902, but the premature termination of occupation was a crucial cause of the ultimate failure of Cuban republicanism.

The United States Government did not believe that the American people would allow the occupation to continue for as long as a decade. Had this been possible, representative government would have been more likely to endure. Despite the remarkable achievements of the Wood administration, there remained enough indications of instability to warrant continued occupation, but the Americans, eager to leave, hoped that the Platt Amendment would act as a stabilizer. However, Cubans and Americans after 1902 rarely understood or employed the Platt Amendment as its authors intended. Cubans, who hampered chances for success by resenting their inability to win independence unaided, allowed hurt pride to lead them to use the Platt Amendment as an excuse for political irresponsibility instead of a springboard to maturity. Americans meddled too often in the island's affairs, forgetting the restraints of the amendment on themselves. In the first intervention, there seemed to be a paradox of authoritarian democracy which imposed self-government with safeguards upon a foreign culture.

The planners of Cuban policy attempted to resolve this conflict between the principles of self-determination and strategic security. Presidents McKinley and Roosevelt, Senator Orville H. Platt, Secretary of War Elihu Root, and General Wood served Cuban-American interests by supporting Cuban independence. They did not believe the islanders were ready for immediate independence in 1898 but believed them capable of it after preparation. The delegates to the Constitutional Convention also demonstrated their desire and faith in deciding for a republic by accepting the Platt Amendment. From 1898 to 1902 Cuban moderates and the military government cooperated to prepare Cuba for nationhood. Their most difficult task was to form unity among Cubans. The only alternative to American assistance in this endeavor would have been continued civil war.

In 1898 Cuba was exhausted. A decade of depression and revolution had reduced the island's population by twelve percent and destroyed two-thirds of its wealth. The economy was crippled by staggering debt. The countryside lay ravaged and towns and cities suffered from famine and pestilence. Water systems and sewers were destroyed, and the only sanitation came from buzzards, dogs, and rain. Malaria, dysentery, typhoid, smallpox, and yellow fever stalked emaciated Cubans. Deaths in Santiago alone exceeded two hundred per day. Bodies littered the shattered streets, while the living crouched in dark and filthy dwellings, awaiting relief. The more fortunate Cubans and Spaniards, unimpressed by this addition to the accumulated filth of centuries, affirmed that life would continue and did little to help. Virtual anarchy prevailed as enmity continued between Spaniards and Cubans.

Of the island's 1.5 million people, two-thirds were illiterate and unemployed. The courts had ceased to function, public funds disappeared in the hands of the Spaniards, and ordinary lines of communication and transportation were severed. The Cuban army had not disbanded and American troops were weakened by tropical disease. It was a critical time, demanding action to feed the starving, tend the sick, clean the cities, plant the fields, and rebuild the island.[2]

But rebuilding required cooperation, and hostility in Cuban society, caused in part by a colonial heritage of corruption and misrule, partly by the enervation stemming from decades of depression and revolution, prevented unity among Cubans. This hostility flared among five groups: the Spanish element, autonomists (Cubans desiring home rule under Spain), neutralists, revolutionaries, and the Negro faction. The latter two groups cooperated with each other and, with the neutralists, composed a majority of the populace. Yet this coalition was too weak to achieve a peaceful, prosperous Cuba, for most of the wealth and talent lay with the Spaniards and autonomists, who avoided political activities. The revolutionaries, given the opportunities, would have enacted severe reprisals against these two groups, who they believed had oppressed the Cuban people.[3]

[2] U. S. War Department, *Report on the Census of Cuba, 1899* (Wn: GPO, 1900), 41, 155, 179; H. Hagedorn, *Leonard Wood* (N.Y., 1931), I, 184-188.

[3] U. S., *Congressional Record*, 55th Cong., 2d Sess., 3969; O. H. Platt, "Our Relation to the People of Cuba and Porto Rico," *Annals of the American Academy of Political and Social Science*, XVIII (July, 1901), 152.

Cuban revolutionary leaders had long recognized disunity as their greatest problem. None had seen this more clearly than José Martí, the apostle of *Cuba Libre*. Martí, the founder and guiding spirit of the Revolution of 1895, was a remarkable man, embodying traits of both unifier and organizer. Under his guidance, the Cuban revolutionary movement changed from a conspiracy to a crusade. In 1892, Martí and others founded the Cuban Revolutionary Party (PRC), whose stated aim was a unified, independent republic. The party platform emphasized the goal of a free Cuba, without faction or oppression.[4] This objective was reemphasized most notably on March 25, 1895, in the Manifesto of Montecristi. In this proclamation Martí, the soul of the Revolution, was joined by the sword of the cause, Máximo Gómez. In addition to dividing civil and military responsibilities between the two men, the Manifesto called on the Cubans to unite. The purpose of the war, proclaimed Martí and Gómez, was not merely to fight Spaniards, but to establish a free, united Cuba. Urging cooperation and hope for the cause, the Manifesto called repeatedly for trust among factions: for treating the Negro as an equal and the Spaniard as a respected former enemy once the war was won.[5]

Unfortunately for the cause, Martí, the one man who could unify the Cubans, was killed in battle in May, 1895, shortly after landing in Cuba. Nevertheless, his ideals inspired Cubans to fight on for freedom.[6] While lacking Martí's compassion and mystic appeal, the remaining revolutionary leaders were still men of ability. Máximo Gómez was an old professional soldier from Santo Domingo, as agile in his seventies as most men in their thirties, who had been one of the leading Cuban generals in the Ten Years' War of 1868-1878. His strategy of attrition was complemented by the daring tactics of the mulatto general Antonio Maceo, one of Cuba's greatest military leaders. Political assistance for the military effort was led in Cuba by Salvador Cisneros Betancourt, who surrendered his Spanish title and vast property to serve as first president of the 1895 version of the Cuban Republic. Logistical support for the Revolution was organized in part by Tomás Estrada Palma, president of the Republic during the Ten Years' War of 1868-1878, who lived in New York and succeeded Martí as Chief Delegate of the PRC. None of these men, however, possessed the ability to unify Cuba.

[4] República de Cuba. Senado. *Memoria de los trabajos realizados durante las cuatro legislaturas y sesión extraordinaria del primer período congresional, 1902-1904.* Tomo 1, *Mención histórica, documentación relacionada con los acontecimientos que dieron, como resultado definitivo, la independencia y el establecimiento en república de Cuba, 1892-1902* (La Habana, 1918), 9-11.

[5] *Ibid.*, 15-22.

[6] Jorge Mañach, *Martí: Apostle of Freedom* (New York, 1950), 355-63.

This became apparent during the war when Cuban apathy retarded the struggle of these leaders for the unity necessary to achieve Cuban independence. Popular sentiment lay with the revolution, but no more than 30,000 men ever served in the field at one time, and most Cubans wanted both Spaniards and insurgents to leave them alone. It was extremely difficult to finance the struggle, to buy arms and ammunition. Furthermore, the Spanish forces so far outnumbered the Cuban army that major victories and the capture of cities were virtually impossible. Nevertheless, Cubans in the eastern part of the island, which had been liberated by the insurgents, elected a transient provisional government which maintained the rudiments of administration during the war. Most of those elected were military officers who represented the army more than the people. The *Consejo de Gobierno,* or executive council, operated a postal system, collected taxes and obtained supplies for the army through local prefects in many areas of *Cuba Libre.* This organization was effective in its limited efforts, but never elicited full support of the people.[7]

Because the provisional government could not unify the islanders to win the revolution unaided, most Cubans desired outside assistance and many actually expected American intervention. General Gómez originally wanted American weapons and munitions, but not American troops; later, however, he estimated that the Cuban army would have capitulated in another six months without the American arrival. Bartolomé Masó, who succeeded Cisneros as president of the provisional government, agreed that Cuba could not have won the war unaided. Cisneros even spoke favorably of annexation to the United States because of the advantages to be gained in security and trade.[8] These attitudes on the part of the Cuban insurgent leaders revealed lack of confidence in Cuban competence to achieve and maintain independence without assistance.

With the war ended, the provisional government knew that Cuban divisiveness stemmed more from inner conflict between conservatives and radicals than from American occupation. On September 1, 1898, President Masó circulated a message in *Cuba Libre* urging Cubans to use restraint in their relations with one another. On November 7 Masó sent a special message to

[7] U.S., *Congressional Record,* 55th Cong., 2d Sess., 293-297; U.S. Congress, Senate, *Report of Committee on Foreign Relations,* "Affairs in Cuba," 55th Cong., 2d Sess., Sen. Rep. 885; G. Flint, *Marching with Gómez* (N.Y., 1898), 222-236. Cf. Calixto García to Gonzalo de Quesada, May 29, 1897, in Gonzalo de Quesada y Miranda, ed., *Epistolario,* 2 volumes in one (La Habana, 1948-51), I, 175.

[8] U.S. Congress. Senate, Letter of Gen. Máximo Gómez to the President, Feb. 9, 1897, 55th Cong., 1st Sess., S. doc. 75; Flint, *Marching with Gómez,* 188-196, 224; D. Méndez Capote, *Trabajos* (La Habana, three volumes in one, 1929-30), III, 140-198, 232.

the Cuban Assembly convened at Santa Cruz del Sur, pleading once more for cooperation. He mentioned the United States as a third party, which had helped to free the Cubans; but the American presence concerned him less than the activities of Spanish and Cuban conservatives who now were encouraging the Americans to remain in Cuba. Masó stated his confidence "in the purity of the intentions" of the United States, asserted the right of Cuba to be independent and claimed that Cubans wanted to enjoy cordial relations with other countries.[9]

Masó's message was prompted in part by the report of Domingo Méndez Capote, vice-president of the provisional government, who had traveled to Washington, D. C., in May, 1898, to ascertain United States plans for Cuba. His report reveals that the United States had a general policy for Cuba before the war ended, that this policy was based on fear of Cuban disunity, and that Cuban leaders knew the outline of this policy long before being presented with the *fait accompli* of the Platt Amendment in 1901. According to Méndez Capote, Attorney General John W. Griggs stated that the United States intended to expel the Spanish troops, establish order, and institute a Cuban government to manage its own internal and external affairs. This achievement would prevent continued American intervention in Cuba. Griggs assured Méndez Capote that Cuba would not be governed as a colony or a territory but by a military government which would protect the lives and rights of the people and allow the Cubans to run the government with American supervision.[10] This was in accord with President McKinley's Cuban policy: "to secure in the island the establishment of a stable government, capable of maintaining order and observing its international obligations, insuring peace and tranquility and the security of its citizens as well as our own." [11]

In the interview Griggs explained that the United States did not recognize the Cuban government because it represented only a fraction of all Cubans. Méndez Capote rejoined that the revolution represented Cuba's best interests and that the United States must govern according to Cuban consent, or the laws of the military government would have no lasting effect. In fact, Méndez Capote misinterpreted the interview, carrying away the conviction that the United States, had no definite policy for Cuba other than to establish peace

    [9] Méndez Capote, *Trabajos*, I, 166-177, III, 243, 255, Masó was often referred to as Masso, but they were one and the same. U.S. Congress, House, *Report of the Secretary of War*, 56th Cong., 1st Sess., 1899, 12-13.

    [10] Méndez Capote, *Trabajos*, III, 201-13.

    [11] U.S. Congress, House, *Message of the President of the United States on the Relations of the United States and Spain*, 55th Cong., 2d Sess., 1898, doc. 405, LXIV 13.

and call upon Cubans to organize a government acceptable to all elements in Cuba. This conclusion resulted from disagreement over the length of time required to pacify the island. The United States Government considered pacification would take several years in order to have a chance of permanence. Upon his return, Méndez Capote recommended to Masó that a temporary commission be appointed to cooperate with the forces of occupation. The Santa Cruz Assembly agreed to this, dissolved the Consejo and disbanded. The United States ignored the new commission, headed by Méndez Capote, and President McKinley appointed Major General John R. Brooke as Military Governor of Cuba on December 13, 1898.[12]

Just before it disbanded, the Assembly was implored by the most influential Cubans in New York City to cooperate with the United States.[13] The plea exasperated the men of the *Asamblea*, who considered themselves closer to the firing line than these self-exiled Cuban men of letters and commerce who financially supported the revolution from New York.

The views of other leading Cubans also reflected apprehension about Cuban viability. Enrique José Varona, a distinguished Cuban man of letters and philosopher, welcomed intervention and counselled cooperation with the Americans. He believed in the Joint Resolution and held that the military occupation would be temporary, because both Cubans and Americans wanted a "Cuban government freely elected by its people." [14] Eusebio Hernández dreamed that Cuba would develop into the commercial leader of the West Indies. A doctor of medicine and one of the more capable men of affairs in the island, Hernández marched with Gómez and later became a leader in the conservative Democratic Union party.[15]

Conservative revolutionaries, like Gonzalo de Quesada, advocated working with the United States to build a unified Cuba. Quesada was the Cuban diplomatic representative in the United States during the Revolution, later delegate to the Cuban Constitutional Convention and then Cuban minister to the United States and to Germany. His correspondent and friend, Emilio Núñez, general in the Cuban army and civil governor of Havana province during the occupation, contended that the Americans had done more for Cuban independence than had his "suspicious" countrymen.[16]

Tomás Estrada Palma, who had succeeded Martí as Chief Delegate of the PRC, suggested that regardless of whether Cuba was independent or

[12] Méndez Capote, *Trabajos*, III, 207-213, 219-224.
[13] *Mención histórica*, 96-100.
[14] Enrique José Varona, *De la colonia a la república* (La Habana, 1919), 198-199.
[15] Flint, *Marching with Gómez*, 191-192.
[16] E. Núñez to Quesada, July 25, 1898, Jan. 2, 1899, Jan. 27, 1899, *Espistolario*, II, 127-132.

part of the United States, the indispensable point was respect for each other; Cuba was assured a hopeless future without the medium of intimate relations with her northern neighbor. Furthermore, Estrada Palma stated, the immediate task was the rehabilitation of Cuba, not arguments about matters which would divide Cubans. More sympathetic to annexation as the solution to Cuba's problems than most of his countrymen, Estrada Palma believed his views would be received unfavorably in Cuba and made the "irrevocable" decision that he would not occupy a place there; [17] however, he was to be elected president of the Republic in 1902.

Meanwhile, the radicals began to blame Cuban disunity on the United States in an effort to expel the Americans and seize power. In July, 1899, the resourceful and doctrinaire Negro patriot, Juan Gualberto Gómez, speaking at a Havana rally, demanded that his audience renew the pledge of independence or death until the Americans departed. Other orators repeated this demand, threatening to "take to the woods." In Santiago, the Maceo club denounced McKinley for trying to deprive Cubans of independence, and Quintín Banderas, a guerrilla chief during the war, called for organization to plan resistance.[18]

Ignoring the basic problems of feeding and clothing the people, of carting off the debris of war and building a new Cuba, Cuban leaders argued about employment, payment of the army of liberation, and how to ensure civilian control of Máximo Gómez and his army. By the spring of 1899 the $ 3 million remaining from the $ 50 million congressional war appropriation was spent to give each Cuban soldier $ 75.00 to help him adjust to civilian life. This payment was not intended to recompense fully the Cuban soldier for his services, but to provide a means for preventing disorder. Gómez endorsed this proposal by Robert P. Porter, who was McKinley's special representative in Cuba. Objecting to the proposal, a group of army officers and former officials in the provisional government met at Cerro, a Havana suburb, in an attempt to assert control over Cuban civil affairs. They opposed Gómez and tried to arrange for a large loan to pay the troops. Taking a further step, the Cerro assembly voted to depose Gómez as General-in-Chief, in what has been termed a vindication of the principle of civil control over the military. In reality this move was an ineffectual attempt at a coup by twenty-six men who were ignored by both the Cuban populace and the American occupation

[17] Estrada Palma to Quesada, May 18, 1899, *Ibid.*, 141-142; Dec. 13, 1899, *Ibid.*, 148; Mar. 14, 1901, *Ibid.*, 149; E. S. Santovenía y Echaíde, *Armonías y conflictas en torno a Cuba* (Mexico, D. F., 1956), 231-232, showing Estrada Palma's appreciation of the fact that while the United States aided Cuba, no Latin American country did.

[18] *New York Times*, June 23, 1899, July 13, 1899; Wood papers, file 248, *Chicago Inter-Ocean*, Dec. 9, 1899.

THE REASONS FOR OCCUPATION, 1898-1899

forces. The flurry of the Cerro sessions drove Gómez closer to the Americans and the frustrated members quickly quarrelled the assembly into oblivion. Possibly the United States triggered this dissension, but with or without the occupation, Cubans disagreed over the means to achieve their goals. Without the United States occupation, disorder and bloodshed possibly would have spread from incidents like the Cerro meetings.[19]

Máximo Gómez, the most influential man among the Cubans after the death of Martí, attempted to reconcile Cuban aspirations with United States occupation. Gómez recognized the necessity of revamping Cuban affairs rather than obstructing the United States. His attitude proved invaluable in rebuilding Cuba during the following years.

We wanted and depended upon foreign intervention to terminate the war. . . . But none of us thought that this extraordinary event would be followed by a military occupation of the country by our allies, who treat us as a people incapable of acting for ourselves. . . . We must make useless by our behavior the presence of a strange power in the island, and must assist the Americans to complete the honorable mission which they have been compelled to assume by force of circumstances.[20]

Here Gómez perceived with characteristic clarity the most beneficial and enduring policy for Cuba. Could it have been effected, United States guidance would indeed have been unnecessary. But the revolutionary, autonomist and conservative factions could neither cooperate nor win support from the people who wanted to be left alone. Apparent from the scant records left by various Cuban men of affairs at the turn of the century is their majority conviction that Cuba needed American assistance to rebuild a prostrate and divided society. Upon this condition the McKinley policy was constructed.

Thus the challenge of winning the peace was greater than that of winning the war, and Cuban-American cooperation was needed before *Cuba triste* could truly become *Cuba libre*.

---

[19] *New York Times*, March 2, 1899, March 13, 1899, March 15, 1899, April 5, 1899, April 7, 1899; R. P. Porter, *Industrial Cuba* (N.Y., 1899), 207-210; O. Costa, *Manuel Sanguily* (La Habana, 1950), 70; A. G. Robinson, *Cuba and the Intervention* (N.Y., 1905), 106-107.

[20] *New York Times*, June 7, 1899; R. Infiesta, *Máximo Gómez* (La Habana, 1937), 213, stresses that during those uncertain days, Gómez used his authority to insist on one theme: union. Since Gómez accepted housing and subsistence from the Military Government, it might be argued that he was unduly influenced, but the old General refused the offer of a sinecure from Wood and possessed too much strength of character to be liable to these accusations. Wood papers, Wood to Root, Dec. 30, 1899; M. Gómez to Wood, Dec. 30, 1899.

But American views on annexation and the governance of Cuba were not unified. The anti-imperialist struggle at the end of 1898 helped to divide American opinion and this lack of unity was evident in the press.[21]

The basic editorial reaction to the troubled Cuban conditions was one of *noblesse oblige*. Most Americans endorsed McKinley's policy of responsible trusteeship which sought to guide unprepared peoples in self-government rather than casting them loose in a hostile world or trying to assimilate them into a society already fraught with assimilation problems. There was a feeling of good will toward Cuba and a wish to see a republic after the American example; this opinion was basically responsible for the American departure in 1902 and the chance for Cuba to be free.

Typifying these opinions about self-government, the *New York Tribune* shifted from impatience with some existing American attitudes to a stoical view of the course of empire.

The islands have been placed in charge of the United States as a trustee. Every civilized nation will expect, and have a right to expect, that the U.S. will assure to these islands as good government as it can give, not only with respect to international obligations, but for the development of the people, their trade and industries. It will be found not a bit of cowardice merely, but an utter impossibility, to evade that obligation.[22]

No one wanted to take Cuba or the Philippines, argued the *Tribune,* but the men who shrank from the task saw it could not be avoided.

The President may not be able to read the future, but he does the duty that lies nearest with the best light he can get. In precisely the same spirit the nation has to face its task, knowing not how great it may be, nor how costly, nor how little or how much of reward may follow.[23]

By mid-summer of 1899, before the gaze of an actively interested public, President McKinley was dealing with belligerent Filipinos, a Cuba which was peaceful but unpacified, and an incompetent Secretary of War who impeded the assumption of reforms and new duties required in the wake of war. During the next six months far-reaching decisions were made. Elihu Root

[21] Some newspapers supporting McKinley administration policy were: *New York Times,* Jan. 3, 1899; *Cedar Rapids Republican,* Dec. 31, 1899; *Scranton Tribune,* Dec. 27, 1899. Among those opposed were the *Indianapolis Sentinel,* Jan. 17, 1899, *Springfield* [Massachusetts] *Republican,* Dec. 1, 1899. Other papers expressed gratitude at clean government in Cuba because they were concerned about the lack of it at home: *Brooklyn Times,* Dec. 15, 1899; *St. Paul Pioneer-Press,* April 27, 1901. With the exception of the *New York Times,* all other papers in this note are located in the Wood papers, scrapbooks 239, 248, 251.

[22] *New York Tribune,* Dec. 16, 1899, Wood papers, scrapbook 248. Whitelaw Reid, the editor, was an expansionist.

[23] *Ibid.*

replaced R. A. Alger as Secretary of War, Major General Leonard Wood relieved Major General John R. Brooke as Military Governor of Cuba and the President decided to retain a temporary military governor rather than install a civil governor as was done in the Philippines.

McKinley's pronouncements on Cuba have been construed by both contemporary and current writers as staunchly guarding the prerogative of the executive against the incursions of Congress in order to maintain a free hand. He has been accused of obscuring his intentions in vague phrases, either because he had no policy or to disguise the annexation desires of business interests on which he relied. Actually, McKinley desired a free, stable Cuba and considered its annexation undesirable. Some Americans believed Cuba would ask to be annexed by the United States after a few years of independence; indeed, minority agitation for such annexation went back at least to the days of Thomas Jefferson. Most Americans did not regard Cuba as a valuable addition to the Union and wanted to leave a free Cuba which would not be a nuisance. McKinley's persistence in establishing self-government in Cuba represented this opinion.[24]

William McKinley had changed his mind about high tariffs and world affairs after he became President and saw conditions from a new viewpoint. As he saw it, United States production needed a world market, and the reciprocity principle seemed to reconcile protection with production. He was fond of the phrase "good trade insures good will." [25] McKinley envisioned rounding out his career by gaining American supremacy in world markets. In the Caribbean, strategic supremacy would be supported by market control. The annexation of Puerto Rico, the Hay – Pauncefote treaties regarding the proposed isthmian canal, and the attempt to purchase the Virgin Islands illustrated this aim.[26] He even hoped for a great power cooperation abroad to complement political combinations and business trusts at home, for pooling power interests seemed to be the essence of McKinleyism.[27] In Cuba, his failure to place the insurgents in charge signified his intention of

[24] Supporting the idea of continuity of policy are Margaret Leech, *In the Days of McKinley* (N.Y., 1959), 170, 182, 188, 272-3; C. G. Dawes, *A Journal of the McKinley Years* (Chicago, 1950), 165. In opposition are Henry Adams, letter to Elizabeth Cameron, Jan. 22, 1899, W. C. Ford, ed., *Letters of Henry Adams*, II, 206, (Boston, 1930); J. H. Wilson, *Under the Old Flag* (N.Y., 1912), II, 479-80; Robinson, *Cuba and the Intervention*, 109; D. F. Healy, *The United States in Cuba, 1898-1902* (Madison, 1963), 88, 125.

[25] Leech, *Days of McKinley*, 142.

[26] T. Dennett, *John Hay* (N.Y., 1933), 264-65.

[27] H. Adams, *Education* (N.Y., 1931), 423-24.

future representative government; [28] the President wished to trade with a friendly, enduring Cuba, not a constant source of trouble.

President McKinley outlined his Cuban policy of trusteeship on several occasions in 1898 and 1899. His directives to the army in Cuba clarified the mission of the military government.

On July 18, 1898, McKinley instructed his commanders as to their conduct of the military occupation.[29] After describing the first effect, by military occupation of an enemy territory, as severance of the former political relations of the inhabitants and the establishment of new political power, McKinley directed the Commander of the Army of Occupation to announce:

that we come not to make war upon the inhabitants of Cuba, nor upon any party or faction among them, but to protect them in their homes, in their employments, and in their personal and religious rights. . . . Our occupation should be as free from severity as possible.

The powers of the military occupants were absolute and supreme, although the customs and laws of the people were not to be abridged unless necessary. The American commander was charged with the duty of adopting measures to keep law and order. The military government could seize and use all public property, funds, securities, arms and supplies. All buildings devoted to religion, the arts, science and education, as well as archives and monuments, were to be protected. Private property could be confiscated, but compensation for its use was payable in cash. Taxes were to be used only for defraying the costs of the civil government under the military occupation. All ports were to be opened to the United States and to neutral nations upon payment of duties.

On December 22, 1898, the eve of the final departure of Spanish troops, McKinley sent to Brooke a confidential letter of "private and unofficial suggestions." [30] Based on the law of belligerent right over conquered territory, the authority of the Military Government, as an arm of the Commander-in-Chief, would continue until Congress provided otherwise or:

until such time as the people shall have established a firm and stable government of their own, capable of performing its international obligations. The government to be maintained under this authority by you on behalf of the United States is not in the interest or for the direct benefit of this country, but in the interest and for the benefit of Cuba and those possessed of rights and property in that Island.

He urged Brooke to mingle with men of all parties, work for Cuban unity and encourage civil reform, especially in sanitation, education and the courts. Corruption, oppression, or violation of public trust would not be tolerated.

[28] Leech, *Days of McKinley*, 273.
[29] General Order 101, L. Wood, *Civil Report,* 1900, I, 1-5.
[30] C. S. Olcott, *Life of William McKinley* (Boston, 1918) II, 196-202.

Explicit in McKinley's policy statements was his intent to build stable independence in Cuba. In December 1898 he told Congress:

As soon as we are in possession of Cuba and have pacified the island it will be necessary to give aid and direction to its people to form a government for themselves. This should be undertaken at the earliest moment consistent with safety and assured success. It is important that our relations with this people shall be of the most friendly character and our commercial relations close and reciprocal. It should be our duty to assist in every proper way to build up the waste places of the island, encourage the industry of the people, and assist them to form a government which shall be free and independent, thus realizing the best aspirations of the Cuban people.[31]

The President elaborated upon this policy statement in his annual message for 1899:

This nation has assumed before the world a grave responsibility for the future good government of Cuba. We have accepted a trust the fulfillment of which calls for the sternest integrity of purpose and the exercise of the highest wisdom. The new Cuba yet to arise from the ashes of the past must needs be bound to us by ties of singular intimacy and strength if its enduring welfare is to be assured. Whether these ties shall be organic or conventional, the destinies of Cuba are in some rightful form and manner irrevocably linked with our own, but how and how far is for the future to determine in the ripeness of events. Whatever be the outcome, we must see to it that free Cuba be a reality, not a name, a perfect entity, not a hasty experiment bearing within itself the elements of failure. Our mission, to accomplish which we took up the wager of battle, is not to be fulfilled by turning adrift any loosely framed commonwealth to face the vicissitudes which too often attend weaker states whose natural wealth and abundant resources are offset by the incongruities of their political organization and the recurring occasions for internal rivalries to sap their strength and dissipate their energies. The greatest blessing which can come to Cuba is the restoration of her agricultural and industrial prosperity, which will give employment to idle men and reestablish the pursuits of peace. This is her chief and immediate need.[32]

The President ended by asking for favorable terms of trade with Cuba.

The President had set a policy, but it was not being implemented to his satisfaction. Desirous of resolving the colonial question more effectively, McKinley appointed Elihu Root as Secretary of War in August of 1899, an event which signified the articulation of McKinley's policy for Cuba. An able corporation lawyer who satisfied both McKinley's patronage requirements in New York and his desire for a legal mind to administer the new possessions

---

[31] U.S. Congress, House, *Message of the President*, 1898, 55th Cong., 3d Sess., doc. 1, lxvi-lxvii.

[32] U.S. Congress, House, *Message of the President*, 1899, 56th Cong., 1st Sess., xxix-xxx.

and trusteeships, Root was destined to be one of the greatest secretaries of war in United States history. No other public figure of the time so incisively perceived the issues or proposed such clearly worded solutions. Eventually, Root successfully ended Philippine unrest, reorganized the Army, and made Cuban independence secure. His immediate measures for Cuba were to order a census and create the Division of Insular Affairs.

Taking the federal government as his client, Root read deeply and widely, seeking the legal basis for the United States position in Cuba. After careful study Root reported,

I assume, for I do not think that it can be successfully disputed, that all acquisition of territory under this treaty was the exercise of a power which belonged to the United States, because it was a nation, and for that reason was endowed with the powers essential to national life. . . .[33]

The law officer of the Division of Insular Affairs, Charles E. Magoon, who later acted as Provisional Governor of Cuba from 1906 to 1909, rendered an opinion on October 19, 1899, to Secretary Root entitled, "the Powers, Functions, and Duties of the Military Governments Maintained by the United States in the Islands Lately Ceded and Relinquished by the Government of Spain." [34] These opinions formed the legal basis for the Secretary's policy in Cuba. Magoon held that military governments resulting from occupations were intended to promote the operations of the occupying army and to preserve the safety of society. The governments maintained in the islands were instituted during time of war, because the invader had to provide another government to replace the defeated one. Magoon found that the United States Supreme Court had determined in the Mexican and Civil wars that the military authority of the United States could govern under certain conditions. The ancient doctrine, "The will of the conqueror is the law of the conquered," shorn of its terrors, was still recognized as a law of nations. Military government replaced, suspended or destroyed sovereignty; martial rule replaced government unable to cope with temporary local conditions. All law and procedures of a locality remained in effect unless altered or superseded by military authority whose duty was to maintain peace and order.

[33] U.S. Congress, House, *Report of the Secretary of War*, 56th Cong., 1st Sess., 1899, doc. 2, vol. I, 24; Root to Attorney General, October 12, 1899, National Archives, Social and Economic Branch, Dept. of Interior Division, Record Group 350, Division of Insular Affairs, file 1102. Hereafter cited as DIA.

[34] C. E. Magoon, *Reports on the Law of Civil Government in Territory Subject to Military Occupation by the Military Forces of the United States*, 2nd ed. (Wn: GPO, 1902), 11-37. Senator Orville H. Platt, of Connecticut, using different sources and the same reasoning, made a similar case in the Senate. Platt papers, 24 page "Memorandum" n.d., n.p. Platt's theme was that pacification required longer occupation.

Magoon held that military government after the peace treaty was legal because it was necessary. Necessity was the basis for such government,

and this necessity justifies and requires the continuance of the military government until there is established in said islands a civil government which comports with the interests and inclinations of the dominant power.

Though the law officer did not discuss how a civil government was to be prepared to replace military government, he did make clear the locus of sovereignty. The sovereignty of Spain was withdrawn, the sovereignty of the United States was not attached, and thus Cuba's sovereignty, Magoon reasoned, "declared by Congress to be possessed by the people of the island, remains dormant." The Military Government of Cuba was a temporary substitute for sovereignty, and as such could exercise such powers as were necessary for the successful conduct of internal affairs, subject to the restraints imposed by the ideas of government prevailing under the sovereignty of which it was created and the orders of the superior officials of the sovereignty by which the military government was sustained. There was an implied contract between the United States and any man who was submitted to dominion, Root added, and Congress would hold itself bound by those limitations which arose from the law of its own existence, which was the Constitution.[35]

Turning to the issue of congressional direction of the conduct of the Military Government of Cuba, Magoon held that Congress stopped itself from so doing by the Joint Resolution. Congress had declared that sovereignty rested in the Cuban people and authorized the Commander-in-Chief to act. To interfere would give sanction and the fixed character of legislative enactment to martial law. Martial rule, according to the American theory of government, arose from necessity and ceased with its demise; thus every act during military occupation had to be justified by necessity. The safeguard against any arbitrary exercise of military government was the liability of the military person in charge before the courts after martial rule had ceased. If the Congress exercised the authority of martial law, the justification of military acts became not necessity, but law. Such a justification could not be impeached, and any injured party would be without remedy.

In making a solid case for the administration, Magoon minimized the possibility of judicial review and of due process of law, which were used for recourse against the Military Government. Actually, the quickest redress could be achieved by direct appeal to the Secretary of War. This was done often, but Root rarely found cause for granting redress. However, the argument for preservation of the separation of powers through executive enact-

[35] Magoon, *Reports*, 11-37; *Report of the Secretary of War*, 1899, I, 24-25.

ment of legislative authorization was sound. More important was Magoon's opinion: "Wherever the sovereignty of the United States may be asserted, the Congress of the United States may prescribe the ways and means, the manner and methods by which such sovereignty is to be asserted.[36] But conduct was left to the executive branch. Significant also was Magoon's exclusion of Cuba from his subsequent discussion of territory and inhabitants acquired. He confined his treatment of Cuba to a discourse on occupation by belligerent right, considering United States intervention to be a temporary situation in fact and in law.

Thus the administration was satisfied that the Military Government of Cuba was a necessary and legal agency to fulfill the Joint Resolution and the Peace Treaty, with safeguards against injustice provided.

In addition to accepting the restraints of United States constitutional and statute law in the administration of Cuban affairs, the Military Government also abided by the provisions of the Foraker Amendment, passed, like the Spooner Amendment (organic act for the Philippines) and the Platt Amendment, as a rider to the annual army appropriations bill. The February 10, 1899 issue of the Washington, D. C. *Evening Star* reported a new government board appointed by the President to investigate and supervise the granting of franchises in Puerto Rico and Cuba. When Senator Joseph Benson Foraker read this, he became apprehensive that a large amount of American money invested in Cuba would delay withdrawal. The Ohio Senator's motives stemmed from two sources. His Cincinnati group fought with Mark Hanna for state control, and any chance to steal a political march enhanced his prestige. Foraker also had a long record of friendship to Cuba. He advocated, in succession, recognition of the Cuban republic, going to war, and quick withdrawal from the island. He assumed an independent, prodding role in Cuban-American relations. His proposed amendment provided that

No property franchise, or concessions of any kind whatever, shall be granted by the United States, or by any other military or other authority whatever in the Island of Cuba during the occupation thereof by the United States.[37]

The Senate, disgruntled at not being consulted by McKinley in the matter, passed Foraker's bill, forty-seven to eleven, on March 3, 1899.[38] Though

[36] Magoon, *Reports*, 55: cf. C. F. Randolph, *The Law and Policy of Annexation* (N.Y., 1901), 173-190, who held that Cuba was a foreign country under U.S. control, was not a protectorate because it existed as an economic, geographical and cultural entity, yet had no sovereignty because it was vested in the representatives of the U.S. who administered the government of Cuba. The military government was not oppressive because it abided by the Paris Peace Treaty and the Joint Resolution. The occupation was terminable at American discretion.

[37] J. B. Foraker, *Notes on a Busy Life* (Cincinnati, 1916), II, 39-51.

[38] *Ibid., New York Times,* March 15, 1900.

the amendment did prove valuable in preventing American carpetbaggery, it was to be an impediment to Cuban economic development.

In the fall of 1899 the McKinley administration flirted temporarily with the notion of a civil governor for Cuba. It advanced a proposal allowing a degree of home rule, yet resting final control with the civil governor to be appointed by the President. (This proposal was to be carried out in the Philippines after Emilio Aguinaldo, the insurgent leader, surrendered.) But it smacked of long-term control, and the administration did not dare try it in Cuba, especially in an election year, and additionally because of the Joint Resolution and the arguments of Foraker, Root and Wood for a military government. The administration Senators and Congressmen were chiefly responsible for quashing the plan, thereby relieving the Cubans of some anxiety.[39] McKinley reverted to the earlier plan of a short-term military government to establish local, then insular self-government. Mayors and civil governors were to be elected in the near future, and then the people would elect members to a constitutional convention to make the fundamental law of the republic.[40] The Cuban program was beginning to develop, but it required a reliable, forceful and capable administrator in Cuba to fulfill it.

General Brooke had supervised a much-needed start. Relief and sanitation measures were carried out, revenues collected, schools established, prison conditions improved and Cuban appointees given authority and responsibility in civil government. On February 11, 1899, Brooke directed the civil secretaries to resume their duties and extend their influence throughout the island, reporting all orders to him for approval and publication. Also, the appointment of provincial governors did much to end confusion in the island as the gears of administrative machinery began to engage once more.[41]

The War Department had already effected administrative accommodations for Cuba. On December 13, 1898, the Secretary of War established the Division of Cuba within the War Department; on January 26 of the following year, seven military departments within the Division of Cuba were formed conforming to the Spanish colonial subdivisions. In July these departments were consolidated into four: Santiago and Puerto Príncipe, Matanzas and Santa Clara, Havana City, Pinar del Río and Havana province. In November 1899, the United States Army in Cuba numbered 334 officers and 10,796 enlisted men, a number which decreased by half during 1900 and was reduced

---

[39] *New York Times*, Dec. 2, 1899.
[40] Estrada Palma to Quesada, Aug. 17, 1899, Nov. 27, 1899, *Epistolario*, I, 145, 146.
[41] U.S. Congress, House, *Annual Reports of the War Department*, 56th Cong., 1st Sess., 1899, doc. 2, "Report of Maj. Gen. J. R. Brooke on Civil Affairs in Cuba," 23-26; Robinson, *Cuba and the Intervention*, 133 ff.

again in 1901 and 1902. This small figure, compared to the 30,000 men in the Cuban army and Weyler's 250,000 Spaniards, indicated that serious friction between Cubans and Americans did not exist.[42]

With organizational, procedural and relief measures operative by February 1899, the time seemed propitious for moving ahead. But nothing happened. *Alcaldes* (mayors), *ayuntamientos* (municipal councils) and decrees from Havana were old institutions in Cuba, and Cubans knew how to abide by them. But actual public education, sanitation and effective administration of justice and government were new matters. Brooke allowed Cuban secretaries and appointees to let the insular government drift along as it had for centuries under Spain; in J. G. Lanuza, he retained a Secretary of Justice and Public Instruction who typified the corruption and impotence of the Cuban administrative past. His report to Brooke for 1899 was entirely inadequate: disputatious and discursive, it revealed a person incapable of acting directly to remedy serious problems. Later, a great scandal in his department was narrowly avoided.[43] The other secretaries, while more productive, still indicated no awareness that they simply were not meeting the great needs of their devastated country.

By August of 1899, the *New York Times* reported that many Cubans criticized Brooke for failing to see the issues, chief of which were preparation for self-government and public education. His reports to Root had been unsatisfactory in their lack of information as to the collection and disbursement of revenues and the progress of civil government.[44] The most significant result of Brooke's passive policy was the failure of the cabinet officials to effectively manage Cuban affairs. It became imperative for Root to find a more tactful and energetic military governor.

Several men eyed Brooke's job. Partly out of concern over Brooke's inadequacy, partly because of individual ambition, his subordinates in the provinces, Generals Fitzhugh Lee in Pinar del Río, William Ludlow in

[42] *Report of the Secretary of War*, 1899, I, 3, 12-13.
[43] "Brooke Report," 247 ff.; cf. Wood papers, Root to Wood, Dec. 22, 1899, enclosing a ten page letter from Charlton T. Lewis to Root. This letter from the president of the New York Prison Association revealed to Root the extent of Brooke's neglect of Cuban prisons and administration of justice. Lewis spent part of November and December of 1899 in Cuba, reported his findings to Brooke and Lanuza and was ignored. Lewis believed, "Nothing but prompt interference by the War Department can stop the intolerable cruelty and injustice which now constitute a national disgrace." The chief ills were confinement without trial or hearing and overcrowded, unhealthy jails. Root to Wood, Jan. 27, 1900.
[44] *New York Times*, Aug. 9, 1899. The Wood papers contain 7 scrapbooks of newspaper clippings from Dec. 1898 through 1899, indicating a widespread concern throughout the U.S. about the Cuban situation.

Havana, James Harrison Wilson in Matanzas and Santa Clara, and Leonard Wood in Puerto Príncipe and Santiago, offered proposals of their own to meet conditions in the island. General Ludlow was an extremely intelligent, articulate and honest engineer whose ability exceeded that of most of his associates. He advocated occupying Cuba for at least a generation, a policy reportedly derived from President McKinley.[45] General Wilson, a spread-eagle expansionist who dreamed of adding Canada, the Antilles and Central America to the American empire, acted at this time as a protector of *Cuba Libre*. He was not selected because he could not be trusted to follow the administration's policy. Wilson advocated immediate withdrawal, a treaty of political relations and a customs union, all designed to make Cuba need annexation.[46]

When Root asked the military governors to submit their ideas about Cuban conditions, General Leonard Wood confined his remarks to limited objectives such as local funds for local expenditure, decentralized government, the need to build schools, roads and harbors, and most important, an effective legal system based upon justice, not politics. He was not so indiscreet as to advocate annexation but wrote that a long occupation was necessary to prepare Cubans for independence. Disgruntled and anxious, he conducted his own campaign in the periodicals of the day with articles on conditions in Cuba and wrote privately to his friend Theodore Roosevelt, telling him of mismanagement in the island.[47]

[45] Wilson, *Under the Old Flag*, II, 490.

[46] *Ibid.*, 416; cf. Wilson papers. He employed Albert G. Robinson, a newspaperman, off and on until 1910 to attack Wood. Wilson to Robinson, May 22, 1899, Nov. 22, 1901, Nov. 29, 1901; John J. McCook to McKinley, May 26, 1898; Wilson to D. W. Flagler, March 16, 1899. Wilson argued to Root and McKinley that he wanted to uphold the Joint Resolution, to Flagler he said that he deemed it an error and that the United States should have declared war and annexed Cuba. Wilson to Goldwin Smith, Dec. 27, 1899. See also his inaccurate recollection of an interview with McKinley regarding his influence on the President's Cuban policy, *Under the Old Flag*, II, 502.

[47] Root papers, Memorandum dictated by Wood in January 1899; Wood, "The Existing Conditions and Needs in Cuba," *North American Review*, CLXVIII (May, 1899), 593-601; *New York Times*, June 24, 1899; Wood papers, Maj. Gen. Adna R. Chaffee to Wood, Jan. 10, 1899; Wood to Roosevelt, July 12, 1899. Wood told Roosevelt that the Cuban cabinet was

simply working to produce friction between the Americans and the great bulk of the Cuban people, believing that if they can show discontent on the part of the Cubans with our administration, that they can, on presenting this fact and supporting it with the 'Mugwumps' at home obtain the withdrawal of our occupation. ... One year or even six months, of decent, candid, courageous government here will turn the public sentiment all our way and the problem will be solved, as far as Cuba is concerned.

The Chaffee letter indicates an incident between Brooke and Wood. Brooke wanted to use the Santiago revenues in the rest of the island, Wood wanted to use them in Santiago. Brooke accused Wood of loose financial methods in a semipublic censure.

Roosevelt had already asked John Hay to discuss the question of Cuban administration with McKinley, hoping the Secretary of State would give it a note of urgency.[48] The New York governor was uneasy about Cuba and the Philippines, fearing increased discontent in the United States over conditions in the islands. Roosevelt linked Wood and the Cuban question to the Republican party and the nation:

A series of disasters at the very beginning of our colonial policy would shake this administration, and therefore our party, and might produce the most serious and far-reaching effects upon the nation as a whole, for if some political cataclysm was the result, it might mean the definite abandonment of the cause upon which we have embarked – the only course I think fit for a really great nation.

Cuba needed a man in command, pronounced Roosevelt, "in whom we can absolutely trust and to whom we give the widest liberty of action." That man was Leonard Wood.

We need tact and judgment just as much as we need firmness in Cuba now. Wood is a born diplomat, just as he is a born soldier. . . . He has a peculiar faculty for getting on with the Spaniards and Cubans. They like him, trust him and down in their hearts are afraid of him. . . . He understands their needs, material and moral, and he also understands their sensitiveness and their spirit of punctilio. Finally, he is able, while showing them entire courtesy and thoughtful consideration, to impress upon them the fact that there can be no opposition when once he has made up his mind.

Though all the military governors performed meritoriously, Wood's exemplary work in Santiago de Cuba stood out in the minds of Cubans and Americans alike. General William Shafter, commanding the American troops in Cuba, considered Wood, along with General Henry Lawton, "the best man in the army at Santiago." By mid-September of 1898 Wood had cleaned up the filth in Santiago's streets and buildings; a month later he was appointed Commander of the Department of Eastern Cuba.

His method was to put Cubans to work cleaning and building roads, streets, bridges and docks, paying them first with rations and then with checks. Tons of refuse were burned and thousands of buildings cleansed by squads of workers fighting the dreaded yellow fever; in his crusade against filth and disease, Wood returned honest payment for honest labor. He canvassed the countryside, urging villagers to give what little they could to their municipality so he could provide them with a mayor, policeman, doctor

Wood demanded a court of inquiry and Brooke backed down. Wood won, but when he became Military Governor of Cuba, a central treasury allocated the insular revenues.

[48] Wood papers, Roosevelt to John Hay, July 1, 1899.

and some sanitation. He distributed supplies throughout the interior, made merchants keep prices down and encouraged farmers to resume cultivation, thereby reducing their dependence upon the Military Government. The accomplishments of Wood and his devoted assistants became legendary, helping to mollify those Cubans who threatened to "take to the woods." He solved the brigandry problem (and also prevented the danger of American troops firing upon Cubans) by forming the better Cuban soldiers into a rural guard and developing their *esprit de corps*. Wood also persuaded leading citizens to nominate Cubans for him to appoint, thereby developing their sense of responsibility and inducing more capable Cubans to assume office. Above all, Wood endeavored to enhance Cuban self-respect by giving the inhabitants of Oriente a bill of rights copied from the first ten amendments to the United States Constitution.[49]

There were objections that Wood was too young for the appointment as Military Governor. Fellow Army officers who resented his meteoric rise from a Captain in the medical corps to Colonel and then Brigadier General of Volunteers – a "medico" who was in diapers when they were in the trenches before Richmond – accused him of receiving unearned favors from Washington. They overlooked the fact that Wood had won the Medal of Honor for his role in catching Geronimo in one of the most physically demanding campaigns in history. He was a hero as a result of his leadership in the battles of Las Guasimas and San Juan Hill, as well as for his work in cleaning up Santiago de Cuba.[50]

To those who protested that Wood was too young, Roosevelt said,

If we are going to try to administer Cuba and conquer the Philippines on the seniority plan, we had better abandon the two jobs at once, and it is not possible to carry either through successfully on such terms. We have got to push up our best men, wholly without regard to seniority, just as they were pushed up in the Civil War.[51]

Certainly Roosevelt wanted his good friend to be military governor, but only because he believed Wood was the best man for a task vital to the Republican party and to the nation.

---

[49] Hagedorn, *Wood*, I, 184-260, *passim*. Wood papers, scrapbook 248, *New York Herald*, Dec. 24, 1899; *Chicago Inter-Ocean*, Dec. 31, 1899.

[50] Wood papers, scrapbook 249, *Atlanta Constitution*, June 28, 1899, where Wood was complimented for rejecting a $ 30,000 a year job in business. More than 40 articles from around the country praised him for staying in Cuba to perform "humane work." E. T. Brewster to Wood, June 26, 1899; Reverend John O. Foster to Wood, March 26, 1899, sources indicating a reform interest in Cuba.

[51] Wood papers, Roosevelt to Hay, July 1, 1899.

Wood was born October 9, 1860, at Winchester, New Hampshire, and raised at Pocasset on Buzzard's Bay, Massachusetts. His ancestors arrived in the New World on the *Mayflower,* served as freemen in Plymouth and later fought at Lexington and Bunker Hill. His father volunteered his services as a doctor in the Civil War. Many of the family attended Harvard; Wood matriculated at the medical school, practiced for a short time and then joined the army as a contract surgeon. After serving with distinction in the Apache campaigns of 1885-1886, Wood settled into the routine of post life in New Mexico, San Francisco, Atlanta and Washington, D. C., reading constantly and developing his military and medical proficiency. In 1890 he married Louise Condit-Smith, the ward of Supreme Court Justice Stephen Field; they eventually had three children.

When the war came, Roosevelt and Wood formed the 1st Massachusetts Volunteer Regiment of cavalry, popularly known as the "Rough Riders." As a result of their prowess in combat, Wood emerged as a strong leader, earning the onerous responsibilities of governing Santiago de Cuba and eventually the Island of Cuba. During his later career he served as military governor of the Moro Province, commanding general of the Philippines Division, commanding general of the Department of the East and Chief of Staff of the Army. One of the leaders of the Preparedness Movement of 1915-1917, Wood was passed over for political reasons and languished in the United States, training troops. As Roosevelt's political heir, he ran strongly for the Republican presidential nomination in 1920, but the Republican Senate leaders wanted a man they could control. Wood accepted appointment as civil governor of the Philippines, mostly because conditions there demanded reform but partly because his political aspirations were thwarted. During an able but stormy governorship, Wood died in 1927 while undergoing surgery for a brain tumor. For many of his generation, he was a hero who embodied the ideal of a stoic, active life that fulfilled beliefs. To others he was to be harnessed because of his ambition and power. During all his life, Wood aroused controversy wherever he happened to be.[52]

Root's decision to replace Brooke with Wood was expected, but few knew just how it came to pass. Wood's biographer, Hermann Hagedorn, thought Wood was appointed because he was the one general interviewed who did not tell Root how Cuba should be governed; he inquired how the

---

[52] Wood papers, Wood to Mrs. Wood, June 13, 1900, box 201 (genealogical materials); Hagedorn, *Wood,* I, Chapters 1-7, *passim*; E. E. Morison, *Turmoil and Tradition* (Boston, 1960), 152-53. Wood was 5' 10" tall, weighed 180 pounds, and a superb athlete.

President and Secretary of War wanted it governed. Moreover, Wood was a doctor and had imagination, needed assets in Cuba.[53]

There were murmurs that Wood was merely clever in agitating for the position, or that he used his influence in Washington. In addition to his close friendship with Roosevelt, he had once been Mrs. McKinley's physician. But Wood did not ask for the appointment, bring influence to bear upon Root, or intrigue in any way. They had met only once, briefly, at a public dinner. Root wrote that he interviewed both Ludlow and Wood, and

formed a high opinion of Ludlow but thought he was inferior to Wood in the quality of patience and imperturbability, so necessary to control and get on with the somewhat excitable and sensitive Cubans. Accordingly I recommended that Wood be made Military Governor. . . .[54]

As Root saw it, "There was not a dozen men in Cuba who believed that the United States was going to keep faith with them," and there was danger that the Cubans, believing they had merely exchanged Spanish tyranny for American, would begin another insurrection. In such a delicate situation, the only answer was "getting the best man that we could to do that most serious and difficult work . . . ." Root was satisfied that Wood was the best man and so informed McKinley. The President replied, "All right, go ahead." Wood received a major generalcy of Volunteers; Brooke moved to the Department of the East; Ludlow, Lee and Wilson were made Brigadiers in the regular line and eventually transferred.[55]

Leonard Wood knew he was making history. In a letter written to his wife just before landing at Daiquiri, Wood pictured transports upon a sea of indigo blue and said,

Hard it is to realize that this is the commencement of a new policy and that this is the first great expedition our country has ever sent oversea and marks the commencement of a new era in our relations with the world.[56]

After it was all over and he had emerged from Cuba with laurels, Wood told an audience at Williams College (where he received his second LL.D.) that his only instructions from President McKinley concerning the purpose of United States government in Cuba were to prepare Cuba for a republican form of government and leave the island as soon as possible. The President wanted "good schools and courts" and directed Wood to "get the Cubans

[53] Hagedorn, *Wood*, I, 259.
[54] Root papers, Root to Lawrence F. Abbott, Dec. 19, 1903; DIA 195-4, General Order 206, Dec. 13, 1899; *New York Times*, Nov. 24, 1899, showing Wood summoned to Washington, D.C.
[55] P. Jessup, *Elihu Root* (N.Y., 1938), I, 286-87.
[56] Wood papers, Wood to Mrs. Wood, June 15, 1898.

on their feet," but left the details to the General.[57] Thus, by December 1899, though the island remained divided and unstable, the appointments of Root and Wood augured well for the President's policy of legal and responsible trusteeship in Cuba.

[57] Wood papers, box 239, *Boston Evening Transcript*, July 12, 1902; Wood, "The Military Government of Cuba," *Annals of the American Academy of Political and Social Science*, XXI (March, 1903), 156-57.

CHAPTER II

THE ADMINISTRATION OF THE MILITARY GOVERNMENT OF CUBA

As Wood went to work in Cuba, Root reported to McKinley:

The rule of administration of the civil government of the island has been to employ the people of Cuba themselves to the fullest extent possible and to furnish to the Cubans, during our occupation, an opportunity for training in the honest and efficient performance of official duties which has never been afforded to them before.[1]

This broad principle set the tone of the military government of Cuba from 1899 to 1902. By the time the new century dawned, Root had crystallized a program built upon McKinley's Cuba policy: preparation for self-government through municipal elections, insular administration under American supervision, a constitutional convention to frame Cuba's government and determine Cuban-American relations, and American tariff reduction to give Cuba a market. Root reasoned that economic viability would ensure political stability.[2] Much of the timing and detail had to be worked out, but the policy was decided in the spring of 1898 and the program established in the fall of 1899. For the Military Government, 1900 was the year of introducing new procedures, 1901 the year of practicing them and 1902 the period of transferring control.

Disinterested administration was the Military Government's most valuable gift to Cuba. The methods and procedures of insular, provincial and municipal government indicated that Wood's administration, characterized by its vigor, boldness, effectiveness and personal control, fulfilled McKinley's injunction to "get the Cubans on their feet." An alternative would have been a longer, colonial administration similar to that of the Philippines. Immediate withdrawal from Cuba would have meant a quicker return, which the McKinley administration wished to avoid.

[1] U.S. Congress, House, *Report of the Secretary of War*, 56th Cong., 1st Sess., 1899, doc. 2, I, 16.
[2] *Ibid.*, 32-34.

American military officials took charge of a devastated island which had lost two-thirds of its wealth and 12 percent of its population, and left it a "going concern" with freely elected officials, 1.7 million dollars in the treasury, 256,000 children in a functioning public school system, disease-free cities, 300 post offices and road connections throughout the island.[3] Courts in twenty-one judicial districts disposed of case loads fairly and quickly, the number of prisoners was reduced by two-thirds, 3,000 schools were built, 3,600 teachers employed at high wages by 121 local boards of education. Eighty-two municipalities were put on a self-supporting basis, and by 1902 only schools, sanitary engineering work and thirty-nine hospitals were supported by the state. The University and *institutos* (high schools) were modernized. A railroad was built to connect the island's producers with means of transportation, and the Signal Corps rebuilt and expanded new cable and telephone connections over the island. Twelve orphan training schools, four vocational trade schools, six nursing schools, six homes for the aged poor, and one insane asylum were in operation where none had existed before. Yet Wood's policy was not to institutionalize the poor, the aged and the orphaned, for they were placed in jobs and with families as quickly as possible. One hundred ninety-four out of 207 sugar plantations were back in action, and thirty-eight new mines were located. Yellow fever was conquered. In all this the Cubans performed most of the actual work.[4]

Wood assumed command on December 20, and changed the atmosphere of Havana almost overnight.[5] Up at 5:30 in the morning and never in bed before midnight, he visited prisons, inspected hospitals, investigated courts and schools, viewed public works projects and directed his staff in a series of sweeping reforms, promulgated in civil orders. He checked his ordered courses of action by frequent inspections, usually traveling by boat, since sealanes were quicker than rural roads and jungle trails at the time. Wood moved ahead, imperturbable to critics, alarmists and men of little faith. He did not immediately tell the Cubans they were capable of self-government; he asked for teamwork so they might learn it. The General met with anyone who wished to see him: formal banquets with merchants and *alcaldes*, chats with *guajiros* (farmers) by the roadside and visits with the hospitalized persuaded Cubans that Wood cared.

Wood's exceptional perception and energy enabled him personally to

[3] *Census of Cuba, 1899,* 152-79; Wood, *Civil Report,* 1902, I, 270-1.

[4] U.S. Congress, House, *Report of the War Department, Secretary and Miscellaneous,* 57th Cong., 1st Sess., 1901-1902, doc. 2, no. 2, 36-53; Wood, "Military Government of Cuba," *Annals,* 153-182; Bureau of Insular Affairs, *The Establishment of Free Government in Cuba* (Wn: GPO, 1904).

[5] Wood papers, Wood to Root, Dec. 22, 1899, Hagedorn, *Wood,* I, 216, 278, 291.

direct and approve virtually every action taken. Inspired by his example, his loyal and capable aides rendered creative service far beyond the call of duty. Patient when the occasion demanded, Wood nevertheless preferred any course of action to inaction, willing to experiment until he found the action that worked. He sought advice and changed plans often in their preliminary stages but rarely wavered once he set out to execute a decision. A Cuban explained Wood's ways from the recipient's point of view:

From the standpoint of Washington, Cuba needed as its head a man more politically minded [than Brooke]; subtle and able to keep his subtleties concealed from the inquisitive eye; endowed with great force of character and personal integrity for the management of affairs, yet possessed of a political conscience reasonably elastic; capable, in the interests of his country, to support as just that which was expedient and, if need be, to favor might over right.[6]

Wood surrounded himself with able, diligent officers. His second in command was Colonel Hugh L. Scott, later Chief of Staff of the Army, a descendant of Benjamin Franklin. Scott helped to temper the ebullience of Lt. Frank R. McCoy, Wood's aide, and the drive of Wood.[7] All orders were promulgated through his office, and his enormous work load increased whenever Wood was away on a trip. Within the War Department, the Department of Cuba ranked third in size, behind the Departments at Washington, D. C. and Manila.[8]

In the main office of the Military Government at the palace reigned the chief clerk, Frank Steinhart. According to Colonel George H. Burton, the Inspector General of Cuba, Steinhart headed the most efficient and hard-working office in the army. He and twenty-four clerks did more work than twice their number performed in the United States. His ability to remain unruffled and reach the direct, frictionless solution, combined with an amazing memory and an accommodating spirit, stamped him as a man of uncommon talents. Steinhart was devoted to Wood and inspired by the work they were doing.

The military section of the office was composed of four clerks. The civil division had these departments: financial and statistical, correspondence, records, translation, order and mail. Scott and Steinhart handled all items for distribution and decision; this office was the center for all business of the

---

[6] Hagedorn, *Wood*, I, 306-307, quoting R. Martínez Ortiz. Brackets mine. Wood could read, write and speak Spanish. Many of the Cuban and American officials were bilingual. Orders were published in both languages. The Military Government employed interpreters and translators.

[7] H. L. Scott papers, Scott to Mrs. Scott, June 25, 1900.

[8] Scott papers, Scott to Mrs. Scott, July 7, 1900, May 7, 1900, Feb. 12, 1900, April 30, 1900.

Military Government. The clerks, mostly Cubans, were paid well, worked hard and were loyal to Steinhart, who was more than a great clerk. He was one of the few who could successfully stand up to Wood, and occasionally he saved his chief from some indiscretion.[9]

It gradually became clear to McKinley's cabinet that a decision must be reached about channeling colonial matters. The first problem to arise after the war was that of customs, because foreign ships immediately began to seek entry to Cuban ports. At first the Department of State handled these matters, but because of Army occupation many inquiries came to the War Department. A clerk was designated to answer and file these inquiries according to the directions of the Assistant Secretary of War, who began to devote part of his time to such affairs. Then, on December 13, 1898, the Division of Customs and Insular Affairs was created in the War Department by executive order. On December 10, 1900, this office dropped the word "Customs" from its title and Puerto Rico from its cognizance, because that island received a civil government. Elihu Root's creation, the Division of Insular Affairs was defined as:

> that branch of the office of the Secretary of War to which are referred all matters pertaining to the civil affairs connected with the governments of Cuba and the Philippine Islands as distinguished from a purely military character.[10]

By 1901 the DIA had blossomed to eight branches and fifty-two clerks. During most of the period from 1898 to 1902, the DIA was headed by Colonel Clarence R. Edwards, a self-confident infantry officer who reported directly to Root in the chain of command and was of tireless assistance to Root and Wood. The DIA prepared trade and population statistics, developed legal opinions, maintained a colonial library, issued publications and

---

[9] U.S. National Archives. Social and Economic Branch, Interior Division, Record Group 140: "The Military Government of Cuba," Civil Division, Department of Cuba file 3854 of Oct. 8, 1901, Report of Col. G. H. Burton on inspection of office of chief clerk. Hereafter cited as CDDC, file no., date, correspondents. The Records of the Military Government of Cuba were shipped to Washington, D.C., in 1903 by Frank Steinhart and stored in a warehouse. In 1913, by Congressional order, for the purpose of saving space, most of the records were destroyed. Those that remain are chiefly the accounts, vouchers, warrants of the finances. The Record Group is valuable also for the large number of letters and other material on administration of the Military Government.

[10] U.S. Congress, House, *Report of the Secretary of War*, 57th Cong., 1st Sess., 1901, doc. 2, "Report of the Division of Insular Affairs," 741-773; H. D. McInnis, "The Bureau of Insular Affairs: an Administrative History," May 20, 1940, in Record Group 350, National Archives, Dept. of Interior. For a helpful survey, see E. S. Pomeroy, "The American Colonial Office," *Mississippi Valley Historical Review*, XXX (March, 1944), 521-532. In May 1902 the DIA became the Bureau of Insular Affairs and cared for Philippine matters until 1939, when it was abolished as the islands passed under the aegis of the Department of the Interior.

records of all types, acted as a comptroller's check of the insular audit, ordered supplies and personnel for Cuba, and developed special reports demanded by Congress.[11] The Adjutant General of the Army, Major General Henry C. Corbin, was an able and efficient officer whose great experience aided the Cuban administration.

The day after he assumed command, Wood met with a group of Cuban leaders in Havana to ask for their cooperation in the march toward independence.[12] Skeptics were mollified by his announcement of joint commissions to frame laws for criminal procedure, taxation, public education and elections. Wood appointed civil officials on the recommendation of a representative group of Cubans, a method designed to develop their sense of responsibility while retaining the privilege of rejecting a nomination or releasing an incumbent. By December 30, Wood named a new cabinet of six instead of four portfolios,[13] and cut each secretary's salary from $ 7,000 to $ 6,000 per year. The new men differed in their backgrounds, but all were responsible revolutionaries.

José Ramón Villalón was named Secretary of Public Works. An American-educated engineer and a war veteran, Villalón was received by Cuban and American engineers as capable, energetic and trustworthy. Diego Tamayo y Tejera assumed the post of Secretary of State and Government. Former president of the Academy of Science and one time autonomist, Tamayo had become a revolutionary in 1895. Enrique José Varona agreed to the post of Secretary of Finance, or *Hacienda*. Luis Estévez y Romero was named Secretary of Justice on the basis of his prominence in legal circles and financial aid to the revolution. Juan Ríus Rivera, an outsproken Cuban general, became Secretary of Agriculture, Industry and Commerce. Juan Batista Hernández y Barreiro, Dean of the legal faculty of the University of Havana, accepted the office of Secretary of Public Education. These men were given complete responsibility and authority in their departments, and the appointments were well received by the Cubans.

Civil Order 29 of January 19, 1900 set forth Wood's managerial policy.[14] Office hours for all hands were to be from nine to eleven in the morning and twelve to five o'clock in the afternoon, Monday through Saturday. The era

[11] *Report of the DIA*, 1901.

[12] Wood papers, Wood to Estrada Palma, Wood to Masó, both telegrams of Dec. 21, 1899; Wood to Root, Dec. 30, 1899, which indicates Wood was taking initiative yet keeping his chief informed; Hagedorn, *Wood*, I, 266.

[13] Wood papers, Wood to Root, Dec. 30, 1899. The offices of Secretary of Justice and Public Instruction, Public Works and Agriculture were split. DIA 195-8, Civil Order 1 of Jan. 1, 1900.

[14] Wood, *Civil Report*, 1900, II. The volume is comprised of civil orders numbered chronologically.

of the three-hour work day vanished. Wood operated around-the-clock shifts in his own office, with Frank Steinhart in charge. After February 1, all correspondence between civilian officials and the Military Government was to go through civil channels. Departmental secretaries and civil officials were charged with the conduct of civil affairs, under the Military Governor's supervision. Wood relied on the United States Army for certain essential duties: Department commanders maintained public order, sanitation, public works of sanitary nature and the rural guard. They inspected, at least monthly, all prisons, hospitals and public institutions in their districts and reported the results to Wood. Schools received quarterly inspections.

Any impairments of the function of the Military Government, such as abuse of authority or neglect of duty, were also to be reported. Interventions of military officers in civil afairs were to demonstrate to the people that complaints of malfeasance would be promptly and thoroughly investigated. Military officiers, however, were to follow Wood's policy of restraint by not interfering with civil authorities except under conditions threatening life, property or public order. Suspension of a civil official could be exercised only in cases of extreme gravity – even then, only when waiting for reply from the Military Governor might incur dangerous delay.

Military officers were to interfere with the press only to prevent continued publication of matter provoking a major disturbance of the public peace or of such obscenity as to subvert public morals. Allowable action consisted of suspension of a paper pending decision by judicial authorities and had to be reported by cable and letter to Wood. Usually the General ignored the Cuban press for he realized that some newsmen sought attention. A few Cuban newsmen boasted to the Governor that they were not afraid to practice abusive journalism because they knew he would be fair with them.[15]

Thirteen hundred rural guards were hand picked and developed into a high state of efficiency, spirit and discipline. While municipal policemen were under municipal authority, the Rural Guard was under control of the Military Governor. *Rurales* were charged with keeping the public peace and were available to judges and civil governors for apprehending suspects, transporting convicts and other law enforcement measures. The state paid for arms and ammunition, but the *Rurale* provided the rest of his own equipment. On practice marches by American detachments, *Rurales* served as guides; and they trained with regulars to let other Cubans see that they could work in harmony with the United States troops.[16]

[15] Wood papers, Wood to Root, Feb. 6, 1900.
[16] U.S. Congress, House, *Reports of the War Department*, 56th Cong., 2d Sess.,

Realizing that the presence of too many troops tended to increase suspicion of American motives, Wood cut the number of army personnel in Cuba. A few detachments sufficed to symbolize United States strength and solidarity, and to signify law and order to Cubans.[17] They did no police work at any time, and all disturbances were settled by *Rurales* or by the mediation of an Army officer. Actually, Wood needed more junior officers and longer tours of duty for surviving officers who had gained experience in Cuba, for continual combat against yellow fever had taken its toll of lives and health. Yet because of Wood's efficiency with few men, by July 1900 the four military departments had been consolidated into those of East and West, and three months later Cuba's administrative status changed to that of a single department. Thus Wood shaped the military establishment into a finely tuned instrument for the purpose of supporting the civil government.

In the month of January, 1900, forty-eight civil orders were promulgated, dealing with appointments, schools, procedures and pardons. Early in February Wood's report to Root, made after a two-week trip through the middle and eastern parts of the island, noted a steady improvement in economic conditions.[18] Many patches of earth were under cultivation, some sugar mills were grinding and there was practically no hunger. Wood estimated that "eight out of ten" Cubans approved of the work being performed under the auspices of the Military Government. Many inhabitants, both conservative and radical, urged Wood to move slowly in establishing Cuban self-government. Still Wood contended:

The time has now come to gradually transfer the conduct of civil affairs to the civil authorities, retaining whatever degree of supervision may be necessary. Under the system existing until recently no real advance towards a government of the people and by the people had been made. We have got to trust them with the handling of affairs under our supervision and in this way teach them.[19]

1900, doc. 2, II, 4; *Reports of the War Department*, 1901, II, doc. 2, 36 ff.; Wood, *Civil Report*: 1900, I, 77, 1902, III, Slocum Report.

[17] *Reports of the War Department*, 1900, II, doc. 2, 4; *Reports of the War Department*, 1901-1902, II, doc. 2, 9. This process also involved the transfer of Generals Ludlow, Wilson and Chaffee, who resented Wood.

[18] Wood papers, Wood to Root, Jan. 13, 1900, Feb. 6, 1900.

[19] *Ibid*. Wood also described prison and hospital conditions that the Americans had to improve:

In the women's prison we found neither beds nor bedding, all the attendants men, the food cooked in an institution quite a distance away. The women had not clothing enough to appear before the Board and had to exchange with each other before they could present themselves. One woman who had been in confinement seven or eight years had a child three years old. ... The *Beneficencia* of between 700 and 800 children would have made you sick to go through it. The beds were immaculate on

The financial organization consisted of separate offices with complementary duties, checked by an independent auditor answerable only to the Military Governor.[20] The customs service was the first unit of government assumed by the United States after the initial relief and pacification measures. A United States Army officer served as collector of customs at each port of entry, but 97 percent of the clerks were Cuban. In May 1899 the Treasury office was removed from the Customs service and established as a separate office. The Treasurer of the Island of Cuba was an American Army officer who actually handled the money, receiving it from internal and external duties and disbursing it through district offices. At the same time the Auditor's office was split from the Treasury to provide the penultimate check upon disbursing and accounting by a separate office. The Department of Finance, chiefly concerned with the general apparatus of tax and revenue administration and headed by a Cuban, collected internal revenue for the Treasury and trained the municipalities in fiscal affairs.

Wood's aide, Lieutenant Frank R. McCoy, collated budgets with income to frame estimates for the overall operation of the Military Government. Under McCoy's system, he received semiweekly statements from the Auditor and Treasurer of the balances on hand and warrants outstanding. McCoy compared balances with warrants and warrants with allotments, and required close, detailed estimates of expenditure from the field. *Alcaldes* had to account for expenditures bimonthly, as did supervisors of public works projects, hospitals and schools. Brooke's method of bloc appropriations to Departments was replaced by departmental requisitioning and paying for individual projects by check. Wood came to rely on McCoy in this field, but inspected him closely on every point and amazed his aide with vast detailed knowledge of the facts and figures of various projects. The General was taking no chances of leaving an opening for criticism of his financial methods.[21]

In May 1900, Leopoldo Cancio replaced Varona as Secretary of Finance, while Varona became Secretary of Instruction.[22] Cancio, a hardworking, serious minded man, organized his departments to provide the supervision, consultation, collection and statistical services required. The *Hacienda's* main function was supervision of the accounts of municipalities; since municipal budgets were required to conform to revenues, the *Hacienda* was forced to

top, but when uncovered were indescribable, containing everything from excrement to pus.
[20] Wood, Civil Report, 1900, I, 5-9, 96; III, Tamayo Report; V, Cancio Report.
[21] Wood, *Civil Report*, 1900, I, 96; McCoy Report, I, 3-9; McCoy Report, 1901, I, 4.
[22] Cancio Report, 1900, V, 4-8.

approve budgets in advance. Other duties were to collect internal revenue, enforce tax laws, pay government employees, care for public buildings and collect rent on government property. Cancio was outspoken in requesting that the Finance Department control the Treasurer, Auditor and Customs Chief. However, Wood maintained the Treasury and Customs separate for a year and two years longer, respectively; the Auditor was not merged until 1902.

Funds were allotted through civilian and military offices. The Department of Finance had the responsibility of allotting funds for civil administration, and the military disbursing officers for the major expenditures of public works and operation of transportation and charitable institutions. All moneys received at Havana were paid over to the Treasurer and deposited by him in the Treasury, to be paid out on warrants signed and countersigned. Moneys received at other points were transmitted in specie to the Treasurer at Havana or deposited to the credit of disbursing officers in authorized depositories. At first the North American Trust Company acted as agent; later the *Banco Nacional* assumed this function. The depository gave securities in the amount equal to the maximum deposits of island funds which it was allowed to hold.[23]

Income to the insular coffers came from four sources: customs, internal taxation, post office and miscellaneous.[24] Of these, the customs revenues were by far the most important, composing over 93 percent of the revenues.

The standard of currency was the United States dollar, which provided a soundness that the previous reliance upon fluctuating values in Spanish and French coins did not. Banks were scarce in Cuba at this time. The former *Banco Español* served chiefly as a subtreasury for the Spanish government, and a few banks acted as an exchange and credit agency for private business.

[23] *Ibid.*, II, Civil Order 127 of March 26, 1900, circular of April 6, 1900. Civil orders hereafter cited as C.O., number, date. These banks were American controlled as was the Bank of Habana.

[24] BIA, *Establishment of Free Government in Cuba*. From January 1899 to May 20, 1902, the Military Government received $ 57,197,140.80 and spent $ 55,405,031.28. While the Military Government derived about 17 million dollars annually, the former Spanish government budgeted 26 million dollars annually, deriving $ 14,705,000 from customs, $ 1,900,500 from lotteries, $ 7,783,000 from internal revenue, with miscellaneous and state revenues making up the balance. Ten million dollars of this revenue went directly to Spain to help pay off the debt Spain saddled on Cuba. Over nine million dollars went to the "Executive" and the army and navy. $ 733,000 went to colonial legislature, churches, justice. Charities received $ 1,612,000; the Treasury operation received $ 708,978; public administration, $ 247,033, public works and communications, $ 1,036,582; agriculture, industry, commerce $ 108,178. All of the latter allocations were chiefly for salaries. See Porter, *Industrial Cuba*, 248, 256-63. Over one-third of these revenues were never raised and little of the money was ever actually used for the allocations. See Porter, *Report on the Commercial and Industrial Condition of Cuba* (Wn: GPO, 1898), 33.

The Cubans were reluctant to adopt a paper system because they had trusted only hard money under the Spanish governors.[25]

The tariff was designed to afford the lowest possible rates on all commodities consistent with sufficient revenue to meet government expenditures. An average reduction of 62 percent below the former Spanish tariff, coupled with an honest and efficient customs service encouraged productivity and importation. Revenues went into the development of Cuba rather than to Spain, the United States, or into the capacious pockets of officials.[26]

To stimulate production, the Military Government greatly reduced taxes of internal nature: these supplied only $ 650,000 to $ 880,000 of an annual insular revenue of over $ 17,000,000. Internal taxes were levied upon conveyances, inheritances, products of rented state properties, various products and licenses. Wood knew that new tax laws were needed. He repeatedly stated that the existing system paralyzed those who produced and favored those who did not; unused or unimproved land was not taxed, while production items were. The main reason he did not tax this unused property, even though he had the power and the desire to do so, was that the Cuban commissions on taxation and undivided property recommended against it. Also, many land titles were not clear, and it would have taken a long time to clear them. The Cuban commissions wanted to leave the ownership and demarcation of rural property to private litigation in the courts, rather than have the government make any sweeping changes. Cuban property holders called any proposal for much-needed reform too involved and volatile an issue to be settled at that time, and Wood refrained from pushing the matter; with so many changes going on and new procedures to be learned, additional major modifications would have created an unmanageable situation.[27]

However, regulations were issued for the formation of assessment records that later served as the basis for direct taxation of real estate.[28] Municipalities were charged with keeping records of urban and rural property. Boards of five councilmen and four rural and three urban taxpayers were formed to collect data for registry of estates, maintain registers, verify and propose saleable and income value of estates, establish average prices of products and draw up assessments. Fiscal zone boards, which were convened to supervise

[25] Wood, *Civil Report*, 1900, I, McCoy Report, 9-10; 1900, V, Cancio Report; 1900, I, 6; U.S. Congress, House, *Report of the Secretary of War*, 57th Cong., 1st Sess., 1901, doc. 2, Appendix I, 315; Porter, *Report on the Commercial & Industrial Condition of Cuba*, 8-9.

[26] Porter, *Report on Condition of Cuba*, 5, 17, 21.

[27] Wood, *Civil Report*, 1900, 93-95; Cancio Report, 1900, V, 11, 28, table I; C.O. 62 of March 5, 1902; Wood papers, Wood to Root, Nov. 4, 1901.

[28] Wood, *Civil Report*, C.O. 335 of Sept. 4, 1900.

and assist in evaluation of cases, were composed of fourteen rural and urban taxpayers, an engineer, agricultural expert and *instituto* (high school) director. Over these boards, supervising and hearing appeals, was the *Hacienda.*[29]

Real property in Cuba was subject to codified statutes dating from the Spanish era. There were 25 to 30 registry districts in Cuba, each with one Registry of Property in which all deeds, mortgages and leases of over six years duration were recorded. Each municipality in the district employed a Registrar who was bonded, a qualified lawyer and a graded civil servant. This official registered deeds, filed the records in appropriate volumes and rendered decisions on claims and documents. The new lists for assessment of real and rural property and the procedures for determining ownership of property held in common were not completed during the tenure of the Military Government.[30]

The Auditor of the Island was responsible for receiving, examining and settling all accounts pertaining to the revenues. The Treasurer rendered a monthly account of receipts and expenditures to the Auditor, with a monthly report to the Secretary of War and a certified true copy to the Military Governor. The Auditor accounted for moneys received and expended, certifying the balance to the Military Governor and preserving the accounts and vouchers. The Military Governor was responsible for a quarterly examination of the books and accounts of both Auditor and Treasurer. By approving all requisitions and signing all warrants, Wood maintained close control over finances.[31]

With the financial apparatus of the Military Government well-organized and closely supervised, the basic industries of the island began to produce again, and a new department was established to coordinate reports and collect statistical data. In May 1900 Perfecto Lacoste replaced Juan Ríus Rivera as Secretary of Agriculture, Commerce and Industry.[32] (Ríus Rivera had resigned after a heartfelt but indiscreet speech calling for immediate American evacuation of the island.) Lacoste was born a Frenchman, claimed United States citizenship and owned extensive agricultural interests in Cuba. While he desired Cuban annexation to the United States, Lacoste was particularly critical of General Wood's refusal to subsidize agriculture. Lacoste recommended a five point program: immigration to increase the labor force, agricultural banks to ease credit, reciprocity with the United States,

[29] *Ibid.,* C.O. 270 of July 5, 1900, C.O. 463 of Nov. 13, 1900.

[30] Wood, *Civil Report,* 1900, I, 93-94; 1901, II, C.O. 139 of May 27, 1901; *Cuba Review,* III, no. 4 (March, 1905); Wood, *Civil Report,* 1902, C.O. 62 in III, Cancio Report, 7.

[31] Wood, *Civil Report,* 1901, II, C.O. 79 of March 22, 1901.

[32] Wood, *Civil Report,* 1900, II, C.O. 183 of May 1, 1900.

reduction in Cuban export duties, and agricultural stations. Cuba's main source of wealth was agriculture, and Lacoste wished to encourage its development as much as possible.[33]

The Department of Agriculture, Commerce and Industry was primarily a data-collecting agency. Most of its information concerned agriculture; Lacoste affirmed that little industry existed beyond the raising of sugar and tobacco. He reiterated the prevalent argument of the day — Cuba had great resources of undeveloped wealth — and advocated the influx of capital and labor. The Military Government did little directly to aid the Cuban farmer beyond providing some tools for the destitute and a chance to buy cattle cheaply. Wood stimulated the farmer's pride and relied upon his initiative. The General knew that the rich soil easily yielded crops. An office force of forty-five clerks in six bureaus issued licenses, supervised the patent, forestry, mining and fishing laws, and issued statistics on land use, mortgages, prices, exports, imports and production. During the tenure of the Military Government the Department of Agriculture, Commerce and Industries advanced from infancy to an agency of ever increasing service to Cuba.

In general, the Secretary of State and Government supervised municipal and provincial administration and foreign affairs, such as consular or extradition cases. Diego Tamayo managed three sections, composed of some seventeen bureaus manned by fifty clerks, that handled the functions of compilation and correspondence dealing with vital statistics, elections, prisoner disposition, passports and even regulation of bullfights. In addition to the important business of maintaining accurate public records, the most onerous task of Tamayo's department was the supervision of municipal government and elections.[34]

Provincial government was an arm of the insular government. The civil governor of a province, appointed by the Military Governor, was responsible for overseeing the affairs of his province; through these governors Wood exercised civil control over the municipalities. There were six provinces in Cuba: Pinar del Río, Havana, Matanzas, Santa Clara (Las Villas), Puerto Príncipe (Camagüey) and Santiago (Oriente). Within there provinces were municipalities, more like countries than single towns. The civil governor's staff corresponded to the Military Governor's cabinet and administered the political, legal, educational, sanitary, agricultural and commercial affairs of the province. The provincial governor approved municipal budgets,

[33] Ibid., I, 89-92; VII, Lacoste Report, 4-14. Wood also wanted agricultural banks but the matter was not completed.
[34] Ibid., I, 5-9; III, Tamayo Report.

granted mining and timber permits, authorized public works of a general character, scheduled public meetings and kept order in the province.[35]

The municipalities, in debt and poorly administered, were a source of concern. Wood remarked that the only men who would take office were men from the Army of Liberation, who were perhaps capable field soldiers but who were ill-fitted to discharge the duties of rebuilding a shattered locality. Wood found too many policemen and a "tendency to an abnormally large personnel and entirely disproportionate outlay for official salaries in comparison with expenditure for public improvements." [36] The municipalities were an old Cuban institution, but never before had they performed such duties as taxation, revenue accounting, school planning and management, and administration of elections. As a result, their staffs expanded. Nevertheless, the state often had to finish jobs normally expected of the municipalities, such as unloading and setting up shipments of school equipment.

After an initial six months of close support, Wood tried to develop self-reliance in the municipalities by directing them to pay the salaries of their own officials, cost of police force and some street maintenance. They were unable to pay for more services and wanted to pay for less. Wood received many petitions requesting that he remove from the municipalities those local taxes which would make them solvent and thus independent. Although Wood understood that this dependency resulted from colonial habits and the war, he believed that the prime requisite for the effective performance of municipalities was increased public spirit which would demand efficient conduct from officials. Gradually Wood reduced insular aid and allowed more local authority (supervised by increased inspections). By the spring of 1902, municipalities were directed to pay for their sanitation and charities, police and fire protection, management of municipal property, public lighting, road and building repair, salaries of officials, and water supplies. The Military Government paid for schools, public works and hospitals.[37] Wood hoped the Cubans would learn self-government by practicing it.

The original 132 municipalities were reduced to eighty-two due to lack of population and resources. These municipalities were subdivided administratively into subdistricts, which were in turn broken down into *barrios* (wards); the Military Government divided *barrios* into electoral districts and sections. *Alcaldes* headed the municipal government and were charged with employment, keeping the peace, representing municipal interests to provincial and

[35] *Ibid.*, I, 8; *Census of Cuba, 1899*, 51.

[36] Wood, *Civil Report*, 1900, I, 3-13, McCoy Report, 9.

[37] *Census of Cuba, 1899*, 46; Wood, *Civil Report*, 1900, I, 13-14, McCoy Report, 10; Wood, *Civil Report*, 1902, II, C.O. 112.

insular officials, accounting for funds and ministering to the needs of the people. An *alcalde* usually was assisted by an assistant mayor and sometimes by *alcaldes de barrio*. Each municipality also had an *ayuntamiento*, or council, of five to thirty members, depending upon population. Mayor and councilmen were appointed until June 1900 and after the date were elected.[38]

The chain of command ran from the Military Governor through the departments to provinces and municipalities. Wood frequently contacted the municipality directly, especially in matters of public works, education, sanitation and charities; even these matters, however, were usually channelled through the Chief of Staff, an aide, or the secretary of the appropriate department. The Military Government occasionally took more acute problems out of the hands of civil government, but this was rare. Restraint was the rule of the Military Government.

In his relations with the War Department, Wood endeavored successfully to receive orders solely from the Adjutant General in Root's name and to retain complete authority over all American governmental agencies in the island. Wood was unwilling to abide by contrary instructions from Assistant Secretary of War G. D. Meikeljohn, whom he considered ignorant of Cuban conditions, and he also attempted to gain control of both the Marine Hospital (Quarantine) Service and the Department of Posts.[39] This insistence centered responsibility and authority on him. In Washington, Root set the policy and allowed Wood to work it out; the secretary specifically refrained from directing action at a distance. He received Wood's loyalty in return. Among McKinley, Roosevelt, Root and Wood, an aura of confidence facilitated the conduct of Cuban affairs.

Wood's desire for control over all United States agencies in Cuba was justified in the spring of 1900 when his chief inspector, Colonel George H. Burton, found discrepancies in the Department of Posts records. Eventually this led to the greatest scandal of the American occupation. Estes G. Rathbone, the Director General of Posts, and C. F. W. Neely, one of his deputies, were tried and convicted by the Cuban Supreme Court for defrauding the government of some $ 300,000. The case was complicated by opposition from the powerful Senator Mark Hanna of Ohio, indebted to Rathbone for past services. Wood and Root, backed by McKinley, ignored such political opposition in the United States; in Root's words, they "scraped to the bone"

[38] *Ibid.*

[39] DIA 765-15, Wood to Agwar, June 20, 1900, C.O. 292 of July 17, 1900; Wood papers, Root to Wood, March 24, 1900; Wood to Root, March 28, 1900; Wood to Root, April 26, 1900; Wood to Root, May 12, 1900; Wood to Root, June 3, 1900; Wood to Root, June 8, 1900.

to solve the case, no matter who might be hurt. McKinley, more pained by this scandal than by any other occurrence during his administration and humiliated by American betrayal of Cuban trust, ordered J. L. Bristow, Fourth Assistant Postmaster, to investigate: "Do no one an injustice but shield nobody who had committed a wrong. I want every offender properly punished. As for complaints against you, do your duty and leave that to me." Root maintained that the only alleviation of the disgrace was Wood's vigorous investigation and prosecution; of course his prompt action was a relief to Republican party leaders.[40] It was fortunate for Cuban-American relations that Wood detected and corrected the neglect in Rathbone's department at an early stage and insisted that the matter be settled in Cuban courts.

Wood was intermittently embroiled in controversies such as the "Runcie affair." James E. Runcie, a San Francisco lawyer and former Army officer, was devoted to Wood because the latter had three times saved his life in delicate brain surgery. Runcie volunteered to aid Wood in Santiago without pay. In Havana he performed extremely valuable work on the various commissions established to write legal, tax and electoral codes in January and February of 1900. Knowing his chief's disgust with Brooke's passive policy, Runcie wrote an article for the *North American Review*, which severely criticized Brooke's administration, and caused an uproar. Wood accused the magazine of abusing Runcie's confidence by using his name, but he dropped his support of Runcie when Ray Stannard Baker and George Harvey of the *Review* and Oswald Garrison Villard of the *New York Evening Post* informed him Runcie had given permission to use his name if they believed it necessary. Runcie's misguided attempt to be of help broke his friendship with Wood, and Runcie resigned, remaining in Cuba as one of Wood's active opponents. Root considered Wood indiscreet but supported the General and did not press the issue. Wood was not so clumsy as to allow such an article to be written and published; he simply did not know about it until after it emerged in print.[41]

Another controversy arose over the claims of Michael J. Dady and Company to the rights of installing sewers and paving Havana's streets. Dady, a Brooklyn Irishman with high political connections, claimed that the Spanish law give him the right of *tanteo*, a first choice on the project, because of his proposals offered before the war. Like the Rathbone matter, the Dady case

[40] Wood papers, telegrams, Wood to Root, May 7, 1900; Wood to Root, May 12, 1900; Wood to Root, May 23, 1900; Root to Wood, June 2, 1900; J. L. Bristow, *Fraud and Politics at the Turn of the Century* (N.Y. 1952), 100.

[41] J. Runcie, "American Misgovernment of Cuba," *North American Review*, CLXX (Feb. 1900), 283-294. Box 28 of the Wood papers, letters between Wood, Root, McKinley, Brooke, Runcie, Villard, R. S. Baker, and Harvey.

dragged on throughout Wood's administration. Wood and his engineers were convinced that Dady's estimate was far too high and his plans insufficient. Between Wood's orders and Dady's bribes the Havana city fathers veered wildly. Finally Wood directed that Dady be paid $ 250,000 to settle his claim and that new bids be requested on the contract. Havana never received a new sewage system during the years of the Military Government. Wood allowed the city council time to reach its own decision, yet he prevented an American from foisting off a lucrative but unsound deal upon the Cubans.[42] He believed the reputation of the administration was at stake and preserved it, at the cost of not finishing a project which could have been achieved under purely American auspices during the tenure of the Military Government.

Cuban ineptitude and American schemers were a constant source of worry to Wood. He too was accused of being involved in deals, but not even the most enterprising agents of his adversaries could find a shred of incriminating evidence. When Wood came up for promotion to Major General in 1902, Rathbone and Hanna charged that he interfered with the courts and accepted gifts from the Havana Jai-Alai Company. Wood's interference had been directed by Root and was strictly administrative, not legal; he made sure cases were brought to trial but did not influence their outcome. Wood did accept a silver service, a gift offered at a public breakfast upon his departure from the island.[43] Wood was more strict with himself than with subordinates. The point is not that Wood was a saint or a hypocrite, but that he possessed a remarkable combination of discretion and integrity.

The church property settlement presented another difficult piece of work. Wood reached an agreement with the Bishop of Havana that rent would be paid for church properties at 5 percent of their approved value of $ 2,000,000 with a five-year option to buy.[44] The state bought the church-held *censos,* or mortgages, and allowed debtors to redeem them at fifty cents on the dollar.

[42] Wood papers, Wood to Root, Jan. 4, 1901; Wood to Root, Feb. 19, 1901; Wood to Root, April 10, 1900; Wood to Mayor of Havana, Jan. 28, 1901; L. E. Quigg to Root, Jan. 17, 1901; Wood to Root, Dec. 19, 1900; Wood to Root, Sept. 26, 1900; Root papers, Wood to Root, May 18, 1900; Hagedorn, *Wood,* I, 279; Jessup, *Root,* I, 292.

[43] Wood papers, McCoy to Wood, March 22, 1902; DIA 2205-68, Rathbone to Root, March 19, 1903, DIA 2205-71, 72, Root to Roosevelt, n.d.; Wood papers, Wood to Root, June 12, 1900. Box 203 of the Wood papers also contains a receipt to Wood from Fred K. J. Davies, dated March 13, 1901, which suggests that Wood and Davies, a transient, capable, English engineer, may have bought 300 acres on the Isle of Pines. This does not prove Wood was a land speculator, for he may have loaned Davies the money for some other purpose. It may also have been a device for transacting some business matter of the Military Government. If Wood had been culpable, his Democratic enemies and personal foes would have ferreted out the evidence.

[44] See D. Lockmiller, "The Settlement of the Church Property Question in Cuba," *Hispanic American Historical Review,* XVII (Nov. 1937), 488-98.

All this amounted to one-third of the church claim. Both sides were content; however, the Americans were more friendly to the Church than the Cubans and the Cuban government. The general effect was to lift a real and psychological burden from Church, state and debtor. The General believed in the separation of church and state, for the good of each. Personally, he accepted and supported the organized forms of Christianity.[45] As an administrator, he desired to resolve the problem and did so.

Wood also dominated relations with labor organizations. If his usual method of allowing labor and management to negotiate a point of issue failed, he sent an Army officer to help the parties reconcile their differences. This usually worked. If there was violence on a plantation by labor organizers, the *Rurales* arrested them. If Havana's health or food supply were endangered, Wood ordered the strike leaders to his office and told them to return to work or the Military Government would operate the city's means of transport and supply. Neither Wood nor Ludlow was sympathetic to labor unions, but their decisions show that conditions were bettered and wages raised as often as strikers were jailed or dispersed. Wood wanted the work of rejuvenating Cuba to proceed without interference and ensured that it did.[46]

Orville H. Platt once said to Henry Cabot Lodge that Wood was the perfect example of the iron fist in the velvet glove. He was firm and patient with a people accustomed to subordination, yet in revolt against such a status. The United States administration made no real cultural changes in Cuba. The Americans cleaned and modernized the island, showing the Cubans how an honest, economical government operated and how free elections should work. Although Wood's government was centralized and he was answerable only to Root, the aim was local and insular self-government; he let the Cubans practice while he supervised. To Wood and Root there was nothing paradoxical in teaching democracy authoritatively; conditions demanded it.[47]

[45] Wood papers, Wood to Root, June 10, 1901; *Report of the Secretary of War*, 1901, 41; Hagedorn, *Wood*, II, 76.

[46] CDDC 223, Jan. 19, 1901; CDDC 18, April 10, 1901, March 15, 1901; Wood papers, subject file 254, *Chicago Inter-Ocean*, Feb. 28, 1900; Hagedorn, *Wood*, I, 306, II, 334-36. In 1919 Wood earned publicity by keeping the peace during strikes in Gary, Indiana, Omaha and West Virginia, actions that helped boost his candidacy for the Republican presidential nomination because he appeared dependable.

[47] See Herminio Portell Vilá, *Historia de Cuba en sus relaciones con los Estados Unidos y España* (La Habana, 1941), IV, 164, 94, 102, 109-110. Portell argues that Wood's methods failed to teach democracy to the Cubans; instead, he demoralized them.

CHAPTER III

THE LEGAL AND EDUCATIONAL SYSTEMS

With physical rebuilding and administrative organization started, Wood and Root began the revision of the legal and educational systems. Both men believed that a fair system of justice and a literate public were indispensable to a free republic. A disproportionate amount of attention centered on the departments of justice and education, because Leonard Wood knew he had to meet the future halfway by training Cubans to manage their own affairs.

Early in 1900 Wood declared that the corrupt legal system was Cuba's most immediate problem.

It can be safely asserted that no department of insular administration was more in need of thorough and radical reform, rigid inspection and constant supervision than this department, [Justice] which was lacking in efficiency, energy and attention to duty. . . .[1]

Judges ignored the long and unnecessary detention of prisoners awaiting trial and "occupied themselves in a leisurely manner for a few hours each day in a feeble attempt to dispose of the enormous volume of business awaiting their attention." Naturally enough, Cubans had little confidence in courts hampered by a procedure so cumbersome that prompt administration of justice was impossible. A man could be incarcerated in numerous ways with a minimum of evidence; in fact, many prisoners awaiting trial were confined for a period longer than the possible sentence. Wood pointed out:

This was especially lamentable when it is remembered that the prisoners were mostly Cubans and the judiciary entirely so, and it indicated a neglect and indifference to the responsibilities of their positions painful to contemplate.[2]

Spanish oppression prior to 1898 resulted in Cuban hesitancy to sign complaints or make charges against offenders during the American occupation. Witnesses in court obstructed the prosecution, and juries invariably acquitted the accused. Wood employed every legitimate method to assure Cubans that

[1] Wood, *Civil Report*, 1900, I, 78.
[2] *Ibid.*, 79.

the influential and those in authority were punishable. He realized that until Cubans believed this, an efficient system of justice would be impossible except under an arbitrary form of government.

The only way to show the poor man in Cuba that he is equal to the plantation owner before the law is to assure him that he will be protected in telling the truth and that his evidence as to facts shall be as good as the evidence of any other man. . . . If we can . . . impress upon the official classes the fact that their offices are offices of public trust and not of personal gain, we shall have laid the foundation of a secure and stable government in this Island.[3]

Spanish law was excellent, its enforcement deplorable. Procedures for handling cases and protecting the accused were clearly defined in the Spanish criminal law of 1889 and the civil law of 1885. Appeals, challenges and jurisdiction were provided and attorneys appointed for the poor. Anyone witnessing a crime had to report it. Even delays were considered: if courts prolonged a decision or handling of a case, complaint could be made to the Colonial Department in Madrid. Yet these provisions were ineffective; more notable were the privileges of prosecutors in selecting cases and the judge's right to hold a person *incommunicado* without explaining his reasons.[4] Practice perverted procedure, with the result that the courts upheld the Spanish colonial government, not justice.

In Wood's day the Cuban court system operated at four levels with varying responsibilities. Each municipality had a court roughly equivalent to an American justice of the peace; it had jurisdiction in civil cases not exceeding $ 200 and in minor criminal cases. Judges and prosecutors of these courts, who were paid by fees, appointed family counsel and guardians of minors, conducted preliminary investigations and registered births, deaths and marriages. The court of First Instance constituted an appellate court in civil and municipal matters. At the same level, in the court of Inquiry, the judge had criminal jurisdiction and investigated cases, recommending them to a provincial *audiencia*. *Audiencias* tried criminal and civil cases arising from courts of First Instance and Inquiry. Over these provincial courts presided the Supreme Court of Cuba, appointed by General Brooke on April 14, 1899 to hear cases previously handled in Spain. Eleven justices sat on the highest court which was divided into civil, criminal and administrative chambers.

The most important person in the system was the *fiscal,* or prosecutor. He could, under Spanish rule, choose to try or ignore a case. He represented

[3] *Ibid.*
[4] DIA, *Translation of the Law of Criminal Procedure for Cuba and Puerto Rico, with Annotations, Explanatory Notes and Amendments made since the American Occupation* (Wn: GPO, 1901).

the government, not the law, and could waive questions of innocence or guilt because of political considerations. Solicitors representing contending parties in civil and criminal cases, with attorneys, were virtual officers of the state because of the way they were required to represent clients. The system was hampered by the absence of courthouses in Cuba. Clerks handled ninety-five percent of the cases in their homes and took them to the judges' homes for signature. The man who added a handsome gratuity (*gratificación*) to the fee paid was likely to receive a quicker, more favorable decision.[5]

To reform procedures, facilitating the trial of persons arrested and protecting their rights, Wood sought a capable, respected and diligent Secretary of Justice. Elderly jurists like Luís Estévez y Romero and J. B. Hernández y Barreiro, who succeeeded him in April of 1900, lent dignity to the Department but lacked the fortitude to enforce disinterested decisions by their judges.[6] When Hernández resigned in August, Wood was fortunate to find Miguel Gener y Rincón, who served until he became mayor of Havana in May 1901. Gener was fearless and independent, a radical in politics and Dean of the College of Lawyers. He expanded the Department's staff, discharged and transferred judges vigorously, and fought the old system with intrepidity. As Gener saw it, the United States regime was no substitute for reform of Cuban legal institutions. These were Spanish designed to maintain Spanish control, and the mere replacement of a Spanish bureaucracy by a Cuban one could be no solution for a society which needed its own rather than a colonial law. Gener maintained that even uncertainty about the date when Cuba would institute its own organisms of government should not prevent Cubans from changing laws. "Only political passion or the spirit of routine could hide such a pressing necessity." A proud and patriotic Cuban, Gener regarded the American intervention as necessary.[7]

Gener was succeeded by José Varela y Jado, who retained his position on the Supreme Court. Varela was a man of unimpeachable character and possessed of high administrative and juristic abilities. These men were instrumental in making Cuba's legal system function efficiently from 1900 to 1902.[8]

[5] Wood papers, Subject file 254, *Chicago Times-Herald*, Feb. 27, 1900, by J. D. Whelpley; Wood, *Civil Report,* 1901, II, C.O. 95 of April 10, 1901; *Census of Cuba, 1899,* 56-59.

[6] Wood, *Civil Report,* 1900, I, 80-81; Wood, *Ibid.,* VI, Report of Secretary of Justice, 7-19; Wood papers, Wood to Root, Aug. 6, 1900.

[7] Wood, *Civil Report,* 1900, VI, Gener Report, 7.

[8] Wood papers, Wood to Root, Aug. 6, 1900; Wood, *Civil Report,* 1900, II, C.O. 364 of Sept. 6, 1900, showing removal of four justices from the Havana *Audiencia,* C.O. 365 showing removal of one Judge of the First Instance; C.O. 508, wherein they request investigation of their removal; C.O. 317 of Aug. 11, 1900; Wood, *Civil Report,* 1900, I, 24; CDDC, 4574, April 3, 1901; DIA 195-12, C.O. 115 of May 1, 1901.

It took only two weeks of the new year for Wood to act regarding the courts. By January 12, 1900, Wood had removed Federico Mora, the *Fiscal* of the Supreme Court, because of inefficiency and corruption. The next day he separated convicts from prisoners awaiting trial and those under 18 years of age. At the same time, the Customs House frauds were broken by Colonel Tasker Bliss, the extremely efficient and able collector of customs. These actions produced a sensation in Havana, because no Cuban had ever before seen any well-connected official or merchant prosecuted. Wood wrote Root to explain:

I sent for the judge and the prosecutors and told them that they would have the full support of the military government in doing what was right, and that they were to allow only one thing to influence them, namely, the evidence in the case. . . .[9]

As a step toward prison reform, Wood relieved the congested conditions by releasing all those whose sentences had expired and those who had no charges against them. In four months the number of prisoners in the Havana jail was reduced from 600 to 180; these releases indicated the results of the work by the Board of Pardons.[10] To administer this area of reform, Wood appointed Carlos García Vélez as General Inspector of Prisons. García, son of the old general of revolutionary fame, visited every *presidio* (penitentiary) and *carcel* (jail) in Cuba once every four months. The main *presidio* was located in Havana and each province had a prison, as did each of the eleven judicial districts. García was instrumental in ensuring that prisons were clean and properly operated; and he tried to correct instead of merely punish. As part of this process, industrial training schools and separate reform schools in the country for boys and girls were established. Additionally, small *beneficencias* existed in nearly every town through private or state aid to the aged and the orphaned.[11]

Under the Secretary of Justice, fourteen clerks were distributed among bureaus of jurisprudence, personnel, criminal affairs and statistics. For the first time reports were required from, and inspections made of, tribunals and courts, and the average time in a criminal case – from arrest to final disposition – was reduced to three and one-half months.[12]

The new correctional court, similar to a police court, or military summary court, greatly accelerated the handling of cases. The judge was empowered to issue arrest and search warrants and subpoenas, and to render sentences

[9] Wood, *Civil Report*, II, 1900, C.O. 12-13; Wood papers, Wood to Root, Jan. 13, 1900; DIA, C685-2, Bliss to Sec. War, Dec. 27, 1899.

[10] Wood, *Civil Report*, 1900, I, 79.

[11] *Ibid.*, 14.

[12] *Ibid.*, 1901, II, C.O. 93 of April 9, 1901; *Ibid.*, 1900, VI, Gener Report, 7 ff.

up to thirty days confinement and $ 30.00 in fines. These correctional courts operated under the Judge Advocate General of the Military Governor. In Havana, Major W. L. Pitcher became famous for the rapidity of cases he decided by "10 days or $ 10." By April of 1900 Wood was able to report that correctional courts had removed 3,000 cases from the dockets.[13]

During the spring of 1900 the Department of Justice took action to place judges and clerks on salaries, removing them from the lure of fees and *gratificaciones*. Perjury was defined and punishment provided for. A marriage law was promulgated which licensed religious marriages and allowed a couple to celebrate a church wedding without the former exorbitant fees to the Catholic Church. This order was extremely unpopular with many Cubans, who, in their antagonism toward the Church, wanted only civil marriages.[14]

Other orders by Gener and Wood established the American version of due process of law, the jury system and *habeas corpus*, protected private property and enabled judges to compel witnesses to appear and testify. Accused persons were informed of charges and supplied with public defenders. Attempts to bribe government officials, at any level, met more stringent laws.[15] The *Fiscal's* office was reorganized, movable *audiencias* were started, and a tribunal of equity, dealing with co-owners, minors and guardians relations was established. Appeals against decisions by the courts were recognized for the first time.[16]

The process of appeal for redress against procedural action of the government was reorganized. This process, known as *contencioso-administrativo*, had been stopped by Brooke to prevent claims upon the Spanish government from falling on the United States. Soon, however, other means for hearing new appeals became necessary. These claims involved property and business, not removal of officials or the nature of the Military Government. Wood decreed that appeals from decisions he made were to be submitted to the Secretary of War or the President. Appeals against other agencies of the government, usually actions for liability, rehearing or revision of a case, were channelled through the administrative chamber of the Supreme Court.[17]

[13] Wood papers, Wood to Root, April 12, 1900; Wood, *Civil Report*, II, 1900, C.O. 152 of April 10, 1900.

[14] Wood, *Civil Report*, 1900, I, 79-81; II, C.O. 487 of Dec. 2, 1900, C.O. 116 of March 17, 1900.

[15] Wood, *Civil Report*, 1900, VI, Gener Report, 6-11; II, C.O. 427 of Oct. 15, 1900; R. H. Fitzgibbon, *Cuba and the United States* (Menasha, 1935), 35.

[16] Wood, *Civil Report*, 1900, VI, Gener Report, 21.

[17] *Ibid.*, 1901, II, C.O. 111; 1900, II, C.O. 2, 163, 208; Wood papers, Wood to Root, Apr. 4, 1901; Wood, *Civil Report*, 1901, II, C.O. 95 of Apr. 10, 1901; DIA 701-3, 4, 5, 6, 7; DIA 2200 Memo of Dec. 21, 1900; CDDC 1731, March 23, 1901, report of Major E. S. Dudley to Wood; Wood papers, Wood to Root, Apr. 6, 1901.

Cubans were not violent or lawless.[18] Only 7.27 persons per 1,000 were indicted for offenses in 1900 and 14 per 1,000 in 1901; [19] 5.08 Cubans per 1,000 were involved in crimes or misdemeanors. A majority of the offenses were against persons, general interests, the government and property; the most prevalent crimes were swindle, gambling, libel, theft and assault. Correctional courts handled ten to eleven thousand cases per quarter, and *audiencias* dealt with as many per year. Roughly two-thirds of those accused were sentenced. During 1901 there were 1,090 prisoners in Cuba, plus 192 serving three-month sentences and a varying number in jail for a few days.[20] These small numbers indicate the lack of friction between Cubans and Americans and among the islanders, as well as the low incidence of crime. The small number also represents an acceptance by the Military Government of Cuban standards, rather than American standards, in the issuance of complaints.

Despite the achievements of the Military Government in judicial matters, not all difficulties were resolved. Many *audiencias* reported that minor judges were poorly trained and a detriment to insular justice; Varela criticized their lack of attention to duty. Cases were often dismissed because of a lack of diligence on the part of witnesses, juries or the Rural Guard. Frequently the *Rurales* reported inability to locate a man wanted by the courts because that was easier than looking for him. The jury system had to be abolished after a year and a half. Courts desired authority to punish a witness on the spot if perjury were proved. In one case, reported by Captain F. S. Foltz, witnesses testified that they saw a notorious ex-convict trying to rob an American woman, yet a jury freed him. Juries would never convict a man charged with gambling, because they sympathized with it. Although some of this recalcitrance stemmed from genuine cultural differences, most of it emanated from fear of reprisal and hostility to government in general, caused by 400 years of Spanish rule, when the courts bolstered the government instead of justice.[21]

During the last two months of the occupation, "threats of agitators to remove them after the transfer of government. . ." [22] caused consternation

---

[18] Wood, *Civil Report*, 1900, VI, Gener Report, 16-18.

[19] *Ibid.*, 16-17; Wood, *Civil Report*, 1902, IV, Report of A. Arostegui, Secretary of Justice, 4.

[20] *Ibid.*, 1901, I, 24-25; X, Varela Report, 112, 195, 202, 255.

[21] Wood, *Civil Report*, 1901, X, Varela Report, 11, 17, 35-41, 67-69; CDDC 1929, Apr. 12, 1901, case of Francisco Esquerra; CDDC 497, Feb. 3, 1902, Captain F. S. Foltz to Scott; CDDC 497, Feb. 19, 1902, Varela to Wood; C.O. 84 of March 31, 1902; CDDC 4106 of Oct. 3, 1901, case of José Magriña; Wood, "Military Government of Cuba," *Annals*, 160.

[22] Wood, *Civil Report*, I, 1902, 9.

among the judges. Article Eighty-Seven of the new constitution supposedly protected judges from the caprice of the public or vengeance from those who had suffered at the hands of the courts, but such protection was of no help. Varela himself was forced from the bench in 1903. Despite Wood's efforts, the independence of the judiciary never became well established in Cuba.

Secretary of War Root periodically made decisions that compelled Wood to rescind certain orders. After the protocol was signed on August 12, 1898, the Spanish government had granted a concession to a company to deepen and widen the mouth of the Matadero River, which flows into Havana Harbor. Brooke had issued an order prohibiting the execution of the concession, and Wood upheld Brooke's decision, not because of the date of the concession, but because it would benefit only a few shippers and force the condemnation of a large amount of private property. Wood believed the Military Government should have jurisdiction in issues affecting the public interest and the courts over cases involving individual rights. Root and Magoon pointed out that Spain and the United States had agreed that concessions made after August 1898 were allowable if made in good faith and without attempt to defraud the United States. They further held that neither the Military Government nor the War Department should rule in the case: the Military Governor had the right under belligerent power to act in a judicial capacity, but questions of law and property were to be referred to the courts whenever possible. Because this was a question of law, not of procedure, the civil courts had jurisdiction over the case. Thus the War Department decided the case on the basis of administrative jurisdiction, not the rights of the concessionaires. The effect enhanced the power of the Cuban courts.[23]

The postal frauds case, in which Estes G. Rathbone, Director General of the Department of Posts, and C. F. W. Neely, Associate Auditor, were convicted for embezzlement of funds, resulted in new precedents and procedures. The case held that Cuba was considered a foreign country by the United States Supreme Court, that Cuban courts had proper jurisdiction, that extradition was proper and that letters requisitional (depositions) could be used in the trial. Wood and Root forced the case to trial, not to influence the decision, but to convince the Cubans that a decision would be reached.

There was no doubt of the guilt of both Neely and Rathbone, but the length of the case surprised and perplexed the prosecution. The arrest, on May 5, 1900, was followed by a reaudit and investigation of accounts. Pre-

---

[23] Root papers, Root to Wood, May 29, 1901; Wood papers, Wood to Root, June 5, 1901, June 10, 1901; Magoon, *Reports*, 579-595. The Military Government rarely overruled Cuban administrators, CDDC 5101, Jefferson Kean to Scott, Dec. 28, 1901.

liminary investigation was not closed until September 30, 1901. The trial lasted from January 4 to March 8, 1902, and the two men were sentenced on March 24 by the Havana *Audiencia* to ten years in prison with fines of $ 35,000 to $ 56,000. William H. Reeves, a third defendant, received a similar sentence but had turned state's evidence. The men were pardoned by the Cuban government in May 1902.

The Federal Circuit Court of New York held that the evidence of embezzlement warranted extradition. The defense protested Neely's detention, and the case was reviewed by the Supreme Court. Mr. Justice Harlan wrote the decision, *Neely* v. *Henkel*, of January 14, 1901. His decision was based in part on the Joint Resolution of 1898, the McKinley war message and the executive policy of civil government supervised by military government. Also Harlan cited Section 5270 of the revised Statutes, wherein Congress on June 6, 1900 had ruled that a United States court could determine if there was enough evidence to warrant extradition. The act was passed especially for the Neely case. The Supreme Court ruled that Cuba was a foreign country held in trust by the United States and that the act of June 6 was in accord with the United States obligation to develop stable government. The Court further found that United States citizenship did not give Neely immunity to commit a crime in another country. The court claimed no jurisdiction over the issue of the duration of occupation but denied the defense allegation that the United States recognized the republic of Cuba, showing that the Joint Resolution merely recommended freedom for Cuba. The Supreme Court found no grounds for granting *Habeas Corpus* and upheld the circuit court decision.[24]

The American contribution to Spanish law protected the individual's rights. Every effort was made to convince the Cuban that all men were equal before the law and that the guilty would be punished. Wood, while no lawyer, vented his indignation at prison conditions and judicial apathy by accelerating the liberalizing proposals of Magoon and Major Edgar S. Dudley, his chief legal officer. Despite the temporary success at operating such a necessary part of stable self-government, disturbing signs remained. Juries and witnesses unjustly shielded the accused, cases were dismissed without decision, judges suffered intimidation. The American changes were significant, but insufficient to ensure a lasting basis for self-government, something only time and practice could achieve.

[24] DIA 1663-97; file on Rathbone case and *Neely* v. *Henkel*, 180 U.S. 109. DIA files 1663, 7300, 3494, 2722, 2652, 2205, *passim;* Wood papers, boxes 28, 29, 31, *passim;* box 203, 8 page memo, n.d.; box 204, depositions and memoranda. Jessup, *Root*, I, 292.

Developing Leonard Wood's theme "Barracks into Schools," the Military Government either built or remodeled an average of one room a day for public school use, working chiefly with the numerous unused Spanish army barracks. Although many new schools were built by the Military Government, and a few municipalities financed their own new schools, most were instituted in rented houses of other buildings.

Wood stated his views on education in Cuba emphatically:

The work has been exceedingly expensive, but the prevailing idea controlling all the acts of the Military Government in Cuba was that if the Cuban republic was to be established and maintained as a stable government, it must not only have good courts of justice, but a well-educated body of people from which to draw.[25]

Tracing Latin American political instability in part to illiteracy, Wood reiterated, "I have always believed that Cuba's future as a nation depended more upon the education of her children than on anything else...." [26]

The improved physical facilities, modernized curriculum, teaching methods, equipment and organization sparked an educational revolution which spread from the University of Havana to the most remote rural school. Comparative figures clarify the importance of Wood's performance. Some money did filter through Spanish hands to an insufficient number of schools, but although 57 percent of the Cubans claimed they could read, it was generally conceded that two-thirds of the islanders were illiterate. Under Brooke, 21,435 pupils were enrolled in the primary and secondary schools of Cuba, compared to 18,000 in 1895 under Spain. In June of 1900, Wood reported 143,120 pupils in 3,000 schools, and by May of 1902 there were 256,000 Cuban children enrolled in 3,800 schools.[27] Approximately 25 percent of the insular budget, $ 4,000,000 per year, was spent on education.

[25] Wood, "Military Government of Cuba," *Annals,* 166.

[26] Wood, *Civil Report,* 1901, I, 26, 1902, I, 17.

[27] Wood, "Military Government of Cuba," *Annals,* 162-3; BIA, *Establishment of Free Government in Cuba,* 23. In 1893 there were 898 public schools with 35,159 students, and 789 private schools with 27,196 pupils. Around $350,000 per year was spent on public instruction while another $650,000 was supposed to be obtained from matriculation fees. These figures obscure the fact that schools functioned languidly, if at all, in Cuba. Wood, *Civil Report,* 1901, IX, Hanna Report, 15; *Census of Cuba, 1899,* 152, 585. On page 150, the *Census* shows that from October 1898 to October 1899, there were 87,935 pupils in school out of a school age population of 552,928, or 15.7 percent. On page 617, the *Census* reported a seating capacity of 114,735 and 47 school buildings unused. The discrepancies are obvious; little was accomplished to educate Cuban youth, until the spring of 1900. A few Cubans tried to help themselves. Marta Abreu, the famous woman patriot, gave a building in Santa Clara for a school. The *ayuntamiento* of Marianao gave the school board funds for a school. Wood, *Civil Report,* 1900, VIII, Hanna Report, 27, *Ibid.,* 1901, Varona Report, IX, 11.

Prior to 1898, Cuban teachers were paid irregularly; they were forced to exist on the fees exacted from their pupils. Because there were no school houses, classes met infrequently, generally where the teacher resided. The work performed consisted of catechism study, recitation, and such tasks as embroidery. Most teachers were untrained, and morale was low; many held their positions as a result of a political favor by some office-holding relative. *Institutos* existed in name only and were the scene of barefaced traffic in degrees given to pupils. During his tour of duty. General Brooke started educational reform. He allocated $ 50.00 per school room to each municipality and wrote a new school law, but the schools established with state money needed supervision.[28]

Wood watched the unorganized proliferation of schools with growing alarm. In May 1900, he transferred Varona to the office of Secretary of Public Instruction, to impart his vitality to the system. By June, Wood had decided to exert more control and direction of public education. He appointed one of his aides, tough-minded and able Lieutenant Matthew E. Hanna, Commissioner of Public Schools, and ordered him to draw up a new school law for the island. The twenty-eight year old Hanna (no relation to Senator Mark Hanna) had four years of high school teaching experience in Ohio prior to attending West Point. His goal was modern instruction and facilities supported by as economical and efficient a system as possible. The new law, put into effect late in July, retained some points from Brooke's old one and added regulatory, reporting principles derived from the Ohio school law.

The new school law established the office of Commissioner of Public Schools, whose responsibilities were strict and impartial enforcement of all orders and instructions pertaining to public instruction, school construction, and the purchase of supplies. He was appointed by the Military Governor and reported to the Secretary of Public Instruction.[29]

The powers of the Superintendent of Public Schools were reduced to planning curriculum, selecting textbooks, directing teaching methods and heading the Board of Provincial Superintendents. The incumbent at the time Wood took control was Alexis E. Frye, a thirty-five year old teacher and writer of geography texts, who had been recommended to Brooke by President Charles W. Eliot of Harvard. Though Frye was enthusiastic, idealistic, and devoted to the Cubans, he proved unstable and difficult to work with.

[28] *Havana Post,* July 21, 1901; Wood, "Military Government of Cuba," *Annals,* 162; Wood, *Civil Report,* 1900, VIII, Report of Varona, Secretary of Public Instruction, 3; Wood papers, Wood to Senator G. F. Hoar, Aug. 31, 1900; DIA 368-18, C.O. 226 of Dec. 6, 1899.
[29] Wood, *Civil Report,* I, 1900, 121-161, C.O. 368 of August 1, 1900.

Instead of cooperating with Wood, Varona, and Hanna, he magnified and distorted issues, organized Cuban teacher protests, appealed to Eliot and Root, and wrote political opinions in the press. His duties were necessarily circumscribed, because he lacked organizational and supervisory ability. Hundreds of letters, unopened and unanswered, were stacked about his office. Records were incomplete; he had little comprehension of actual conditions in some schools. For example, several *alcaldes* were found to have maintained their mulatto mistresses as school teachers; certain school boards squandered funds; some teachers were actually illiterate, while others met their classes as seldom as once a month.[30] Unable to abide Wood's disapproval, Frye resigned in January 1901, much to the General's relief.

Under the new school law Cuba was classified into 135 school districts, with first and second class cities, together with municipalities, constituting districts. Cities of the first class had seven-member boards of education elected for two-year terms by the people of the district. These boards had the usual powers to employ, own property, open and close schools. Municipal districts had one director for each subdistrict. These directors formed a board of education and reported to the provincial superintendent. There was an average of one teacher per fifty students. Teachers were paid $ 50.00 per month in the rural districts, a salary that compared favorably with the highest in the United States. Their pay continued through the summer, but they were required to attend school for training.[31]

A board could establish its own number of schools, with separate schools for boys and girls if desired. By law, schools had to be clean and conveniently located, with adequate lighting, toilets, playground space and supplies. The building or room could be used only for public instruction; teachers and janitors had to find lodging elsewhere. The school year lasted for thirty-six weeks, five hours a day (excluding recess), and parents had to send children aged six to fourteen at least twenty weeks of the period. Schools were free to all unmarried youths from six to eighteen years of age who were children, wards, or apprentices of district residents. If twenty-five students petitioned

[30] *Ibid.;* DIA 2339-7, Dec. 15, 1903, statement of Alexander W. Kent (former chief clerk in the office of Commissioner of Public Schools); DIA 2339-10, Frye to Root, Sept. 26, 1900; DIA 2080-2, cable Frye to Root, Jan. 9, 1901; DIA 2339-1, 2, 3, Dec. 21, 1900, Dec. 26, 1900; Wood papers, Wood to Root, June 18, 1900; C. W. Eliot to Wood, July 31, 1900; Wood to Eliot, Aug. 6, 1900; Wood to Root, Jan. 8, 1901.

[31] C.O. 368. For example, primary teachers in Chicago received $500-$800 per year, New Orleans $ 420-$ 660, New York, $ 504-$ 900, Havana $ 900. The average Cuban salary was $ 50 per month or $ 600 per year, which was higher than the United States average. Wood, *Civil Report,* 1900, VIII, Report of Hanna, table 2, also page 13; *Ibid.,* IX, 1901, 52-53.

and twelve attended, night school was operated in the district. Boards were directed to establish a school in the district children's home or orphan asylum if requested to do so by the directors of those institutions. One truant officer per district was authorized and given police powers; the board was responsible for placing any of his charges before the local correctional court. The board of superintendents provided provincial institutes for teacher training.[32]

To ensure implementation of this law, an army officer visited every Cuban school at least once a quarter. He reported through his commanding officer such matters as health, rent and equipment. To effect Civil Order 368, Hanna sent four Cuban special inspectors to every municipal district in the island. These inspectors spent two months thoroughly checking every item in the detailed order. They reported that a few boards tried to adhere to the order, some misapplied it and the vast majority made no attempt to enforce it. Hanna immediately began a second inspection to ensure compliance with the orders of his inspectors by the municipalities. The Cubans balked at the complexity of the order but later appreciated the way it supported effective education.[33]

In 1901 grading of the Cuban schools began for the first time. Although classes continued to meet in one room in rural areas, teachers were directed to divide their students into grades according to age and level of preparation. Provincial inspectors trained teachers in this process and in utilization of uniform courses.[34]

Students over fourteen years of age who had completed the elementary course could attend one of six provincial *Institutos.* These provincial schools offered the preparatory course, which amounted to a terminal junior high school preparation, and the collegiate institute course. Varona believed the latter to be the most important in the entire Cuban educational system, for it constituted the final education of the bulk of Cuba's thinking, responsible citizens. Until 1900 some of the *Institutos* were closed; the remainder provided very little instruction. Military Government officials reopened the *Institutos,* modernized the curriculum, examined the professors and placed one in charge of organizing the modified approach of each department toward one subject. Schools of arts and trades, stenography and typewriting, commerce, cosmography, pilotage and sailing, painting and sculpture were

[32] *Ibid.*
[33] Wood, *Civil Report,* 1900, VIII, 8-11; CDDC file 2102 contains many inspection reports. The chief complaints were truancy, janitors living at school, lack of supplies, not enough students in district to warrant school.
[34] Wood, *Civil Report,* 1901, I, 27, Varona Report, IX, 1901, 3. *Ibid.,* 1900, I, 118. Initially, $ 750,000 were spent for books, supplies and furniture.

inaugurated to meet the demand of Cuban society for practical training.[35]

Beyond the *Institutos*, for the student who successfully passed the collegiate institute course and who wished to matriculate further, lay the University of Havana. To Secretary of Public Instruction Varona, the University was merely a hollow institution at the head of Cuba's education system.

The university dragged on a sickly existence, without influencing in any way public culture. It never showed that its faculty was composed of men who lived in contact with outside civilization. Not a single work can be mentioned, as having been written by them, except for some compilation without criticism and they cannot be credited with original work of any kind. Most of them looked upon themselves as privileged office-holders, members of an irresponsible bureaucracy.[36]

The University had 381 students and 96 professors, but many of the professors lived in Spain and paid substitutes to deliver their lectures, while others remained on extended leave; still more had no students whatsoever. The poorly trained doctors, lawyers and chemists spewed out by the University were no help to Cuba.

The amazing reform of the Universtiy was due chiefly to Varona and the professors who assisted him. Varona promptly suspended the salaries of all professors with less than five pupils and put his plan of modernization into effect, first opening the schools and then systematizing their procedures. He sought to achieve what he termed a scientific approach to knowledge, stressing the objective, practical, and experimental aspects of inquiry.

To make the youth grasp his knowledge in a principally direct manner, and not by reflex action through books and verbal lessons, is to prepare men for the active competition involved in the multiplicity of relations of modern life, and not make of them creatures inclined to fantastic speculation.[37]

The former faculties (colleges) of Philosophy and Letters, Science, Law, Medicine and Pharmacy were regrouped for more practicality and direction in instruction and experimentation. Courses focused on preparing leaders for Cuban society.[38]

From 107 professors, twenty-seven were selected by examining boards made up of the more active and competent professors. Entrance requirements were raised so only those over eighteen years of age who had either graduated from an academic department of the University or passed a series of examinations showing they had a liberal education would be admitted to

[35] *Ibid.*
[36] Wood, *Civil Report,* 1900, VIII, Varona Report, 3-4.
[37] *Ibid.,* 9.
[38] *Ibid.,* 10, 12. Appendix A of Varona Report.

professional schools. Qualifying marks in the stiffened *Instituto* curriculum were raised for entrance into the University. Student fees were reduced to $ 60.00 per year, and students were allowed to take courses outside their school or major field. Varona wished to interest Cuba in the University, which was to be the "exponent of its higher culture, and the laboratory of men who are primarily to direct its social work." To that end he appointed a council of inspectors to keep the University in the public eye. Despite the modifications, the annual budget of the University for faculty was reduced from $ 206,370 to $ 125,450, and its total annual budget dropped slightly to $ 329,460.69.[39]

Physical additions to the facilities aided Varona's war on ignorance. The University was moved from its dreary location in downtown Havana to the remodeled *Pirotecnica Militar* on the southwest heights between Vedado and Havana, overlooking the ocean. Wood's personal interest as a doctor appeared in the large sums of money spent on equipping laboratories in physical and natural sciences in both the *Institutos* and the University. The old University building was renovated for use by the school of engineering and for dissection and dental surgery. A new building was erected in Havana for a museum and modern laboratories in histology, bacteriology and applied chemistry. Wood also made available buildings in Havana for the Academy of Medical Science, and a national library.[40]

As a result of the 1900-01 educational reforms, University enrollment increased from 381 to 662, and *Institutos* jumped from 310 to 672 in enrollment. The new schools of painting and sculpture enrolled 490 and the arts and trades school 322. Private schools were encouraged but were required to meet curriculum and health standards set by the Military Government. During 1900 and 1901 about 610 of these schools enrolled some 20,000 pupils, a figure less than that of the Spanish days and destined to become still smaller due to the reduced expenses at the University. During 1901-1902, however, University enrollment dropped to 576 and that of the *Institutos* increased to 823.[41] The chief reason for the decrease was higher University entrance requirements, coupled with higher requirements for graduation from the *Institutos*. There was also an economic depression at the time, and as a consequence, many students were unable to attend the University.

The courses standardized for elementary schools and *Institutos* were as

[39] *Ibid.*, 9, 12, Appendices A and M of Varona Report.
[40] Wood papers, Dr. Gustavo López to Wood, May 27, 1901; Wood, "Military Government of Cuba," *Annals*, 164.
[41] Wood, *Civil Report*, 1900, VIII, Varona Report, 4-5, 12, 22-24; 1901, IX, Hanna Report, Appendix K, 142, Varona Report, 17; Wood, "Military Government of Cuba," *Annals*, 166.

pertinent, relevant, and modern as the Department of Public Intruction could make them; but no attempt was made to Americanize Cuban youth. Wood avoided using American teachers. If Cubans requested administrative or technical specialists, he obtained them, but plenty of eager young Cubans responded to the call for teachers and performed well. Courses in the English language and in Cuban and American history were elective; enrollment was very low. Only 14,000 out of 160,000 pupils were studying English during 1900-1901.[42]

As Commissioner of Public Schools, Hanna called for bids on curriculum materials and he received most of the offers from American publishers, who proposed translations of American texts. These would be made available in a hurry, to meet the deadline of the opening day of school in 1900. Hanna bought American texts, contending that they were superior to others submitted for examination. Yet he pointed out that translations were cumbersome at best and encouraged Cubans to write their own texts. The reading materials, as well as the curriculum, indicated that the Military Government sought to educate Cubans, not to indoctrinate them.[43]

American philanthropy aided the Cuban educational endeavor. Wood was besieged by well-wishers, who offered ideas, money and service, in person and by mail. Some were eccentrics, some productive humanitarians. The most notable instances of benevolence were the Harvard summer session for a thousand Cuban school teachers in 1900 and a gift from H. L. Higginson of Boston.[44]

Wood thought the Harvard trip, conceived by E. L. Conant, Cameron Forbes and Alexis Frye, was a sound idea and helped put it into effect. Army transports carried the teachers, who had been selected by the boards, directors and superintendents and gathered by the Military Government. Harvard provided the instruction, and Boston philanthropy paid for subsistence. The Cubans toured the eastern United States, thoroughly enjoying the entire experience. Hanna later contracted with the New Paltz, New York,

[42] Wood, *Civil Report*, 1900, I, 143; VIII, Varona Report, Appendix B, pp. 17, 24; Hanna Report, Table 11, p. 64.
[43] Wood, *Civil Report*, 1900, VIII, 17, Hanna Report, Table 9; *Ibid.*, 1902, I, 17-18; *Ibid.*, Hanna Report, 52-54. DIA 1497 file; Hanna Report, 1901, IX, 32-34. Wood papers, Sam W. Small to Wood, Sept. 26, 1900.
[44] DIA 368-38 file; DIA 1445 file, Wood papers, H. L. Higginson to Wood, May 16, 1900; CDDC 1653 file: Hermann Hagedorn papers, McCoy to Hagedorn, n.d. (probably 1929). Wood, *Civil Report*, 1900, VIII, Hanna Report, 27. Wilson Gill came to Cuba to promote his "school-city" program, but this was an experiment in community citizenship, not a governmental attempt to "brainwash" a country's youth.

Teachers College to train sixty teachers a year, but the Cuban government stopped this practice in 1902 due to the climate and the expense.

Higginson was so impressed with the work of his friend Wood that he contributed $ 20,000 for the Military Governor to use as he saw fit. Wood considered various projects and finally decided on a model school. In 1901 it was planned and built in Santiago. The Military Government added $ 30,000 to Higginson's gift to meet the total cost of $ 50,000.[45]

Some persistent difficulties remained unsolved in Cuban education. Class attendance at the University, despite all improvements, still lagged. Truancy in the lower schools bothered Hanna so much that he devoted most of his final report to it. He explained the advantages of attendance in circulars, dismissed truant officers and board secretaries, induced the courts to interpret the law stringently and had parents fined in court, but he never considered the problem solved.[46]

Average daily attendance remained low. This was explained by Wood's subordinates as being due to the thin spread of population, the difficulty of communications, parental indifference and the habit of not walking to school, even in town. If the walk to school was even one quarter of a mile, or uphill, or if it happened to be raining, pupils stayed away. Also, families kept children out of school in order to use them in agriculture. Lax discipline prevailed, because teachers did not use their authority. Basically, Cubans hated corporal punishment or any form of coercion because of their recent experiences, and this attitude manifested itself in the permissive schoolroom atmosphere. Tardiness indicated that, in addition to resenting any form of regimentation, Cubans were less eager for education than had been anticipated. In 1900 the enrollment amounted to 172,273, but the average daily attendance was only 123,362. In 1901 daily attendance rose to 132,688 out of an enrollment of 264,742. There were forty-eight pupils per teacher with an average attendance of thirty-four. These attendance figures were lower than those in many sections of the United States but compared favorably with those in the South.[47]

Boards exercised favoritism in appointing teachers, and some were dismissed without pay because funds had been expended elsewhere; board reports were often late and usually inaccurate. People showed little interest in local school elections, and often *alcaldes* continued to control school boards. Hanna issued orders to protect teachers in their jobs and keep

[45] *Ibid.* Wood papers, subject file 254, *Syracuse Post Standard,* Feb. 19, 1900; Wood, *Civil Report,* 1900, I, 165.

[46] Wood, *Civil Report,* 1902 I, Hanna Report, 19.

[47] *Ibid.,* 1901, IX, Hanna Report, 37; *Ibid.,* tables I, II; 1900, VIII, Hanna Report, 25.

school employees out of politics, applying remedial action in as many cases as possible. These examples, in themselves petty and typical of all bureaucracies, combine to form a picture of indifference.[48]

Hanna maintained only those schools large enough to permit an average daily attendance of at least forty to fifty pupils, allowing more support for teacher pay and school budgets. He cut back on the number of schools because island revenues decreased in 1901, and also because population in some rural areas was too sparse to support schools.[49] Hanna and Wood wanted to cut salaries on the expectation of more students and less revenue, but outcry from the teachers, Frye, President Eliot and Senator G. F. Hoar of Massachusetts temporarily prevented it.[50] To offset the reduced customs revenues, Hanna asked the boards of education to curtail expenses by reducing janitorial salaries and dismissing truant officers during summers.[51] He still recommended more appropriations for buildings and teacher training. In the overall view, considering that one-eleventh of all Cubans were in school and that 99 percent of the pupils were in grades one to three, it is apparent that a decade or more was needed before the effects of literacy would be noticeable in Cuban society.[52]

One tendency was frightening. The provincial superintendent of Pinar del Río recommended to Hanna that the Island Commissioner of Public Schools appoint local school board members on the recommendation of provincial superintendents, and inspectors on the recommendation of political parties. Because of the sparse population in rural areas, the superintendent argued, people were ignorant of official duties if appointed to office, and voters were indifferent. Such dissatisfaction with local apathy was understandable, but the opportunities for patronage in the proposed system were obvious. Hanna refused these recommendations and attempted to train school boards to handle their own affairs.[53]

From 1900 to 1902 the legal and educational systems of Cuba were drastically overhauled and renovated in twin reform movements deemed vital to the establishment of a Cuban republic. For such a short period of time, the accomplishments were phenomenal; consideration of the eventual results elicits doubt of their net worth. After 1902, the new Cuban Republic allowed

[48] *Ibid.,* Hanna Report, 1901, IX, 81-82, 84. *Ibid.,* 1900, VIII, Report of E. B. Wilcox on study of Santiago schools.

[49] *Ibid.*

[50] Wood papers, Wood to G. F. Hoar, Aug. 31, 1900; DIA 368-27, Hoar to Root, July 24, 1900.

[51] CDDC 2850 of Aug. 12, 1901, Hanna to Scott.

[52] Wood, *Civil Report,* 1901, IX, Hanna Report, 16; *Ibid.,* 1902, I, 80.

[53] *Ibid.,* 1901, IX, Hanna Report, 87.

schools and courts to deteriorate, thereby lessening its own chances of sur-
vival. Whether the methods of forced feeding destroyed any benefit of the
reform in the minds of the Cubans is a matter more of judgment than of
evidence. For the men of the Military Government, this was not a valid
question. They intended no affront to Cuban pride or human dignity, but
they did believe Cuba needed quick reform to become a relatively satisfied
society. They had no desire to remain in Cuba; virtually all of them wished
to return to the United States and other tasks as soon as possible.

Consequently Wood and his well-meaning advisers tried to do everything at
once. In both Cuba and the Philippines, the Americans experimented. Graft-
ing American legal and educational practices on former Spanish colonies required time, for there were not enough educated persons to man the courts
and school boards proposed by Americans habituated to decentralized
institutions. Cubans, accustomed to Spanish unitary rule and rural traditions,
could not cope with such radical changes as functioning courts and schools
in so short a time. The mistake lay not in the institutions proposed, but
in not allowing them time to take hold in Cuba.

Renovation of the educational and legal systems comprised only part of
the larger task, however, as Wood turned also to the problems of establishing
an economic base for Cuban aspirations.

CHAPTER IV

THE ECONOMY OF CUBA

In 1900 Cuba was an agricultural country with only three percent of its twenty-eight million acres under cultivation. Despite its unsettled economic and social conditions, Cuba's rich land presented enticing opportunities. General Wood adopted economic measures to stimulate agricultural production as quickly as possible. Wood relied on Cuban initiative to begin raising crops and assisted the process by reducing taxes, building a transportation system and a communications network to link the farmer with the market. This market was finally assured in 1903, when the United States and Cuba signed a reciprocity treaty which consummated a long struggle by Roosevelt, Root and Wood to support Cuban political stability with economic prosperity.[1] Since the United States exercised control over Cuba for four years, the possibility loomed that the attempt to rebuild Cuba's economy might degenerate into exploiting the island's resources for the benefit of American entrepreneurs. Perhaps Wood failed Cuba by not redistributing the land or diversifying the economy; but tasks of this sort require years to accomplish. He worked within the existing social and economic structure and attempted no revolution.[2]

During the 1890's the Spanish-American tariff conflict and the Cuban Revolution combined to ruin the island's economy by destroying two-thirds of her productive capacity.[3] The Cuban debt was three times the size of Spain's: $ 400,000,000 or $ 283.54 per capita. By comparison, in 1900 the United States had a gross debt of $ 1,263,417,913 and a per capita indebtedness of $ 16.60.[4] The 90,960 plantations and farms in Cuba before the war

---

[1] Wood, "Military Government of Cuba," *Annals*, 175 ff. Wood's detractors criticized him for failing to subsidize agriculture and for lavishing funds on public works.

[2] Wood papers, Wood to Root, Jan. 13, 1900; Porter, *Industrial Cuba*, 412-15.

[3] *Census of Cuba, 1899*, 41.

[4] L. H. Jenks, *Our Cuban Colony* (New York, 1928), 37-40; U.S. Dept. of Commerce, Bureau of Census, *Historical Statistics of the United States*, Series Y368-379, 721 (Washington, GPO, 1960); Dept. of Commerce & Labor, Bureau of Statistics #1,

had dwindled to 60,711 by 1899. Sixty-three and one-half percent of the farms were eight to ten acres in size; only five percent ranged over 333 acres. The average size of a Cuban farm was 143 acres, but the average area cultivated was only thirteen acres. Clearly agricultural output needed reviving and the quickest, most profitable method of doing so was to expand sugar production.[5]

Although Cuba produced tobacco, fruits, sponges and fish, sugar was the staple of her economy and presented the quickest means of income. Nearly one-half the cultivated area was in cane, with 11.3 percent in sweet potatoes and 9.3 percent in tobacco. The 1899 *Census of Cuba* reported other industrial endeavors too trivial to warrant tabulation of statistics.[6]

Sugar had come to dominate Cuba between 1834 and 1867, replacing the principal products of tobacco, coffee and livestock. Cane had only to be planted once every ten years, and in the extremely fertile soil yielded 12 to 50 tons of sugar per acre. Increasing markets and the decline of competition enhanced this prosperity. By the 1860's Cuba was the chief sugar producer in the world, with over 1,500 sugar estates in operation.[7]

The real revolution in the sugar industry – social as well as economic – occurred from 1878 to 1898. Refining techniques improved, and the world price of sugar dropped from 10 cents per pound in 1870 to 3.2 in 1884 and less than 2.0 in 1902. European beet sugar rose to control 53 percent of the market by 1884. By 1900 the number of mills had dropped from a high of 1500 to approximately 175.[8] In 1901 32 million dollars worth of sugar was exported, compared to 12 million dollars of leaf tobacco and 12 million dollars in cigars.[9]

Limited land ownership also hampered the Cuban economy. A few

Series 1903-4, *Monthly Summary of Commerce & Finance,* "Commercial Cuba," (Wn:GPO, 1903) 369.

  [5] *Census of Cuba, 1899,* table XLIV, 553, table XXIII, 403, 155. There were 299,197 Cubans engaged in agriculture, fisheries and mining, and 950,467 without gainful occupation. There were 79,427 in trade and transport, 93,034 in manufacturing and mechanical pursuits; 8,736 in professional service and 141,936 in domestic and personal occupations. "Commercial Cuba," 401; Porter, *Report on the Commercial and Industrial Condition of the Island of Cuba,* 14.

  [6] *Census of Cuba, 1899,* 541, 543, 547; cf. Wood, *Civil Report,* 1900, VIII, 55, where Lacoste agrees that sugar and tobacco were the first and second crops and that other industries counted for little or nothing.

  [7] Jenks, *Our Cuban Colony,* 21-36; "Commercial Cuba," 363, 401; Wood, *Civil Report,* 1902, III, Bliss Report, 12. Labor was scarce and necessitated concentration on existing industries rather than new ones. Immigration was encouraged and a laborer could earn $ .76 to $ 1.00 per day.

  [8] Jenks, *Our Cuban Colony,* 26-30.

  [9] *Ibid.,* 30-33, 35; Wood, *Civil Report,* 1902, I, Lacoste Report, Statement 32.

Spaniards, Cubans, Americans, and Englishmen owned most of the land.[10] Close to 80 percent of Cuba's urban and rural property was encumbered by mortgages. This problem, common to disrupted societies, was met by a series of stay laws and assistance by the Military Government to enable debtors to attain solvency. To help debtors without ruining creditors, Wood eventually established a four-year payment plan by which mortgages would be redeemed.[11]

The currency used in Cuba required stabilization. Spanish currency involved three fluctuating media: gold, silver and bank notes. To simplify collection and exchange, and to end the inflation, the Military Government installed United States currency and directed that the Cuban peso be worth 60 cents on the dollar. Rates were fixed on the *alfonsino* (25 *peseta* piece) at $ 4.82 and the *louis* (20 *francs*) at $ 3.86, dropping them from $ 5.30 and $ 4.24 respectively. This action worked against the debtor, but wages rose, and values became more representative.[12]

Wood's actions regarding mortgages and currency indicated an impartial attempt to help stabilize the Cuban economy by encouraging production and investment, within the existing Cuban social and economic framework. As the Military Government assisted Cuban economic development with measures regarding the currency and debt questions, the McKinley administration also framed a tariff favorable to Cuba.

Immediately after the war, the President sent Robert P. Porter to Cuba to inspect commercial and industrial conditions, with instructions to consider tariff reduction. McKinley wanted a tariff for revenue instead of protection. Porter was advised that there were to be no discriminations in the tariff rates in favor of the United States.[13] The tariff revised by the United States for Cuba indicated an attempt to develop Cuban stability without shackling her to the American economy.

Porter recommended an average decrease of 62 percent in the Spanish tariff, a reduction which actually came to 52 percent, because the United States currency replacing the Spanish was more valuable.[14] He interviewed all classes of Cubans, concentrating chiefly on those whose immediate in-

[10] Wood, *Civil Report,* 1900, I, 94; Wood papers, Wood to Root, Nov. 4, 1901; *Census of Cuba, 1899,* 544-5.

[11] Wood papers, Wood to Root, May 18, 1901, May 30, 1901. Wood, *Civil Report,* 1901, X, Varela Report, 113.

[12] Porter, *Industrial Cuba,* 195-96; Porter, *Report on Cuba,* 5.

[13] Porter, *Report on Cuba,* "Special Report on Revenue and Customs Tariff, Internal Industrial and Professional Taxation of Cuba," etc., 21. (Pamphlet included in *Ibid.*)

[14] Porter, *Report on Cuba,* 16.

terests were affected by the tariff. From their statements, Porter concluded:

It soon became apparent that the most urgent need of the island was a tariff that would bear lightest in directions where the people could least afford the burden of taxation and heaviest on commodities which the well-to-do and those engaged in large enterprises required. The Spanish tariff was made by Spaniards, for Spain, in the interests of the Spanish. That seems to be the only principle in it.[15]

Porter recommended reduction of exorbitant duties on commodities Spain could not supply; increase of duty on spirits, wine and malt liquors; change of rates to encourage local Cuban industry; change from specific to *ad valorem* duties in cases where the former method caused disadvantage for importers and consignees. In general, Porter suggested keeping specific duties below 25 percent of the market value of an imported commodity.[16]

Wood had shown in Santiago that the United States could cut the tariff by two-thirds and by efficient administration collect as much as Spain. Fraudulent classification and smuggling had diverted much of the revenue away from the insular and Spanish treasuries. Porter believed the increase in importation induced by tariff reduction would aid the entrepreneur, the consumer and boost revenue. For example, a railroad company which had previously hesitated to import an engine because the duty equalled the price, could import five or six engines under the new tariff. If Cuban home industries were capable of supplying a product, requisite raw materials were made duty free, while the duty on a competitive foreign product remained relatively high.

In his first annual report as Secretary of War, Root wrote:

The revenues of the island of Cuba have been treated as a trust fund for which the United States was accountable to the people of Cuba. . . . [N]ever before in the history of these islands has there been so small a proportion of the revenues applied to the cost of collection and the expenses of government, or diverted to private uses, or so great a proportion of the revenues applied to the benefit of the people of the island.[17]

In 1901 Root tried to revise Porter's tariff, stating,

The policy which we are following is, that the Cuban tariff shall be made in Cuba, in the interests of Cuba, as nearly as possible as it would be made by a legislature elected by the Cubans; that when a permanent Cuban government has been established, the two governments will enter upon the negotiation of a reciprocity treaty. . . .[18]

[15] *Ibid.*, 4, 17.
[16] *Ibid.*, 53-54. Some commodities needed to encourage development were admitted free such as coal, wearing apparel, books, plants.
[17] *Ibid.*, 5-6, *Report of Secretary of War*, 1899, 19.
[18] Wood papers, Root to Wood, May 16, 1901. Root went so far in his sense of

Despite these efforts, no new tariff resulted. Cubans were reluctant to serve on a tariff commission because of their sensitivity to criticism from opposing factions, and the Military Government was forced to leave the old tariff to the eventual Cuban government.

Porter also argued for abolition of many onerous internal taxes such as those on food consumption, marriages and *cedulas* (personal or head tax). He hoped that rehabilitation of the sugar industry, revival of work on tobacco plantations and a full complement of men in the mines, in that order, could renew Cuban prosperity [19] and achieve industrial freedom: "the right to buy in the most advantageous markets in the world, and sell where the natural demands for its products exist. . . ." [20] Thus, the effect of tariff reduction was to divert trade from Spain and introduce a freer import flow with other nations, notably Great Britain, Germany and France.[21]

Colonel Tasker Bliss, the Cuban customs chief, and some Cubans believed that the Cuban tariff allowed a natural flow of trade but worked to the disadvantage of the United States. Foreign flags held the carrying trade, because cheaper wages and operating expenses, lower investments on a given carrying capacity and governmental subsidies made lower rates possible. Foreign hulls brought goods to Cuba cheaper, then underbid American shippers for carrying Cuban sugar to the United States. In American ports they secured a return cargo to Europe at a price three to four times higher than those charged on previous legs of the voyage, making their profit on the United States export trade. Bliss calculated that the United States paid $ 15,000,000 monthly to foreign shipping.[22]

The United States controlled 45.9 percent of the Cuban trade, but Bliss contended that America should sell even more to Cuba. Cubans exercised no prejudice against American products, but American manufacturers failed to cater to Cuban tastes, sizes and customs regulations. They attempted, instead, to sell surplus stocks produced originally for American tastes. For

responsibility that he prevented placing F. B. Thurber of the U.S. Export Association on the tariff commission. Thurber could not be expected to work for Cuba's interests. Later, Root employed Thurber to work for reciprocity, a natural action that caused an uproar in Congress. See chapter on reciprocity. Root to Wood, March 6, 1901; Wood, *Civil Report*, 1902, Bliss Report, 11; DIA C1104-9, Wood to Root, March 16, 1901; C.O. 75 of March 16, 1901; DIA C1104-11, Bliss to Edwards, April 2, 1901.

[19] Porter, *Report on Cuba*, 9, 13.
[20] Porter, *Industrial Cuba*, 10.
[21] Wood, *Civil Report*, 1902, III; Bliss Report, 12.
[22] Porter, *Report on Cuba*, "Special Report," 21; Wood, *Civil Report*, 1902, III, Bliss Report, 18-19; J. D. Whelpley, "The Trade of Cuba," *Harper's Weekly*, XLV (May 25, 1901), 541, agreed that the decrease of American trade in Cuba was due not to friction between Americans and Cubans, but to the decrease in the number of American buyers of goods in Cuba.

example, the American cotton prints were of better quality at the same price than similar goods provided especially for Cuba by English firms. But the duty was specific on cotton prints, not *ad valorem*, depending upon the relation between the number of threads and the weight. The British cloth was designed to meet the tariff requirement and so sell cheaper to the Cubans. The Colonel stated:

Nothing more is needed to show that the United States have not been competing on fair and equal terms with other nations for the trade of Cuba. They have given to Cuba a tariff which allows no discrimination for or against any nation but they have failed to do what other nations have done to take advantage of that equal and uniform tariff.[23]

Bliss urged reciprocity and concessions but believed recommendation of government aid to merchants in order to control a market was outside the purview of his report. He intended to call attention to the fact that the United States, in securing less than one-half of the Cuban export trade and carrying little more than one-half under the American flag, had reached the limit of trade development under the existing tariff. For Bliss, Cuba was the first and most necessary market in a struggle for trade supremacy in Latin America: he maintained that if the United States did not capture the trade, Europeans would. The profit to be derived by the United States would benefit rather than exploit Cuba, the Caribbean and Latin America. Irrespective of the merits of Bliss' economics, as Chief of Customs he was sufficiently worried about the United States' failure to compete in Cuba to report it to his superiors. His gloomy words refute any charges of tariff domination.

In three and one-half years, Cuba exported $ 190,327,474 worth of goods and imported $ 237,641,944. This adverse payments balance of $ 44,314,470 was chiefly due to procurements needed to rebuild a devastated country. Military Government spending partially offset this deficit, but never completely overcame the depression of 1900 and 1901.[24]

When importing clothes and textiles, Cubans bought mainly from England and Spain; food, wood, oil and metal products came from the United States. Root and Colonel Clarence R. Edwards, chief of the Division of Insular Affairs, became alarmed at the decrease in United States exports to Cuba and the increase of British, German and French trade. The War Department claimed that from 1899 to 1900, American trade fell off by ten and one-half percent, while Britain's increased 38.5 percent and Germany's 73 percent. Cuba's exports to the United States decreased 18 percent, to Spain 73 percent; yet to Britain they increased 246 percent, to Germany 454 percent and

[23] Wood, *Civil Report,* 1902, III, Bliss Report, 16-21.
[24] *Ibid.,* 12, 14-15, table 38.

to France 94 percent. It seemed as though the United States had failed to compete with British and German importation of Cuban tobacco and sale of steel rails to Cuba, commodities that could have been controlled by the United States. The War Department worried about lack of economic control, because American economic predominance in Cuba meant keeping Cuba stable and secure.[25]

During the fiscal year 1902-1903, the decline in United States trade continued. The Republic of Cuba imported even fewer goods from the United States (41.1 percent), while importing 14.7 from England, 6.2 from France, 16 from Spain, 5.8 from Germany and 12.8 from Latin American nations. However, Cuba exported the great percentage of her goods to the United States, 80 percent, compared to 8.2 to Britain, 1.5 to France, 2 to Spain, 4 to Germany and 2 to Latin American states.[26] The United States imported more from Cuba than it exported because Americans desired Cuban sugar and tobacco. In short, the Cuban tariff left the island's trade unfettered to such an extent that the United States Government worried about economic domination of Cuba by other countries; the United States did not control the Cuban economy.

Irrespective of the War Department's apprehensions, the percentage of United States trade ranked far above that of any other nation and the gains by competitors, while impressive in percentages, presented little threat in total dollars and cents.[27] Root and Edwards seemed more worried about German and English trade increases in certain items than the totals, for domination in key items of trade was more important than total volume. Cuban imports of British cotton and cotton manufactures jumped 112 percent from 1899 to 1900 (from $ 978,317 to $ 2,078,032). Cuban imports of United States cotton and cotton manufactures for the same period decreased from $ 990,310 to $ 279,865, or 72 percent. Cubans exported less tobacco to the United States, decreasing from $ 10,629,374 to $ 7,108,548 from 1899 to 1900. The Cubans exported more tobacco to Britain and Germany in the same period: from $ 236,293 to $ 2,875,536 and from $ 132,119 to $ 1,868,943, respectively. The figures for 1901 show a decline in both exports and imports for most nations involved in the Cuban trade. The overall losses of the United States were not too great and the rise of trade by other powers suf-

[25] Wood, *Civil Report*, I, 1902, Lacoste Report, Tables 4a, b, c, Statement 33; *Ibid.*, III, Bliss Report, 14-15. F. R. McCoy papers, Bliss to Scott, July 8, 1901. Wood papers, "Memorandum for Colonel Edwards," March 13, 1901; Root papers, Edwards to Wood, March 14, 1901.
[26] República de Cuba. Secretaria de Hacienda, Estadística General. *Comercio Exterior*. July 1902-June 1903. "Commercial Cuba, 1903," 376.
[27] Wood, *Civil Report*, I, 1902, Lacoste Report, Statements 33 and 4C.

fered decline in 1901, but still threatened the United States trade in several key products. The English and Germans were trying to cultivate the Cuban trade and the War Department was alert to foreign economic penetration of Cuba. European trade control could lead to major political influence in the island, and this would constitute a threat to the United States security interests.[28]

As with the Cuban tariff, the navigation policy of the United States enhanced Cuban economic growth. The extent to which a country controls its coastal trade is one test of its sovereignty. The United States did not open Cuba's coastal trade to all countries but did not restrict it to United States vessels. Any Cuban resident who owned a vessel, no matter where built or under what flag, upon renouncing his allegiance to his former state, might obtain from the Military Government a permit to engage in coastal trade. The United States provided a temporary flag (blue with white union) for this merchant fleet. It would have been easy under the war power to arrogate this right for United States shipping interests, but only military transports and vessels of the Military Government received temporary privileges.[29]

The Military Government also aided the Cuban economy by abolishing or settling debts and turning over a large sum of money in the treasury to the new Cuban government. During its tenure, the Military Government received $ 57,197,140.80 and expended $ 55,405,031.28, leaving the new republic a balance of $ 1,792,109.52.[30] In abolishing the staggering "debt" owed to Spain by Cuba, the United States realized that political and economic freedom went hand in glove. Porter and McKinley perceived the need to safeguard Cuba from debts which might infringe her sovereignty and bring foreign powers into the Caribbean. This apprehension about indebtedness to foreign powers runs throughout the period and appears in the second clause of the Platt Amendment in 1901.[31]

While the Military Government framed tariff and navigation policies favorable to Cuba and abolished or settled debts, further indication of the lack of American economic exploitation of Cuba prior to 1902 may be seen in the small amount of investment that occurred.[32] Although it is not pos-

[28] Wood papers, "Memo for Col. Edwards."
[29] Porter, *Industrial Cuba,* 362-65.
[30] BIA, *Establishment of Free Government in Cuba,* 31.
[31] Porter, *Industrial Cuba,* 207-210.
[32] For samples of the charge of exploitation, see Portell Vilá, *Historia de Cuba,* IV, 119, 317; E. Roig de Leuchsenring, *La enmienda Platt* (La Habana, 1935), I, xxv, 203; Robinson, *Cuba and the Intervention,* 166.
Then, as now, a segment of United States opinion took it for granted that the United States has always exploited Cuba. The evidence seems to indicate that this did not take place during the Wood administration.

sible to search all the local district registers in Cuba for transactions and ownerships, available evidence indicates that contrary to the supposed rush of American investors, capital investment in the island lagged. Even a hostile critic of subsequent American economic interests in Cuba believed that the Military Government sincerely attempted to build a republic and that Americans invested far more money in Cuba before and after the first intervention than during its tenure.[33] Americans had invested 50 million dollars in Cuba by 1898, and another 30 million dollars by 1902. Wood generally encouraged private investments that would develop Cuba's productivity and discouraged carpetbaggers. But investments were few and schemes abounded.[34]

As sugar sold, Cuba prospered. Her sugar production rose from 325,668 tons in 1899 to 850,181 in 1902, but the 1894 peak of 1,054,214 tons was not surpassed until 1906.[35] By June, 1903, Americans owned all or part of twelve sugar centrals out of 184 and produced thirteen percent of Cuba's sugar crop.[36]

Sugar production began to revive Cuba by 1903. Even more significant than the exact percentage of the Cuban sugar crop Americans produced, the exact number of American centrals and the amount of land purchased is the fact that less of this economic activity went on during the Military Govern-

---

[33] Jenks, *Our Cuban Colony*, 63-9, 85, 161.

[34] A. Brownell, "The Commercial Annexation of Cuba," *Appleton's Magazine*, VIII, (Oct. 1906), 406-11. By 1906 American investment grew to from one-third to one-half of total foreign investment in Cuba. Americans owned one-quarter of the banking industry, shared railroading with the British, and monopolized the mines, electric railways, fruit and cattle industries. Cf. DIA 15294 translation of *Economista*, Oct. 6, 1906, Wood papers, Wood to R. P. Hallowell, Dec. 26, 1903.

[35] "Commercial Cuba," 400.

[36] Cuba. Secretaria de Hacienda, Seccion Estadística, *Industria Azucarera y sus derivados*, primera parte, Riqueza Agricolo-Industrial, Zafras de 1901-1902, 1902-1903, 37-40; DIA, C390-90, Wood to Magoon, May 8, 1902; *Cuban Sugar Sales* (Wn: GPO, 1902), testimony of Hugh Kelly, 140-181, Robert J. Browne, 324-332, Truman G. Palmer, 370-380; E. Atkins, *Sixty Years in Cuba* (Cambridge, 1926), *passim*; Jenks, *Our Cuban Colony*, 129-131, 284; Willett and Gray, *Weekly Statistical Sugar Trade Journal*, XXX, March 8, 1906; R. Guerra Sánchez, *et al.*, *Historia de la Nación Cubana* (La Habana, 1952), VII, 228-29; U.S. Congress, Senate, "List of Claims now being defended before the Spanish Treaty Claims Commission," (Atty. Gen. to Senate) April 10, 1902, 57th Cong., 1st Sess., doc. 299; *Cuba Bulletin* [later *Cuba Review*] June 1903, I, no. 1; March 1904, II, no. 4; May 1904, II, no. 6; June 1904, II, no. 7; July 1904, II, no. 8; August 1904, II, no. 9; Feb. 1906, IV, no. 3; March 1918, XVI, no. 4. See Richard Daniel Weigle, "The Sugar Interests and American Diplomacy in Hawaii and Cuba, 1893-1903," unpublished Ph. D. dissertation, Yale Univ., 1939 190-9, 260n. For an analysis of ownership by central, see J. H. Hitchman, "United States Control over Cuban Sugar Production. 1898-1902," *Journal of Inter-American Studies and World Affairs*, XII, #1 (Jan. 1970), 90-106.

ment than before or after its tenure, and that 13 percent was a small proportion of the total sugar production. The large American market for sugar was probably more of a controlling factor than American ownership of centrals. American investment in Cuba by a few men increased with the tacit approval of the Military Government, and the basic problem of *latifundia* was not solved.

The Military Government accelerated another phase of the Cuban productive effort. The achievement forming the linchpin of the Cuban economy was the Cuban railway. Before this railroad linked Havana to Santiago, the trip from one end of the island to the other took as long as that from New York to San Francisco, some ten days. Because the high road was a dust bin in summer and a quagmire in winter, water travel prevailed where possible. Politics, communications and trade were immeasurably advanced by this new railroad, which after its completion reduced travel time to Santiago to twenty-four hours.

In January of 1900 Sir William Van Horne, builder of the Canadian Pacific railroad, visited Havana. He rode over the island with Percival Farquhar (representative of an electric tramway group), grasped immediately the economic necessity of communication between the cities of the east and Havana, and understood the War Department's opinion that a railroad would be desirable on strategic grounds. The adventure seemed blocked by the Foraker amendment, which prohibited granting of franchises by the Military Government to private entrepreneurs, but Van Horne, basically a builder and an innovator, loved a challenge. Certainly private land could be bought up by private parties, and building could proceed on private property. When General Grenville M. Dodge introduced Van Horne to Wood, the Military Governor encouraged the project of a railroad, if it would benefit Cuba and not merely enrich a few already wealthy men. Van Horne traveled to Washington to talk with McKinley and Root; then to New York, where in less than a week he found enough big takers to capitalize his corporation, the Cuba Company, at eight million dollars. By March of 1900 he was back in Montreal.[37]

His assistants set to work immediately. Land was surveyed for resources, and acreage was bought at Nipe Bay, in addition to a short railroad running out of Santiago. Materials were ordered, and survey engineers began their work. Van Horne personally employed great courtesy and tact with the Cubans, assuring them of the good will and benefits of the project. Impres-

---

[37] W. Vaughan, *The Life and Work of Sir William Van Horne* (New York, 1920), 277-82; Hagedorn, *Wood*, I, 287; Wood papers, Wood to Root, Feb. 16, 1900, Van Horne to Wood, March 6, 1900.

sive, forceful, cosmopolitan, he took the Cubans to heart and deplored American attitudes of superiority. Americans trusted his American birth, Cubans his status as a British subject. Through the summer of 1900, Van Horne's agents bought parcels of land from private owners. By fall a nearly continuous strip thirty meters wide and 350 miles long (Santa Clara to Santiago) had been patched together, and grading began.[38] Six thousand Cubans were employed on the railroad, with free hospital and medical service, and the best meals that could be provided.

Up to that time, private transactions had evaded the Foraker law. Van Horne had proceeded without a charter, rights of way cost him nothing, and he had no power of expropriation or of eminent domain. But the necessity of crossing public roads and streams clearly involved the Foraker rule. To surmount this obstacle, Root devised a permit giving the company the right to cross public property, revocable at any time by the government, without compensation and at the expense of the railroad. It had been said that Van Horne exhibited great faith in Wood and Root to sink millions of dollars in a railroad on the basis of such a flimsy proposition. Van Horne also took the chance that the future Cuban government might revoke or confiscate the project.[39] Considering the value of the railroad to Cuba and the influence Van Horne could bring to bear, the risk he took was minimal. Still, viewing the instability of the time, the arrangement was an amazing one, predicated on faith in the Military Government and in the Cubans.

On December 1, 1902, the railroad was opened for traffic. With the best of stock, well built track, easy grades and few curves, the railroad was a quality job. When it was finished, Percival Farquhar said:

The Cuban Railway was the purest big enterprise I've ever heard about in North or South America. There was not one dollar spent directly or indirectly in influencing legislation or the people. Sir William relied on the fact that he was supplying a desirable public utility. He merged the company's interests with the community's, and went ahead, buying no man.[40]

The Cuba Company bought a great deal of land and planned to develop sugar plantations and subdivisions for communities.[41] Efforts were made to

[38] Vaughan, *Van Horne,* 285-289; *New York Times,* May 12, 1900.

[39] Vaughan claims that Van Horne conceived the idea of a revocable permit, see p. 290 of *Van Horne.* Jessup argues that Root did, *Root,* I, 297. Hagedorn agrees with Jessup on p. 330 of *Wood,* I, and so does Fitzgibbon on p. 56 of *Cuba and the U.S.* Jessup thinks that the consent of the Cuba Relations Committee was obtained, though no records exist. *Root,* I, 298. Wood's *Report* for 1902, 155, 158, says that Root originated revocable permits. Wood papers, Wood to Root, Feb. 16, 1900. Root papers, Villalón to Wood, Feb. 26, 1902.

[40] Vaughan, *Van Horne,* 296.

[41] Vaughan, *Van Horne,* 300; Platt papers, Van Horne to Platt, May 10, 1902.

create traffic for the railroad, and the Cuban Republic worked closely with the railroad's directors. During the building period, Van Horne wrote to Wood a classic statement of the North American view of the relationship of land to taxation and stable society.

A system of land taxation is the most effective and equitable way of securing the greatest possible utilization of lands, and affords at the same time the best safeguard against holding lands in disuse for speculative purposes. It affords, moreover, the most certain and uniform revenue to the state. Freedom from land taxation or merely nominal taxation comes from landlordism, which you certainly do not wish to continue or promote in Cuba. The country can only reach its highest prosperity and the greatest stability of government through the widest possible ownership of the lands by the people who cultivate them. In countries where the percentage of individuals holding real estate is greatest, conservatism prevails and insurrections are unknown. . . .[42]

The building of the railroad coincided with Wood's growing irritation at the Cuban Central railroad, a British company that charged excessive rates to planters. Wood had allowed operation at the old rates for nearly three years, on the ground that the railroads had lost heavily during the war, but they had for 1901-1902 paid handsome dividends. The charge to haul a bag of sugar from the plantation to the seacoast was seventy-five to eighty cents, while it cost only eighteen cents to ship it to New York. The railroads did not pay for loading or unloading. Even when tax rates were cut from 10 to 5 percent, and freight and passenger taxes were reduced, the railroads did nothing to lower rates or increase their stock. When railroad rates went up – in some cases over 100 percent – Wood decided to act.

A commission composed of Cubans, railroad officials and United States experts devised a thorough code that received the unalloyed praise of all parties involved and was the envy of the United States Interstate Commerce Commission. Highly regulatory, the code was published in three parts during February, March and April of 1902. The first law established a railroad commission composed of three cabinet secretaries, which was to be financed by the railroad companies, whose incorporation, organization and limits of powers were defined. Public and private roads were differentiated, and the principle of eminent domain was included, allowing expropriation of lands for rights of way through court procedures. The second law prescribed rules of practice and the powers of the railroad commission; the third promulgated a full schedule of railway tariffs.[43]

[42] Vaughan, *Van Horne*, 286-87.
[43] Fitzgibbon, *Cuba and the U.S.*, 55-56; Root papers, Wood to Root, Jan. 21, 1902; Wood to Sec. War, cable, Feb. 11, 1901; Edwards to Wood, Jan. 11, 1902; Wood papers, Root to Wood, Feb. 23, 1901; Wood to Root, Jan. 12, 1901; Wood to Roosevelt, Oct. 28, 1901.

The new code regulated rates on loading, switching, use of private roads, and moving and stopped loads. Rates were placed on product types, with no preferred rates allowed. No secret rebates, drawbacks, concessions or high rates to persons or localities were tolerated. The commission could alter and amend rates, control traffic, subpoena, investigate, hear and decide upon cases. Supervision of mortgages and appeals was provided for and rules for maintenance standards codified.[44]

Root was pleased. He wrote to Wood regarding his views on regulating enterprise.

The New York Legislature some years ago passed a law reducing the price of gas in New York City five cents a thousand for each year until it came down to one dollar a thousand. There is no reason why you should not do the same thing in Havana, although the price there would have to be higher. There is one limit to the exercise of power; it is that the price charged must not be fixed so low as to deprive the owners of the property of a reasonable return upon their investment. That is to say, regulation must not go to the extent of confiscation.[45]

The mining industry was not regulated by the Foraker Law or any regulatory commission. The Military Government upheld the Spanish law allowing civil governors in the provinces to execute and deliver deeds to mine claims when locators complied with the necessary steps of registration and demarcation. This was considered to be not a special franchise but a universal right of citizens in all countries. Charles E. Magoon, Root's legal officer in the Division of Insular Affairs, held:

To hold otherwise would be to hold that by a provision appended to an appropriation bill, passed by the Congress of the United States, the law of the land for the Island of Cuba could be modified to the serious prejudice of many individuals, Cuban and foreigners alike; and there is no reason to believe that it was the intention of Congress to withdraw the rights and privileges previously existing to Cuba.[46]

The finding in this case as with others, indicates that the guide of the Military Government and the Division of Insular Affairs was whether a project would advance the Cuban economy without undue prejudice to the future government of Cuba or to property holders.

Wood had been trying to revoke the Foraker amendment since 1900, writing to Root, Platt, Foraker, Lodge and N. W. Aldrich. His argument ran as follows: many municipalities wanted to enter into contracts for water sys-

[44] Wood, *Civil Report*, 1902, I, 25-35; II, Civil Orders 34 of Feb. 7, 1902, 61 of March 3, 1902 and 117 of April 28, 1902.
[45] Wood papers, Root to Wood, Nov. 14, 1901.
[46] Wood, *Civil Report*, 1900, II, C.O. 53 of Feb. 8, 1900.

tems and sanitary improvements but believed the resolution stopped them. Alhough he disregarded it in such cases, believing it did not apply, the Foraker law kept money out the island because investors feared future attempts to invalidate municipal contracts.[47] The Secretary of War and the Senators sympathized with Wood's predicament but maintained that public pressure and political opposition would not permit revocation.[48]

The Cuba Relations Committee received many complaints about construction of Van Horne's railway. Senator Platt wrote to Wood for the facts of the situation, enclosing a letter which criticized the Cuba Company for being a monopoly.[49] In reply, Wood summarized the nature of the Van Horne project, and recommended that the Foraker amendment be withdrawn because it retarded work.

I have always interpreted the Foraker Resolution as intended to apply to giving away any of the inherent rights of the people or of the state and that its interpretation was intended to be on these lines and that no concession in which the rights of the state were involved should be given. . . .[50]

The law remained in force. The Cuba Relations Committee did not act against the Cuba Company.

Several cases arose concerning the Cuba Company and municipal lands. Wood requested opinions from Villalón, Fernando Vidal (his legal counsel), Cancio and Tamayo, then sent the papers to Root for his decision. In the case of the municipal lands of Sancti Spiritus, Tamayo believed that no *ayuntamiento* could give or sell land to a private contractor because of the Foraker act. Vidal held that the city council could not sell its *ejidos,* or public lands held in common with the people of the municipality, but that the private lands of the council itself could be sold. Because the problem was complicated by the different nature of lands adjacent to or surrounding the private lands, Vidal agreed with Tamayo. On February 13, 1902, Scott approved the grant by the municipality of Sancti Spiritus to the Cuba Company on the grounds taken by Cancio that the Foraker law applied only to American concessions or franchises, and that an *ayuntamiento* controlled the land for the people and could authorize the passage of the railroad if it so desired. Earlier, Magoon had rendered an opinion that a municipality could en-

---

[47] Wood papers, Wood to Root, Dec. 22, 1900.

[48] Wood papers, Foraker to Wood, Jan. 7, 1901. Here Foraker said that it was likely the Cuba Company was not violating the prohibition against franchises because no one was giving a franchise. Platt to Wood, June 1, 1900, informed Wood that repeal of the Foraker law was political dynamite because the Democrats would accuse the Republicans of planning to stay in Cuba.

[49] Wood papers, Platt to Wood, Dec. 14, 1900.

[50] Wood papers, Wood to Platt, Dec. 19, 1900.

cumber or convey land and other property by following the Spanish law, and that the Foraker law could not prevent a municipality from exercising the ordinary rights of ownership. Municipalities usually clamored for railroads in their areas, and a legal way was found for them to cooperate with Wood and Van Horne.[51]

Far from exploiting Cuba, the Military Government tackled the complex problem of developing the island's productivity without letting adventurers run amok. The Military Government regulated the all-important railroads far in advance of the Elkins and Hepburn acts. Other large investments were too slow and too few to cause worry about American economic imperialism. The problem was instigation of more American investment, in order to stifle the burgeoning European economic interest in Cuba. America controlled 13 percent of the key sugar industry; Cubans, Spaniards and Englishmen held the balance. In 1900 Cuba had the choices of becoming a colony, an independent entity within the private trade and investment system then current, or starvation. Cubans and Americans in leadership positions chose the second alternative, and Cuba became as free as any small nation could be.[52]

Tariff and navigation laws favored Cuban development, actually working to the disadvantage of the United States. A few Americans bought into sugar, fruit and tobacco plantations, beginning a trend that became a monopoly after World War I. Yet foreigners controlled Cuba's economy before the war of 1898, and the Military Government at least retarded the trend. The Military Government applied all its revenues to Cuban welfare and left a surplus in the treasury. The American officials connected the island's producers with markets and fought for that all-important market even after the establishment of the republic in 1902. Cuba gravitated into the United States economic sphere as a result of the Spanish-American War; what is significant is the degree of American indifference and restraint shown until after 1902. For Wood and Root, a viable economy was essential to political stability.

[51] Wood papers, Wood to Root, June 21, 1901 for case of municipality of Jiguani; Root papers, "Opinion of the law officer of the DIA on the Right of Municipalities in Cuba to grant permission to railroad companies to Cross or Occupy Highways, Streets and Property Belonging to Said Municipalities," April 20, 1901; CDDC 4737, Nov. 27, 1901. Magoon, *Reports on the Law of Civil Government*, 374-389.
[52] A. A. Berle, Jr., "The Cuban Crisis," *Foreign Affairs*, XXXIX (October 1960), 40-55.

CHAPTER V

SELF-GOVERNMENT AND STRATEGIC SECURITY,
JANUARY THROUGH JULY, 1900

During the first six months of 1900, the United States combined initial attempts at self-government in Cuba with steps to ensure its own strategic
interests. The story of the Military Government of Cuba from 1900 to 1902
was largely one of the reconciliation of these two principles. On the one hand,
Americans, believing in representative government, considered themselves
committed to leave Cuba to the Cubans because of the Joint Resolution of
1898. Many Americans felt uneasy at ordering the lives of other people.
On the other hand, most Americans would not ignore the inability of Cubans
and Filipinos to manage their own affairs. Furthermore, other interests were
involved. In an age when navies depended on coaling stations and plans for
an isthmian canal titillated imaginations, Cuba and the Philippines assumed
a strategic interest. Cuba, only ninety miles from Florida, could never be
allowed to constitute a threat, or harbor the threat of another power, to the
security of the United States.

Late in 1899, Secretary of War Root had based his program for Cuban
self-determination upon three considerations: the form of government to be
established and the people's participation in that government, reconciliation
of existing municipal law with American ideas, and the ensuing Cuban-
American economic relations. Although this third question underlay the
others, Root approached first the legal aspect and then the nature of government, leaving the economic question until after 1902. He always considered
the Cuban occupation a temporary period in which the task of the United
States was training the Cubans to govern themselves; nevertheless, he feared
that a people accustomed only to authoritarian corruption would not easily
adopt constitutional restraints and acquiescence to the majority.[1]

Root contended that government derived its powers from the consent of
the governed only if the people were capable of making free, intelligent and

[1] U.S. Congress, House, *Report of the Secretary of War*, 56th Cong., 1st Sess., 1899,
doc. 2, 1, 25-34; Jessup, *Root*, I, 287, 300.

efficacious decisions and willing to maintain just government. To Root, the "immutable laws of justice and humanity require that people shall have government, that the weak shall be protected and that cruelty and lust shall be restrained, whether there be consent or not." [2] Even though government for the Cubans did not depend upon their consent, Root maintained that the Bill of Rights, the Constitution and moral law prevented certain governmental actions against any man.[3]

The decision to turn local appointive offices into elective ones necessitated establishing voting qualifications. The Secretary outlined his views to Wood in December of 1899 in Washington, D. C., stressing the lack of Cuban preparation for voting and holding office and his belief that the new census would reveal a high percentage of illiteracy. Consequently Root believed a conservative and thoughtful Cuban government during the formative period was vital to make the suffrage and its results respected. He envisioned the franchise as a reward for thrift (indicated by ownership of property), for self-respect and ambition (indicated by education) and for patriotism (by letting the Cuban veterans vote).[4]

Self-government was to be initiated at the municipal level. In February, 1900, Wood planned to hold municipal elections throughout Cuba on June 16, to elect *alcaldes,* councilmen, municipal treasurers and judges for terms of one year. He appointed a commission of thirteen Cubans, aided by James Runcie and Horatio Rubens, to draw up an electoral law,[5] although its promulgation hinged on the results of the census.

Wood selected the commission's minority plan, which with its greater detail and broader specifications carried the marks of the American lawyers. In the plan, which became Civil Order 164 of April 18, 1900, each *barrio,* or ward, had a board of registration composed of three officials, all qualified electors, elected by the voters of the district of which the ward was a part. A supervisor appointed by the *alcalde* administered this election; voting qualifications are unknown, although it is probable that the universal manhood suffrage practiced during the war was continued. This board registered electors from May 6 to 16 and submitted certified lists to the *alcalde,* the

    [2] Jessup, *Root,* I, 332. Root made this statement in a campaign speech at Canton, Ohio, on Oct. 24, 1900.
    [3] *Ibid.,* 345.
    [4] *Ibid.,* 304-305, in a letter from Root to Paul Dana, his friend and editor of the *New York Sun,* dated Jan. 16, 1900.
    [5] DIA 1327-1, C.O. 73 of Feb 16, 1900. The Cubans composed a representative group: Diego Tamayo, Luis Estévez, J. B. Hernández y Barreiro, E. J. Varona, Manuel Sanguily, Ríus Rivera, Fidel Pierra, J. M. Gálvez, A. Govín, Rafael Montoro, J. G. Montes, Eusebio Hernández, Martín Morúa Delgado. Three were radical revolutionaries, most were revolutionary war veterans, except Pierra and Montoro.

civil governor of the province and the polling places. Nomination required 250 signatures per petition in Havana, 100 in other cities and 50 in rural areas. Members of the registration board could not be candidates. No petitions were accepted after May 26, when the civil governor printed ballots listing candidates in vertical columns under party symbols.[6]

On election day, the board of registration was to act as an election board, following the prescribed directions for opening and closing polls and ballot boxes, and taking oaths before the local judge. The Australian ballot system was utilized for the first time, and each of a municipality's several *barrios* had one polling place and fifty to one hundred fifty voters. *Alcaldes* and election officials were responsible for bringing charges against any persons who violated the election law by false registration, fraud and other offenses.[7]

The only significant addition to these procedures to come in 1901 was the provision that no voter could vote for more than two-thirds of the councilmen of an *ayuntamiento*. This maintained Wood's policy of requiring minority representation upon elected boards and councils and also prevented a one-sided administration. Wood encouraged participation in government by both conservatives and radicals, desiring members of a defeated party to continue in civic affairs instead of quitting when they lost an election.[8] Wood aimed at cohesiveness and stability, not one party rule.

The Military Governor received protests from municipalities and organizations against limiting the suffrage; but he continued to believe universal suffrage premature.

Any change now would be regarded as indicating a lack of policy on our part and would be taken as an indication of decided weakness. The few agitators who have been howling would consider that the American government has been intimidated and their influence would be increased in proportion as the influence of the people – on whom you must depend for the future government of Cuba – would be decreased.[9]

Wood also urged completion of voter registration without the results of the census, but Root maintained that the statistical evidence contained in the census would be important in determining policy and winning Cuban support for that policy.[10]

---

[6] Wood, *Civil Report*, 1900, I, 45-49, 55-63; Wood papers, Wood to Root, April 12, 1900.

[7] Wood, *Civil Report*, 1900, I, 49-52.

[8] Wood papers, Wood to Root, June 3, 1900.

[9] Wood papers, Wood to Root, Feb. 23, 1900; Jan. 19, 1901, where Wood argued that universal suffrage should be withheld for at least ten years to allow the school system to prepare responsible citizens; CDDC files 1305, 729.

[10] *New York Times*, Feb. 28, 1900, approved the experiment of limited suffrage.

Wood sought conservative, able and responsible men to participate in civil government. He preached one policy, that of all people uniting for good governance. The General maintained, "There is not a sensible man in the country who thinks we can leave for a long time, not measured by months, but by years; several of them at least." He believed that all classes of people in Cuba trusted that the Americans would not leave until a stable government was established, "whose credit is good and under whose administration money will seek investment at rates on a par with those in other well established countries." Wood asserted that leaving Cuba before then would betray "the cause of civilization" and turn Cuba within three months into a shambles not unlike Haiti and Santo Domingo. "All the results of the war would be lost and its purpose defeated." [11]

When Wood talked with radical politicians, conservative planters, the *guajiros* in the fields, the vendors and dockmen of the cities, he represented their views to Washington and sought their cooperation. But he relied upon Cuban men of moderation to provide the leadership he sought. Wood pointed out that a large portion of Cuban conservatives represented the Cuban revolutionary party, who genuinely served Cuban interests and who believed in the formation of an independent government as the next step to be taken. They also desired closer commercial relations with the United States. Considering these men "honest in their convictions," Wood maintained that, "as a class they have co-operated loyally and faithfully with the Military Government in the work that it has done." The General further explained his working relationship with the conservative revolutionaries: "My views have differed with theirs many times in regard to policy and plans, but the differences were only natural ones, incident to complicated public affairs." [12]

Despite occasional criticism, Wood appreciated Cubans. He believed that too many American writers had criticized the Cubans as irresponsible advocates of disorder. To counter this charge, Wood pointed out that at no time had troops been used to maintain public order, that general elections were held in orderly manner, and that Cubans had lifted themselves from poverty and idleness after the war to active employment. "There must be something in the people themselves to have brought about this result. . . ." While Wood thought the Cubans sometimes "impatient and suspicious," he always "found them orderly and obedient." [13] The General agreed that the conditions surrounding the occupation had been trying to both Cubans and Americans, and

[11] Wood papers, Wood to Root, Feb. 16, 1900.
[12] Wood, *Civil Report*, I, 1901, 21. Of course Wood sought to generate good will, ally Cuban support and impress Congress, but his remarks were sincere.
[13] *Ibid.*

was convinced that the Cubans needed only leadership and time. But time was short.

On April 14, Root cabled to Wood that he had mailed to him that afternoon the first five condensed tables of the Cuban census. He directed Wood to publish them in the *Official Gazette* concurrently with their announcement in Washington. For Root, the results fully justified the proposed order, and Wood was allowed to publish Order 164 on the same day as the census tables.[14]

While the high illiteracy rate forced Root to establish suffrage qualifications, these qualifications placed the voting power with native Cubans. Eighty-nine percent of Cuba's population was born in the island, eight percent in Spain. Eighty-three percent of Cuba's population claimed Cuban citizenship and one percent Spanish; eleven percent were in suspense (meaning that disposition had not yet been made upon their claims). There were 417,993 Cuban males of voting age, proportionately a little less than in the United States. Of these, 200,631 could read and fifty-nine percent of this latter number were native Cubans. The suffrage limitation still left the vote, and thus the power, in the hands of the Cubans instead of transferring it to a small class of naturalized citizens. Those disenfranchised supposedly did not know enough to be responsible voters.[15]

To qualify as a voter, it was necessary to be a native Cuban or the son of one, at least twenty-one years old and a resident of a municipality thirty days. Spaniards could vote if they renounced Spanish and requested Cuban citizenship, which most of them did. Voters also had to be either literate, owner of real or personal property valued at $ 250, or holder of an honorable discharge from the Cuban army prior to July 18, 1898.[16]

Registration, which proceeded without disturbance, was high. But because of apathy, habit and the feeling that any election must be rigged to favor the government, the actual vote (68 percent) was not particularly heavy. Of the 150,648 who were eligible (almost one-third of the adult males in

[14] DIA 1327-33, Root to Wood, cable of April 14, 1900; DIA 1327-4, Wood to Root, April 19, 1900, advising of publication of election law; DIA 1327-8 of May 18, 1900, 1327-12 of June 16, 1900.

[15] Wood papers, Root to Wood, Feb. 28, 1900; *New York Times,* Feb. 28, 1900; *Census of Cuba, 1899,* 100-112, 218, 194-95, 96-97; CDDC 869, Enrique Parrdi to Root, Feb. 6, 1900, protesting the soldier vote because the army unlawfully collected rents during the war. He urged annexation to the United States. It affords a sample of the variety of views requiring the attention of the Military Government.

[16] Wood, *Civil Report,* 1900, I, 43-44; Wood papers, Wood to Root, Dec. 30, 1899, Feb. 8, 1900, Feb. 23, 1900; Root to Wood, Feb. 28, 1900. In December Wood reported that the Cubans were beginning to accept the idea of property qualifications and literacy in order to vote.

Cuba), 110,316 voted.[17] Most Cubans expressed gratitude for their first free election, and the turnout and performance in the first election were encouraging.

The revolutionary element, represented by various regional parties, won the elections. The conservatives, headed by the Democratic Union party elements and composed of former autonomists and some revolutionaries, foresaw defeat and withdrew from the contest, despite the fact that the minority representation provision of the electoral law allowed them to hold office.

Regional factions were dominated by *caciques*. Generally, there were three main political groupings: the Democratic Unionists, the Nationalists and the Republicans. None of the three could be termed national parties, but various groupings around the island usually assumed one of these three titles. The programs of the *Nacionalistas* and *Republicanos* were similar; the *Nacionalistas*, the better organized party of Máximo Gómez, possessed more of the leaders and conservative revolutionaries in the island. They held adherents from all over the island and in Havana. The more radical Republicans, an offshoot of the *Nacionalistas*, were generally strong in Santa Clara, Matanzas and portions of Santiago. Both parties emphasized Cuban independence, but while Republicans called for immediate independence, the *Nacionalistas* stressed Cuban unity. A reflection of national sentiment can be seen in that both parties, to gain votes, campaigned on anti-Wood and anti-occupation platforms. Yet most politicians admitted privately that the occupation was needed for some time to come, though few could agree how long.[18]

Despite Wood's intention to encourage conservatives, he did not lend his support to the Democratic Unionists. What influence he did employ at key times supported the conservative revolutionaries, mostly *Nacionalistas*. His attitude toward Cuban politics during the first elections is shown by the following report to Root:

The improbability of a proper conduct of political affairs here, until a change has come over the spirit of the people, is apparent when you look over the present situation. There is only one party in each province all others having withdrawn from the contest rather than suffer the humiliation of possible defeat at the polls. I do not know a more cowardly outfit than the Autonomist party of Havana. They are men of ability, but sycophants, afraid to come out and work for what

[17] Wood, *Civil Report*, 1900, III, Tamayo Report, table 8. Cf. Mario Riera, *Cuba política, 1899-1955* (La Habana, 1955), 12-16, lists 110,816 voting out of 160,648, indicating a printing error.

[18] There were no insular or national parties, however factions could be considered to align themselves on certain candidates and issues. The best accounts of Cuban politics at the turn of the century are to be found in Martínez Ortiz, *Los primeros años*, I, 128-80; Portell Vilá, *Historia de Cuba*, IV, 137-47; Riera, *Cuba política*, 1-66; Wood, *Civil Report*, I, 1900, 63ff.

they believe to be right. They took hold of the elections with interest until they saw they were going to be defeated; then they published a manifiesto [*sic*] in sounding terms, withdrawing and accusing everybody else of fraud. The substance of the whole thing is that they do not want to submit to the will of the majority. Registration has not been heavy, a fact which demonstrates what I have always maintained. That the great bulk of the people are quiet, orderly and want to be let alone and allowed to work, and have very little interest in the political situation. They are satisfied with the condition of security and have had all they want of excitement.[19]

Critics have protested that Wood's authoritarian methods could not possibly have taught the Cubans democratic ways.[20] But the instances of Wood's interference with elections or official decisions were few and of an administrative nature, to ensure that elections would be properly held, not to influence the outcome. Wood secured free elections and abided by their results, a rare occurrence before and after his tenure in Cuba. He altered the election law at the request of hostile Republicans to give them more opportunity to nominate candidates. In Cienfuegos, Colonel Scott negotiated an agreement in a disputed mayoralty election; a new election was held, from which the opponent of the Military Government emerged the victor. That the Military Government would allow an opposition candidate to take office was a revelation for the Cubans.[21]

Despite uncertainties in applying election procedures and although several towns asked for United States assistance to insure legality and order in the elections, no violence occurred.[22] As a precaution the *Rurales* and some American troops were deployed near towns where voting took place, but were not used. On June 23, 1900, Diego Tamayo transmitted to Colonel Scott the returns for all the island's municipal elections. Some recounting of votes and claims of fraud had occurred; the election board, supported by the Department of State and Government, investigated and decided most cases.

[19] Wood papers, Wood to Root, May 23, 1900.
[20] Portell Vilá, *Historia de Cuba,* IV, 137-40. An opposing case could be made, however, on the tactics of other Americans in Cuba who resisted Wood. General Wilson, for example, employed a friend of his, J. H. Drake, from Morgan Park, Chicago, to tour Matanzas and Santa Clara, advising *alcaldes* and former army officers to oppose the proposed suffrage plan. Drake was also to secure information for congressmen. Wood papers, Wood to Root, Feb. 8, 1900.
[21] Martínez Ortiz, *Los primeros años,* I, 137-41; *New York Times,* May 27, 1900; H. L. Scott, *Memories of a Soldier* (New York, 1918), 248; Wood papers, Wood to Secretary of State and Government, March 26, 1900.
[22] CDDC 1305, May 11, 1900, Report of 1st Lt. C. H. Conrad, Jr.; CDDC 1305, June 29, 1900, Wilson to Scott, enclosing twelve reports of post commanders on elections, and on June 23, copies of Wilson's orders to *Rurales* and troops; CDDC 1305, June 25, 1900, Scott to Wilson; July 2, J. M. Gómez to Scott.

Usually the Americans intervened only when the Cubans could not settle a case.[23]

According to Wood, "The assumption of office by the newly elected municipal officials was the beginning of a period of great difficulty for the general government." Unfulfilled promises, favoritism and general ignorance of administration, taxation and accounting elicited criticism of the new office-holders. Since business and professional people placed little confidence in the new municipal governments, money transactions slowed to a barely perceptible rate. Inspectors for the departments of State and Finance, laboring to straighten out abuses in municipal accounting, reported unbonded officials, illegal transactions, money transferred into wrong categories and unauthorized expenditures. The more serious of these situations resulted in the removal of *alcaldes*. Wood remarked that he hoped the people had profited by their mistakes and would exercise more care in the selection of candidates for the next election.[24]

The American and Cuban concepts of town government illustrated basic political differences between the two societies. Where American towns prided themselves on their self-reliance, Cuban towns wanted the support of the insular government. Municipalities were at first without revenues sufficient even for maintenance. After the initial redevelopment period they paid their own officials, but the state continued to underwrite public education, administration of justice, police, sanitation, public works, jails and hospitals. Even though the state temporarily assumed these expenses, the municipalities' deficits increased by $ 300,000 during the last six months of 1899 because revenues were not being collected. Although in 1900 the state refused to pay the debts of the municipalities and assumed only the costs of operation mentioned above, Cuban municipalities were still in debt at the end of the year. By paying the expenses of the towns, the Military Government hoped to relieve municipal taxation so all energies might be devoted to reconstructing agriculture. Nevertheless, the Military Government directed the institution of light tax laws in order to pay local officials and provide some maintenance. General Wood stated in his annual report that there were too few instances of local initiative for local improvements.[25] Far from preferring authoritarian methods, Wood yearned for more local initiative.

Even Leopoldo Cancio, the critical and outspoken Secretary of Finance, called the administration of the municipalities "a public disgrace." *Alcaldes*

---

[23] CDDC 1305, June 23, 1900, Tamayo to Scott; July 14, 1900, Tamayo to Wood.
[24] Wood, *Civil Report,* 1900, I, 62-64; CDDC 1295, April 22, 1902.
[25] Wood, *Civil Report,* 1900, I, 12-13.

ignored budgets, spent and hired according to fancy.[26] Municipalities had always employed more persons than necessary who had "worked" three hours a day or less. These tendencies worsened after the termination of Spanish rule. In Havana (where one might expect a greater percentage of educated and able officials), the city administration after July 1900 had been one of most incompetent in the island; it required constant supervision.

Wood singled out the ingredient lacking for improvement of municipal administration: "What is more needed than anything else for the proper performance of municipal affairs is the formation of a public spirit looking to the economic and efficient conduct of all municipal business." People were unwilling to protest formally or make charges of extravagance against their officials. Because only at state level could any restraint be exerted, the Military Government was the only feasible way to impart ideas of disinterested government. After July 1, 1900, municipalities were expected to support themselves in granting permits and licenses, making budgets, keeping records and paying salaries of officials, and collecting taxes on property and public services. A vigorous system of state inspections reminded the cities of their duties.[27] In April 1901, an order revoked the prohibition of suits against municipalities, and claims were to be addressed to the courts.[28] Gradually, with these measures, Wood attempted to make municipalities self-sustained.

Elihu Root knew that no plan for Cuba could be totally successful. Weighing the differing temperaments of the two peoples, American political attitudes and the state of Cuban society, the McKinley administration attempted first to establish successful local self-government and then to hold a constitutional convention.[29]

On June 3, 1900, General Wood took up this subject with Secretary Root:

There is one very important matter which I wish to speak of and that is the calling of a Constitutional Convention sometime this Fall, provided of course that the elections go off quietly. I am going to work on a Constitution for the Island similar to our own and embody in the organic act certain definite relations and agreements between the United States and Cuba. This, of course, is only preliminary work and the whole thing will have to be subject to the most careful consideration before presented to the Assembly as a model for adoption. For

[26] *Ibid.*, 1902, III, 5-6.
[27] *Ibid.*, 1900, I, 13-14; II, C.O. 355 of Sept. 12, 1900 (budgets); C.O. 123 of March 24, 1900 (tax collection); C.O. 356 of Sept. 13, 1900 (registry of vehicles and loads allowable); C.O. 252 of June 27, 1900 (treasurers of municipalities).
[28] *Ibid.*, II, 1900, C.O. 254 of June 28; Wood papers, Wood to Root, April 4, 1901.
[29] *New York Times*, April 2, 1900, April 3, 1900, March 15, 1900; Wood papers, subject file 248, 249; *Washington Post*, Jan. 9, 1900; *Detroit Journal*, Jan. 24, 1900; *Detroit News*, Jan. 19, 1900; *Erie Times*, June 13, 1900; *Concord Monitor* (N.H.), Feb. 8, 1900; *Wilkes Barre Record*, Jan. 11, 1900.

this purpose, it will be necessary for me to be given a full and explicit statement setting forth the conditions which our government is going to insist upon. I believe that we should not delay unnecessarily the assembling of this Convention and the establishment, under the Constitution adopted, of a local government under our control and supervision for such time as will be deemed proper; but the government should be completely organized as a Cuban government with the exception of the Governor of the Island, who should remain for the present an American commanding the Military Forces of occupation and holding an absolute power of veto. Such a form of government would not differ materially from the present, the only distinction being that it would be under a definite constitution and we could throw upon these people the burden of making their own laws, which procedure, so long as the governor holds the power of veto would be an absolutely safe one.[30]

This revelation of Wood's plans for Cuba is chronologically the first place of evidence specifically listing the immediate calling of a convention and the drafting of a constitution containing an agreement about Cuban-American relations. The idea of a military officer with absolute veto was never carried out and only illustrates that the Cuban policy of the McKinley administration was not made by Wood. Ever since the fall of 1899 Root had intended to call a constitutional convention when conditions seemed favorable, but Wood must be given credit for instigating the actual preparations for the Cuban Constitution of 1901 and the Platt Amendment.

Wood knew of the problems connected with installing municipal self-government and had spoken in 1898 and 1899 about the need to remain in Cuba for a long time, but by June of 1900 he had decided to act quickly. The Boxer Rebellion, which had trapped his wife's sister in Peking, certainly aroused his ambition for service and promotion in active combat. Politically, he knew a longer occupation would mean more opportunities for Democratic criticism. Although Wood recognized the danger signs in the Cuban municipalities, he optimistically believed they would be in satisfactory running order by the time the United States was ready to leave the island.[31]

[30] Root papers, Wood to Root, June 3, 1900. Nothing was found in any of the sources to indicate an earlier call. Jessup, *Root,* I, 306, agrees on this point about Wood's instigation. Healy, *United States in Cuba,* 145, believes the idea was a scheme to allow the Cubans to feel a sense of self-government while the United States retained control of the island. The *New York Times* of Feb. 27, 1900 printed an article suggesting that officials in Washington had no idea of a definite timetable or how long the occupation would last. The point is that the Military Government and the War Department wished that Cubans could govern themselves so they could leave the island.

[31] Hagedorn, *Wood,* I, 302-02, and Healy, *The United States in Cuba,* 145-46, stress Wood's desire to serve in China. However, Wood's optimism and progress in Cuba were equally important factors.

Personally, the General feared that at the expiration of his commission he would lose his volunteer rank and revert to a captaincy in the medical corps. Active service in China seemed a quicker way to a regular commission; to that end, Wood wrote to his friends Theodore Roosevelt and Henry Cabot Lodge, who attempted to assist him in Washington.[32] While ambition weighed heavily, Cuban conditions more than balanced the scale of decision for Wood. He was fulfilling orders to prepare the Cubans for self-government as soon as possible.

Root congratulated Wood for the successful completion of the elections. The Secretary had planned much of the election, and had visited Cuba in March for a personal view of the situation. Senators Aldrich, Platt and Teller also visited Cuba that spring, apprising themselves of Cuban conditions as members of the Cuba Relations Committee. Root regarded the successful election as "an event of the first importance" for the future of Cuba and asked Wood to come North to make future plans.[33] Wood replied that quick action to hold a constitutional convention "will do more to draw Cuba to the United States than anything else and it will produce such a feeling of confidence and friendship that the future will not remain long in doubt." [34]

Wood traveled to Washington in July to plan for the convention that would frame a constitution and define Cuban-American relations. His own words provide part of the meager evidence found for the origins of the decision regarding the convention.

During my visit to the United States in the month of July, 1900, the situation in Cuba was presented in full to the President and Secretary of War and it was decided that, everything considered, the time had arrived for taking the pre-liminary measures for a general election to be held throughout the Island for election of delegates to a convention to be assembled for drawing up and adopt-ing a Constitution for the Island of Cuba and agreeing on the relations which were to exist between Cuba and the United States and providing an electoral law.[35]

While the phrase "everything considered" is vague, the statement helps con-firm the timing of the decision. The conferees believed their initial success warranted taking a further step in preparations for Cuban independence. When General Wood arrived in New York on July 17, he asserted to the press that Cuban conditions were satisfactory, that municipal self-govern-

[32] Wood papers, Wood to Roosevelt, June 7, 1900; Wood to Lodge, Aug. 8, 1900; Wood to Nelson W. Aldrich, June 21, 1900; Wood to Edward O. Walcott, June 21; Wood to Henry M. Teller, June 21, 1900; Wood to McKinley, June 22, 1900.
[33] Wood papers, Root to Wood, June 20, 1900; Wood to Root, July 6, 1900.
[34] *Ibid.* Wood cabled Root a formal request for China duty on July 7.
[35] Wood, *Civil Report,* 1900, I, 64.

ment had succeeded and that the people looked forward to a constitutional convention, probably to be held in the fall.[36] On the evening of the 18th Wood attended a dinner given by Secretary Root for President McKinley, with the other cabinet members, several generals and friends of the President also in attendance. When the conversation turned to Cuba, it appeared that Cubans would have an early opportunity to experiment with self-government.[37]

The President, Root and Wood conferred several times from the 18th to the 20th of July. Indirect reports in the press are, in addition to a few magazine articles, the only records found which indicate any of the specific conclusions reached at this time. The conferees decided to hold the convention in the fall, to request of the convention written specifications of the relations to exist between the two countries, and to accelerate the steps toward Cuban independence.

The *New York Times* speculated "that in less than nine months Cuba probably would be governing herself, and all the United States troops would be out of the island." [38] According to the *Times*, the administration hoped to convene the convention in October. Wood was quoted as saying that in nine months general elections would be held, after which the Cubans would begin to manage the government, their performance determining when the Military Governor would leave the island. Wood thought that he and 4,000 troops would have to remain for some five months after the constitutional government was established, but that this retention of troops amounted to "only another precautionary measure like the clauses in the constitution to be adopted." McKinley and possibly Congress would scrutinize the proposed constitution before it went into operation, "for it is the settled conviction of the officials that Cuba should not be permitted to make treaties with foreign nations except through the United States, nor should the people be allowed to involve the island in debt unless authorized to do so by this government." [39] This statement, embodying the familiar requirements dating back to 1898, indicates one more step in development of the government's plans for Cuba.

In Havana, the press announced the coming convention, and Cubans discovered that the United States probably would not allow any debts or treaties

[36] *New York Times,* July 18, 1900.
[37] C. G. Dawes, *Journal of the McKinley Years,* 238. Charles Gates Dawes, youthful Comptroller of the Currency who had delivered Illinois to McKinley, later formulated the Dawes plan to aid German reparations payments in 1924, and served as Vice-President of the United States from 1925 to 1929.
[38] *New York Times,* July 21, 1900.
[39] *Ibid.*

to be contracted with foreign nations, that they would not have an army and would be defended by the United States. The Military Governor was quoted as saying that he believed Cubans were competent to govern themselves and would demonstrate it after the convention was held.[40] The islanders knew what the United States was planning in the way of Cuban-American relations. Some acquiesced, others remonstrated, but none offered a feasible alternative.

E. L. Godkin and Oswald Garrison Villard, editors of the *Nation,* pointed out that United States control of Cuba's foreign relations and finances would not leave much sovereignty for the Cubans. The editors of the *Nation* contended the most influential segment of American public opinion believed Cuba should be granted her promised independence, and that annexation, if any, would result naturally, through "gratitude, friendly intercourse and trade." The *Nation* claimed that the Monroe Doctrine was a sufficient statement of United States security interests, and concluded that the right to intervene would make Cuba irresponsibly dependent.[41]

Most leading magazines, like the *North American Review,* Albert Shaw's *Review of Reviews* and Lawrence F. Abbott's *Outlook,* supported the administration's Cuban policy. These publishers differentiated between exploiting subject peoples and bringing them the blessings of republican government.[42] They simply did not believe that either the motives or the results of republican adventure could terminate in anything but beneficial progress.

The Cuban question was not discussed in the national election of 1900. The issue of imperialism centered upon the Philippines; if the people did not express approval of the expansion policy, they did not condemn it, for McKinley won impressively. Possibly Cuba was not a campaign issue by mutual consent. Congressman John R. Dalzell (Republican, Pennsylvania) and Senator N. B. Scott (Democrat, West Virginia) agreed that the Cuban question was a national one, and few Americans disagreed over basic Cuban policy.[43] The incumbent administration reasoned that the question was not debated because it could not have received a fair hearing in a time of heated campaigning.[44] This was wide of the mark and perhaps a cover for other reasons;

[40] *Havana Post,* July 21, 1900.
[41] *Nation,* "Control of Cuba's Foreign Relations," LXXI (Aug. 2, 1900), 85-86; Wood papers, subject file 254, with clippings from the *Chicago Times Herald* opposing any failure to fulfill the terms of the Teller clause, and the *Minneapolis Tribune* of July 23, 1900, with a description of the foreign policy, debt, treaty and naval base requirements that were discussed in Washington and later appeared in the Platt Amendment.
[42] Wood papers, Abbott to Wood, March 17, 1900.
[43] Jenks, *Our Cuban Colony,* 321n; *New York Times,* Sept. 20, 1900.
[44] Walter Wellman, "The Cuban Republic – Limited," *Review of Reviews,* XXII (Dec. 1900), 708-12.

McKinley wanted the Cuban question disposed of quickly, because he had a surfeit of other political worries.[45] Cuban matters were silenced by the Republicans and Democrats until after McKinley's reelection. His announcement of the constitutional convention stemmed partly from Cuban readiness, partly from political expediency. This step toward Cuban self-government may have mollified the Democrats, or at least left them little chance to criticize the administration's loose interpretation of the Teller Amendment.[46] Warding off the Democrats was probably a major factor in McKinley's decision to call the convention in October. The Cubans were not deceived; they realized that neither a Republican nor a Democratic administration would establish a Cuban republic in 1900.[47]

The President retained another reason for his interest in Cuba: strategic security. Cuban disunity endangered America's strategic position, and this danger was magnified at the time by plans for the isthmian canal, the navy's need for coaling stations and German designs in the Caribbean. McKinley hoped to establish an independent Cuba which would not threaten future peace. His determination guided American-Cuban relations until his untimely death in the fall of 1901.[48]

Admiral Alfred Thayer Mahan, who had written and spoken for years upon seapower's influence on history and nations, had called for a naval base in Cuba to protect the isthmian approaches. When war threatened in 1898, McKinley feared that the European powers would aid Spain. In the summer of 1900 loomed the pressing foreign issue of the Boxer Rebellion, which Root did not wish to see repeated elsewhere. By December of 1901, the Venezuela debt dispute (with the possible incursion by Germany and Great Britain) worried Root, Secretary of the Navy John D. Long and John Hay. The unstable world situation dictated precautions in Cuba. The national interest demanded that the United States maintain the advantage it retained. Complete Cuban independence was unrealistic; Cuban independence with American safeguards was practicable.

The Secretary of War's fundamental premise was that the United States

[45] Leech, *Days of McKinley*, 569.

[46] E. Stanwood, *History of the Presidency* (New York, 1928), II, 51-58, 73, 77; Pedro V. Vergara, "The Attitude of the United States Toward the Question of Cuban Independence, 1895-1902," unpublished M. A. thesis, Univ. of California, 1934, 93; Portell Vilá, *Historia de Cuba*, IV, 143, points out that no date was set for leaving the island; Robinson, *Cuba and the Intervention*, 207, contends that the decision to hold the convention was due to political considerations and not to recognition of Cuba's immediate readiness to assume control.

[47] Martínez Ortiz, *Los primeros años*, I, 171.

[48] Leech, *Days of McKinley*, 393-94.

could never tolerate a foreign country's occupation of Cuba. As a lawyer he attached importance to the establishment of a solid legal basis which would enable the United States to thwart foreign interest in Cuba. Root's official biographer has summarized the Secretary's outlook:

Throughout this period, the Washington Administration seems to have been worried by the bugaboo of German aggression. There is no question but that Root looked upon Germany as a "predatory nation" with designs on naval bases throughout the Caribbean. Years afterward, Root said, "You cannot understand the Platt Amendment unless you know something about the character of Kaiser Wilhelm the Second." It would be rather more accurate to say that it was necessary to know something of the estimate which Root and other American officials contemporaneously formed of the character of the Kaiser and of German policy.[49]

From the 1870's onward, American and German naval planners conjectured and speculated about possible war between the two countries. The big prize was economic control of Latin America, accompanied by the possession of naval stations. Unreality marked the plans, particularly on the German side, but enough sparring went on to make the United States wary of Germany. In 1896, Ernest von Halle, a big navy advocate, pointed out the desirability of the Danish West Indies, while Admiral Tirpitz eyed Curacao, St. Eustatius, Dutch Guiana, and Galapagos. Fears of German restiveness influenced America's Cuban policy, but the machinations of big navy men, Junkers and pan-Germanists, never quite overcame the restraints applied by the Kaiser

[49] Jessup, *Root*, I, 315, 374. The documents printed in *Die Grosse Politik*, and those microfilmed after the Second World War, together with the thorough research of Alfred Vagts in *Deutschland und die Vereignigten Staaten in der Weltpolitik* (New York, 1935), reveal that Germany would take no action in the western hemisphere to incur the enmity of the United States between 1898 and 1902 without European support. Vagts saw the United States interest in Cuba as primarily economic and secondarily as missionary (pp. 1283, 1320). On p. 1311, Vagts claims that another reason for leaving Cuba was to avoid the appearance of threatening Colombia and Nicaragua with whom the United States wished to negotiate for an isthmian canal. The microfilm of the German Foreign Ministry Archives, Series I, Reel 119, vol. I, Part 10, frames 409-491, B1112/1 *"Die Monroe Doktrin"* and Part 4, frames 305-421, vols. 2, 3 G 1380/1 and 2 *"Die Allgemeine politik der U.S.,"* Reels 108, 109, deal with reports incoming to the *Auswärtige Amt* from the United States. Series III, Reels 4 and 5 are incoming reports from the ministers in Central America. No German plans for the area were noticed in these documents. No outgoing instructions were found in these reels. See L. B. Shippee, "Germany and the Spanish American War," *American Historical Review*, XXX (July, 1925), 754-777, and L. M. Sears, "French Opinion of the Spanish-American War," *Hispanic American Historical Review*, VII (Feb. 1927), 25-44.

[50] A. Vagts, "Hopes and Fears of an American-German War, 1870-1915." *Political Science Quarterly*, LIV (Dec. 1939), 514-535, and LV (March, 1940), 53-76; D. Perkins, *A History of the Monroe Doctrine* (New York, 1955), 208-09; B. Schwertfeger, *Die*

and the German foreign secretary, Bernhard von Bülow.[50] Great Britain, looking for assistance in the Orient and possible aid to remain outside the Triple and Dual Alliances, cultivated the United States on issues in China, Alaska, and Panama. The Germans, heavily committed elsewhere with their *Weltpolitik* and "Risk Fleet" policies, had no desire to provoke the United States unaided.

No competition for Cuba's favors could be allowed to jeopardize the delicate tension between European powers in Africa, Asia, the Balkans and Alsace-Lorraine. Nevertheless, both Germany and Britain had increased their volume of trade in Cuba. In direct response to this situation, Wood urged measures against this influx. On one occasion Root drew Secretary Hay's attention to the attempts of British and German consuls to prevent agreement between Cuba and the United States. He commented, "I should be glad if proper steps could be taken to secure either a change of conduct or a change of residence on their part.[51] By opposing German and British commercial thrusts, the United States Government managed to blunt European political overtures in Cuba.

Root also utilized the Monroe Doctrine as precedent for shielding Cuba by citing the noninterference and no-transfer principles on several occasions.[52] He continued to seek a Cuban-American agreement which would give legal treaty status to the security principles of the Monroe Doctrine. This, however, waited until 1901.

Root's immediate measures regarding Cuban-American security dealt with real estate at Guantánamo Bay. On May 14, 1900, he transmitted to Wood a letter from the Secretary of the Navy.[53] Root stressed the importance of securing the point of land forming the eastern shore of the entrance to Guantánamo Bay for a naval coal depot. Root asked Wood to begin negotiations, keeping the purpose confidential.

Long's letter said in part:

Since the termination of the war with Spain, the Department has had under consideration the selection of a site for a naval coal depot somewhere near the east end of Cuba. In view of the probable construction of a trans-isthmian canal, the

Diplomatischen Akten des Auswärtigen Amtes 1871-1914 (Ein Wegweiser), III (Berlin, 1924), 90, corresponding to *Kapitels* 4201, 4202, 4203, 4204 of *Die Grosse Politik*. See also the marginal notes and letters of the Kaiser and Bülow of April 7, 1898 and April 15, 1898, where they wish to avoid arousing distrust among the other powers and the United States. See also E. T. S. Dugdale, ed., *German Diplomatic Documents, 1871-1914*, II, 507-11; III, 151.

[51] Wood papers, Root to Hay, Feb. 25, 1901.

[52] J. A. Logan, Jr., *No Transfer: An American Security Principle* (New Haven, 1961), 265-66.

[53] Wood papers, Root to Wood, May 14, 1900.

possession of Porto Rico, and the necessity for protecting the island of Cuba from foreign aggression, it is necessary that the United States should control the windward passage through which commerce and our transports and war ships must pass on the way to the canal from northern ports. The strategic value of this passage is very great.

In 1899, the *U.S.S. Eagle* surveyed the area and a geodetic survey charted the entire island of Cuba. On June 20, 1900, Root wrote Wood again on the subject. He maintained that the United States had to retain bases in Cuba in order to require the Cuban government to protect life and property.[54]

Negotiations proceeded during the summer and fall of 1900, lapsing in 1901 due to political complications which arose from the length of time required for acceptance of the Platt Amendment. The sparse evidence indicates that Wood located the land and the owners at Guantánamo, and that some attempt to buy the land was made through a third party. The Navy urgently pressed Root and Wood to gain control of certain harbors, chiefly Guantánamo, Nipe, Havana, Bahia Honda and Cienfuegos. Strong Cuban opposition to American bases was the most important deterrent to leasing specific sites before May of 1902; however, during the debate on the Platt Amendment, general consent of the Constitutional Convention was obtained. The matter was finally resolved by the conclusion of a treaty in 1903 between the Republic of Cuba and the United States, specifying Bahia Honda and Guantánamo as the bases.[55] It is a tribute to President Tomás Estrada Palma, who fought the proposal for a base at Havana, and to Root for his restraint in awaiting a treaty instead of simply taking the land on conqueror's rights. Quite obviously, concern for American security overrode interest in Cuban self-determination on this particular point, even though American demands were quite lenient.

As a result of Wood's trip to Washington, the political campaign at home, and apprehension about foreign interest in the Caribbean, President McKinley directed that on July 25, 1900, an order be promulgated by the

[54] Wood papers, Root to Wood, June 20, 1900.

[55] Wood papers, Hay to Wood, Jan. 15, 1901, Admiral Hackett to Root, Feb. 21, 1901; Root papers, Root to Wood, Feb. 25, 1901; Gen. N. D. Miles to Root, Nov. 15, 1900; Fitzgibbon, *Cuba and the United States*, 105-07. In the eventual treaty, the United States was given the right to use and occupy adjacent waters, to improve and deepen the entrances and anchorages, but not to use the premises for any other purpose than as coaling and naval stations. Cuban trading vessels were given free passage in such waters. The United States recognized the "continuance of the ultimate sovereignty of the Republic of Cuba" over the area and Cuba agreed to the "complete jurisdiction and control" of the area by the United States. No base was ever established at Bahia Honda and the land was relinquished by the United States in exchange for larger acreage at Guantánamo.

[56] U.S., Congress, House, "Annual Message of the President," doc. 1, xli, 56th Cong., 2d Sess., Dec. 3, 1900.

Military Governor of Cuba for holding a constitutional convention.[56] Civil Order 301 cited the Joint Resolution as its precedent and stressed the success of municipal self-government.

The Military Governor of Cuba directs the publication of the following instructions: Whereas the Congress of the United States by its joint resolution of April 20, 1898, declared
"that the people of Cuba are, and of right ought to be, free and independent;
"that the United States hereby disclaims any disposition or intent to exercise sovereign jurisdiction or control over said island except for the pacification thereof, and asserts its determination, when that is accomplished, to leave the government and control of the Island to its people."
And whereas, the people of Cuba have established municipal governments, deriving their authority from the suffrages of the people given under just and equal laws, and are now ready, in like manner, to proceed to the establishment of a general government which shall assume and exercise sovereignty, jurisdiction and control over the island;
Therefore it is ordered that a general election be held in the Island of Cuba on the 3d day of September, in the year nineteen hundred, to elect delegates to a convention to meet in the city of Havana, at twelve o'clock noon on the first Monday of November, in the year nineteen hundred, to frame and adopt a constitution for the people of Cuba, and, *as a part thereof, to provide for and agree with the Government of the United States upon the relations to exist between that Government and the Government of Cuba,* and to provide for the election by the people of officers under such constitution and the transfer of the government to the officers elected.
The election will be held in the several voting precincts of the Island under and pursuant to the provisions of the electoral law of April 18, 1900 and the amendments thereof.
The People of the several provinces will elect delegates in number proportioned to their populations as determined by the census, viz: The people of the Province of Pinar del Rio will elect three (3) delegates. The people of the Province of Havana will elect eight (8) delegates. The people of the Province of Matanzas will elect four (4) delegates. The people of the Province of Santa Clara will elect seven (7) delegates. The people of the Province of Puerto Principe will elect two (2) delegates. The people of the Province of Santiago will elect seven (7) delegates.[57]

This order met widespread opposition among Cuban politicians.[58] *La Discusión,* a prominent Havana newspaper which frequently criticized the Military Government, reported rumors from Washington that the United

[57] DIA 1947-2, C.O. 301 of July 25, 1900. C.O. 316 of Aug. 11, 1900 established the rules for the election, which paralleled those of the first electoral law (italics mine).
[58] Martínez Ortiz, *Los primeros años.* I, 161-68; Portell Vilá, *Historia de Cuba,* IV, 166-67, contends that order 301 was intended to continue the United States policy of dividing Cuban society and thereby ruling it. Actually, unity would have delighted the War Department and Wood.

States would control Cuba's debts and international policies. Juan Gualberto Gómez, a leading Negro radical, instantly demanded that the question of relations be separated from that of making the constitution. The Republican party of Havana concurred, and the Nationalists issued a statement rejecting Order 301. At one point, the members of nine groups joined in a telegrammed protest to McKinley. They received no reply and later discovered that the member delegated to send the telegram had failed to do so.[59] The *New York Times* qualified its misleading statement that all Cubans hailed the call for the convention by adding that the radicals wanted to double or triple the specified thirty-one delegates to meet in convention. Many Cubans who could not reconcile themselves to including relations with the United States in their constitution withdrew from politics, refused to campaign or changed parties. Yet through the barrage of protests and the murk of apathy emerged the desire of most Cubans to utilize the opportunity in Cuba's best interests.[60]

The first eight months of Leonard Wood's administration had been full of confident action, hope and promise. Self-government had begun with success and only a handful of doubtful signs. Nevertheless, the conflicting principles of American national security and Cuban self-determination had not been reconciled. The next ten months would bring hardening divisions of interest and concrete results with enduring consequences for Cuba.

If Cuban politics seemed a mixed success, one great achievement marked the period from May to October 1900. Drs. Walter Reed, William C. Gorgas, Jesse Lazear, James Carroll and Aristidos Agramonte had at last begun to eradicate the yellow fever menace by following the theory of Dr. Carlos Finlay. The story is familiar; it is enough to say that this was probably the most brilliant achievement of the Military Government of Cuba. As a doctor, but more because of his leadership qualities, Wood had the vision to give the support of the Military Government to the experiment of these army doctors. Wood said that the whole Spanish-American war was worth this discovery alone.[61]

---

[59] Martínez Ortiz, *Los primeros años*, I, 168.
[60] *New York Times,* July 30, 1900; Robinson, *Cuba and the Intervention,* 209.
[61] See Hagedorn, *Wood,* I, 323-28; Fitzgibbon, *Cuba and the United States,* 37-44.

CHAPTER VI

THE CONSTITUTIONAL CONVENTION, AUGUST, 1900 THROUGH JANUARY, 1901

On General Wood's return from Washington, Cuban politicians met him with a storm of controversy over the terms of Civil Order 301. Radicals objected violently to considering relations with the United States simultaneously with their constitution, and many petitions flooded the Governor's Palace requesting that the number of delegates to the convention be doubled. The imperturbable General moved ahead, preparing the Cubans for their Constitutional Convention.

Wood recommended to Root that the Cubans be allowed to consider their constitution and relations with the United States separately. He observed that whenever the Cubans were dealt with frankly, they moved closer to the United States; every string attached to independence merely intensified their desire for it. He contended that the separation of relations and the constitution would lessen criticism from agitators and reduce suspicion among the moderates.[1] Wood also mentioned that all parties had requested continuation of the rule that a voter could vote for only four-fifths of the candidates, thus assuring minority representation from each province.[2] When no action was taken by the Secretary of War on the delicate subject of Cuban-American relations, Wood raised the issue twice more in September, but as election time approached, the question remained unsettled.

On August 13 Wood embarked upon a three-week trip around the island, to implore Cubans to send their best men to the convention. Wood wrote to Root that he planned to warn party leaders all over the island that if they sent "a lot of political jumping jacks" to trifle with the convention, their work would be discounted in Washington.[3]

General Wood, greeted warmly wherever he went, received a tumultuous

---

[1] Wood papers, Wood to Root, Aug. 6, 1900.

[2] *Ibid.*, Wood to Root, Sept. 8, 1900, Sept. 14, 1900.

[3] *Ibid.*, Wood to Root, Aug. 13, 1900; Box 239, *New York Evening Post*, Aug. 9, 1900; *New York Times*, Aug. 6, 1900.

welcome in Santiago. His speech at the dinner given there in his honor is typical of the message he brought to the Cubans.

I am here as your friend, and in no other capacity.... Whatever the ultimate destiny of Cuba may be, its immediate future is independence. This is no political move on the part of the United States, but a sincere desire to do what is right. Therefore, I beg you, as a personal favor to me and to the United States Government, to sink your political differences and passions and to send men to the convention who are renowned for honor and capacity, so that the convention may mean more than the Cubans even now anticipate.[4]

During Wood's absence from Havana, two of his antagonists contacted President McKinley. Salvador Cisneros Betancourt and José Lacret Morlot, the latter a general in the army of liberation, objected to the provisions of Order 301 and to the infringements upon Cuban independence by the United States.[5] Cisneros urged modification of the electoral law to allow wider suffrage, and more convention delegates. He contended that the time had come for the United States to remove its troops and allow the Cubans to frame a constitution by and for themselves. Assuring McKinley that the Cubans would look to the United States for guidance, Cisneros also mentioned Cuba's dependency upon the United States for trade. No United States reply appears in the records.

Cisneros and Lacret subsequently informed the press that they had appealed to the United States to leave Cuba. They described the Military Government as the worst possible and remarked ominously that only time could tell whether a revolution against the United States would be necessary.[6] While Cisneros had influence in Puerto Príncipe and Lacret among his ex-soldiers, the two men in no way represented a consensus.[7]

Root saw no harm in doubling the number of delegates to the convention if popular pressure so desired, but he deferred to Wood's judgment. When Wood returned to Havana from his trip around the island, he rejoined that the parties petitioning for additional convention delegates were in the minority, that the satisfaction with thirty-one delegates was general, and that

[4] *New York Times*, Aug. 27, 1900; Wood papers, subj. file 253, *St. Louis Republic*, Aug. 27, 1900; Hagedorn, *Wood*, I, 322; Martínez Ortiz, quoted in Hagedorn, *Wood*, I, 321.

[5] DIA 1947-4, Aug. 18, 1900, Cisneros Betancourt to McKinley, copy. DIA 1947-5, cablegram dated Aug. 17, 1900, from Juan Valenzuela, the Mayor of Guanabacoa, to McKinley.

[6] *New York Times*, Aug. 19, 1900.

[7] Wood papers, Wood to Root, Sept. 8, 1900.

it was already too late to change.[8] A little silence and delay gave the General his way.

At the end of August, one of Wood's frequent letters to President Mc-Kinley pictured everything in good order.

The general sentiment is for Independence provided such independence can be obtained under an absolutely stable and equitable government. That such can be obtained under some of the men now presenting themselves is seriously doubted by members of all independent classes. While they talk independence to each other and in public, in talking with me they all say that we ought to go slowly. They wish to put the burden of going slowly upon us and are not willing themselves to frankly advocate such a course.[9]

In attempting to ensure the success of the coming election, Diego Tamayo, Secretary of State and Government, sent a circular letter to the civil governors, a copy of which Wood forwarded to Root to show that "a lot of men here are trying to do what is right." Tamayo called for a united, patriotic front of all social elements in Cuba to be represented in the convention and prove themselves worthy of independence.

The convocation by the intervening government of a Constituent Convention is the most momentous step made in the political history of Cuba, being at the same time the noblest act of the American Nation because it appears of all this that a foreign government whose military forces occupy the territory, holding in its hands all the reins of power, spontaneously notified the people intervened, of its desire to deliver to them their sovereignty. . . .[10]

Máximo Gómez, the most influential man among the Cubans, consistently supported the *Nacionalista* party, which campaigned for unity as well as independence. Gómez declared that no one who had not fought against Spain should be elected to the convention; let the Spaniards and counter-revolutionaries stand aside and join the patriots later, on equal terms under the republic.[11] This position did not rally the various factions.

Enrique José Varona explained the moderate position. When asked by the Republican party of Puerto Príncipe to be a candidate for the convention, he declined.[12] Basically, Varona believed that in a modern age, countries were

[8] Root papers, Root to Wood, Aug. 18, 1900, cable; Wood to Root, Sept. 3, 1900, cable; DIA 1947-12, copies of Wood cables.

[9] Wood papers, Wood to McKinley, Aug. 31, 1900; Wood to O. H. Platt, Dec. 6, 1900.

[10] Root papers, Wood to Root, Sept. 15, 1900, enclosing Tamayo's letter which was dated Aug. 25, 1900.

[11] *New York Times,* Aug. 21, 1900.

[12] Varona, *De la colonia a la república,* 205-8. The letter was dated Aug. 21, 1900 and addressed to General M. Ramos, President of the Republican Party of Puerto Príncipe (Camagüey).

interdependent. Because of the difference in size and the geographical proximity of Cuba and the United States, it was necessary to consider American interests in the convention. Varona feared the delegates would not do this and therefore felt he could not serve in the convention. Varona preferred cultural freedom to strife-ridden political freedom and sought for Cuba a position similar to those of Belgium and Switzerland, who were protected by the greater powers. "*La intervención vino porque tenía que venir,*" Varona said, the intervention came because it had to come. From the days of the Grant administration, it was clear in Washington that a nation as close to American doors as Cuba could not remain in insurrection. Varona agreed that the delegates should give legal form to a constitution, but contended that resistance to the United States was suicide. He thought it better to devote his life to Cuban culture as a simple citizen and an administrator in the Department of Education, as long as he was asked to do so. Both the Nationalists and the Republicans ignored such advice and issued strong platform statements against the United States, in a popular but unrealistic vote-getting strategy.[13]

While many Cubans were apathetic, and a few hostile to the move, most of those who were active hailed the opportunity they saw in the convention. Manuel Márquez Sterling denounced Varona's letter for "throwing cold water" on a great project. He ridiculed as "remarkable stupidity" the complaint of J. A. G. Lanuza, the deposed Secretary of Justice and Public Instruction, that the United States merely replaced Spain as a colonial power instead of preparing Cuba for independence.[14] The Cuban political spectrum contained intransigent radicals led by Juan Gualberto Gómez and Salvador Cisneros Betancourt, amenable radicals like Domingo Méndez Capote, conservative revolutionaries typified by Diego Tamayo, and Democratic Unionists such as Eliseo Giberga and Eusebio Hernández. Some influential men, like Varona, had left politics. There were, in addition, the almost voiceless Cuban people.

There existed another point of view held by some merchants, planters and professional men. These conservatives disliked the United States for social and cultural reasons, resenting the incursion of "inferior" ideas and attitudes. Enrique Casuso denounced the separatists for their "myopic" clinging to the United States before the war, blaming them for American distrust of Cuba's capacity for independence. Expansion, however, he considered natural to America's federal system; territories all too quickly became states. He ac-

[13] Martínez Ortiz, *Los primeros años de independencia*, I, 168.
[14] Quesada, *Epistolario*, II, 53, Márquez Sterling to Quesada, Sept. 4, 1900; Portell Vilá, *Historia de Cuba*, IV, 146-47; *Havana Post*, Aug. 21, 1900.

cused the Spaniards and Autonomists of prizing Spain too highly and caring too much for public office. Casuso believed that neither autonomy nor a protectorate could stop the Americanization of Cuba and that complete independence should be demanded.[15] Critical of other factions, he offered no constructive program, while his group aided Cuban disunity.

On September 15, people voted quietly throughout the island. The campaign had been marked by occasional disturbances such as a crowd in Marianao breaking up a meeting of the Democratic Union party with the tacit consent of the *alcalde,* who was a *Nacionalista.*[16] The vote was light and its outcome regarded as a victory for the revolutionary element of the Republican and Nationalist parties. Alfredo Zayas, one of the new delegates (fifth president of the republic in 1921), issued a statement that the convention would pursue an independent course, allowing no influence by the American representatives, and would refuse to consider relations with the United States. Alejandro Rodríguez concurred with Zayas that relations with the United States should be considered by a separate commission.[17] The statement, intended for popular consumption, reflected the futile objections of most of the delegates to the inexorable demands of the Military Government. At the end of October, just before the convention, the *New York Times* editorialized that the United States planned to spend two more years preparing the island for self-government. Some delay was expected, because the convention probably would be unable to prepare a constitution before Congress recessed in March, and the new Congress could not consider it until the spring session of 1902. After that it would take time to verify the stability of the Cuban government under the new constitution.[18] Events were to prove this estimate too long.

Máximo Gómez hoped the national convention might heal dissension, preferring this to the obstacles which Cubans had placed in the way of the Military Government. The old General did not blame the Americans for delay in achieving independence and was confident that the promises of the Secretary of War would be kept.[19] Yet Cuban skepticism can be appreciated. Despite the promises of the Joint Resolution, the President and the Secretary

---

[15] E. Casuso, *Politica cubana y sistema americano* (La Habana, 1901), 1-36 ff. Also see *Havana Post,* Aug. 18, 1900, reporting the Havana Democratic Union party meeting as the biggest in years where businessmen and men of letters met for the first time since the occupation. Eliseo Giberga spoke against any ties to the United States and urged Cubans to stay away from the polls.

[16] CDDC 4592, Sept. 15, 1900, report of Major George Dunn, JAG of Dept. of Western Cuba to the Adj. Gen. (Col. Scott).

[17] *New York Times,* Sept. 5, 1900, Sept. 19, 1900, Sept. 17, 1900.

[18] *Ibid.,* Oct. 28, 1900.

[19] *Ibid.,* Sept. 28, 1900.

of War, the political-minded Cubans feared American security and economic interests would dictate some form of subservience regardless of the stability of Cuban society.

Most of the delegates were revolutionaries, veterans of service in the war against Spain, men who had repeatedly been asked by the people to serve their country or who had thrust themselves into leadership positions. Only two of the thirty-one delegates could be called pure conservatives; the others ranged from conservative revolutionaries to extreme radicals.[20]

Twelve were generals or colonels in the Cuban army of liberation, ten were lawyers or judges, one a planter, three doctors of medicine, three men of letters, one a diplomat and one a newspaperman. Twenty-eight had served Cuba in the revolution. More than twenty were employed by the Military Government. Although some local groups allied for this one election, there was no national party, and party affiliation meant little in convention. Men with a Republican leaning outnumbered the Nationalists seventeen to thirteen, and one former autonomist, Giberga, was elected by a Republican-Democratic Unionist coalition.[21] The Republicans drew most of their support from Santa Clara, Matanzas and Puerto Príncipe; Nationalists were strong in Pinar del Río, Santiago and Havana.

Leonard Wood wrote to Root that ten of the delegates were men of the first class, fifteen of doubtful quality and six among "the worst political rascals and fakirs in Cuba." Not over 30 percent of the qualified voters appeared to have cast their ballots, which Wood attributed to their increased liberty and reluctance to "take another leap in the dark. . . . In other words, they lack confidence in their own people." He predicted that the convention speeches would represent both the good and bad sides of Cuba and would justify future United States supervision. Realistically, the convention represented the class which would govern Cuba when the Americans withdrew, for the highly intelligent Cubans of land owning, industrial and commercial classes avoided politics. Cuban politicians, according to Wood, were "doctors without patients, lawyers without practice and demagogues living on the subscriptions of the people and their friends." [22]

Actually, the election was not a failure. Out of a possible 185,501 eligible and registered, 131,627 Cubans voted; only 150,648 had been eligible to

[20] DIA 2229-5, list of delegates and alternates elected to the Cuban Constitutional Convention. For a table on the names of the delegates, their backgrounds, party, vote on the Platt Amendment and career under the Republic, see Appendix D.

[21] Riera, *Cuba política*, 23-67.

[22] Wood papers, Wood to Root, Sept. 26, 1900.

vote the previous June.[23] Hope could be voiced that each voting experience increased the chances for Cuban confidence in the franchise and peaceful political change. It was undoubtedly true that the people were enjoying a better living than before and were sick of violence and war. Some simply assumed the United States would control the convention and therefore stayed away from the polls. Others believed that the convention presented Cuba with a great opportunity.

During the third week in October, Wood again met with Root in Washington. When he passed through New York, the *Sun* quoted him as saying the Cubans would be permitted to manage every detail of making their constitution and therefore could construe nothing as American coercion. He would declare the convention open and leave the *convencionales* to their own devices. No draft of a constitution or any person would be sent by the United States Government to the convention to force the delegates to copy the American Constitution. Wood refused to forecast when the United States would leave Cuba, because departure time depended upon the outcome of the convention.[24]

With high hopes, the members of the Constitutional Convention of the Island of Cuba met at the Martí Theater in Havana at 2:00 P.M. on November 5, 1900. Everyone in the crowded public session felt the excitement of embarking upon a great enterprise for Cuba. General Wood called the convention to order and made the following statement:

It will be your duty, first, to frame and adopt a Constitution for Cuba, and *when that has been done, to formulate what, in your opinion, ought to be the relations between Cuba and the United States.*

When you have formulated the relations which, in your opinion, ought to exist between Cuba and the United States, the Government of the United States will doubtless take such action on its part as shall lead to a final and authoritative agreement between the people of the two countries to the promotion of their common interests. . . .

Under the order pursuant to which you have been elected and convened, you have no duty and no authority to take part in the present government of the Island. Your powers are strictly limited by that order.[25]

Apparently the General lingered for a moment to stress the fact that relations and the constitution could be considered separately,[26] then left the convention hall and the delegates entirely to themselves.

[23] Wood, *Civil Report,* 1900, III, Report of Sec. of State and Govt., (Tamayo) table 8, p. 14; Riera, *Cuba política,* 24.

[24] Wood papers, box 239, *New York Sun,* Oct. 21, 1900; *New York Times,* Oct. 21, 1900.

[25] Wood, *Civil Report,* 1900, II, C.O. 455 of Nov. 9, 1900 (italics mine).

[26] Robinson, *Cuba and the Intervention,* 213, quoting the *Havana Post.*

It is not known whether Root authorized this changed wording, which seemed to separate the hated question of relations from the constitution. Wood wanted to mollify Cuban feelings on the subject, but semantic niceties meant little to him; certainly he did not intend for the convention to ignore the issue. One way or another, Root and Wood planned to evoke a proposal of special Cuban-American relations from the convention. Cubans complicated matters by seizing upon Wood's alteration as an excuse for delay.[27]

One of the first acts of the convention was appointment of a committee to call on General Wood and "manifest the satisfaction with which the delegates have seen him carry out the delicate mission entrusted to him." The same committee was also to request the General to telegraph the President that the assembled delegates

greet with profound gratitude and affection the President of the United States of North America and they are satisfied with the honesty demonstrated in the fulfillment of the declarations made in favor of the liberty and independence of the Cuban people.[28]

The eighty year old lawyer Pedro González Llorente, as the oldest delegate, was asked to take the chair and served as president pro tem until November 24, while the convention was organized. After the credentials of the members were approved, the delegates authorized the rules of procedure from the 1895 Constitution of Yaya and created two standing committees and five sections composed of convention members.[29] They also agreed to limit the number of

[27] Albert G. Robinson, who was present during most of the sessions, contends in his *Cuba and the Intervention,* 212-13, that order 455 changed order 301 in that it separated relations from the constitution. According to Robinson, Wood allowed them to do this, therefore the Cubans should not be blamed for violating instructions and not considering relations promptly. Robinson errs in thinking Wood held there was any intrinsic difference in the outcome intended and also in forgetting that the Cubans tried to delay the question of relations. He even says that Americans at home knew nothing of the order change and thus erroneously blamed the Cubans for delay. Actually, copies of all orders were in the hands of the War Department, Senate and House committees.

[28] Wood papers, Wood to Root, telegram, Nov. 5, 1900; DIA 2229, Wood to Root, telegram, Nov. 5, 1900, "Convention opened promptly at two immense enthusiasm and cheering for United States absolutely harmonious every evidence that satisfaction of the people was entire and complete."

[29] BIA Library, Box 208A, "Record of Sessions of the Constitutional Convention of the Island of Cuba," vol. I, sessions 1-8, Nov. 6 to Nov. 22, 1900. The seven volumes, covering only the public sessions, are probably the only complete, verbatim records in English that exist. Miss Jane F. Smith, Chief, Social and Economic Branch, National Archives, to author, March 18, 1963. See also, *Mención histórica,* 172-73. This volume is especially valuable because it contains summary minutes of the thirty secret sessions held during the debate on the Platt Amendment. No stenographers were allowed in

speeches relative to a motion, although the time and number could be extended by vote. The Constitutional Convention met ninety-two times from November 5, 1900 to September 30, 1901, in sixty-two public and thirty private sessions. The private sessions were held mainly in the spring of 1901 during the debate on the Platt Amendment.[30]

The delegates sat at desks ranged in a semicircle around the president. Carrying on above the noise of street traffic, they took an oath of office whose words were to haunt them in June of 1901, as they voted on the Platt Amendment:

We, the delegates elected by the people of Cuba to the National Constitutional Convention, swear and promise to fill our positions faithfully. We renounce publicly and solemnly our fidelity or contract, past, direct, or indirect, to any other State or nation; swearing the solemnity of the freedom and independence of Cuba, and accepting and obeying the constitution which this Convention adopts as well as the government thereby established.[31]

On November 24, Domingo Méndez Capote was elected President of the Convention, Juan Ríus Rivera First Vice-President and Llorente Second Vice-President, with Enrique Villuendas (the youngest delegate, in his mid-twenties) and Alfredo Zayas as secretaries. A committee on the constitution was composed of Ríus Rivera, Llorente, Berriel, Quesada and Bravo Correoso. From the end of November to January 22, in seven public meetings and many committees, the convention considered numerous drafts of proposals. Llorente and Berriel, who knew most about the academic side of the law, bore the brunt of the drafting.[32]

Men like Berriel, Llorente, Sanguily, J. G. Gómez, Méndez Capote, Giberga, Morúa, Villuendas and Portuondo, schooled in philosophy, history and the law of nations, valued form and style in speech, but tried to avoid academic abstractions and strove to be as practical as possible. All agreed upon having a written constitution, three branches of government, a bicameral legislature, strong checks and balances upon each of the branches. References were chiefly to the United States Constitution – very rarely to those of European or Latin American countries.[33] The idea of a written

the sessions and the two secretaries, Villuendas and Zayas, kept a summary record. The Library of the Department of State has a copy of *Mención histórica*.

[30] *Mención histórica*, 702.

[31] Robinson, *Cuba and the Intervention*, 214.

[32] BIA Library, Box 204 A, "Record of Sessions" 9-15, Nov. 23, 1900 to Jan. 22, 1901.

[33] E. Hernández Corujo, *Los fundamentos históricos y filosóficos de la constitución de 1901* (La Habana, 1953), stating that it was a product of the principles of 18th century bourgeois law and natural rights. 1-32, ff. See Ramon Infiesta, *Historia constitucional de Cuba* (La Habana, 1942). He states that the Constitution of 1901 was

constitution which limited the powers of government and guaranteed civil liberties was superimposed upon centuries of Spanish paternalistic government; while the result represented the wishes of the Cubans of the time [34] and was the best Cuban constitution ever written, still it lacked sufficient balance and authority. There was continuity in the many ideas and clauses carried over from previous constitutions (particularly that of Yaya in 1895).[35]

When it was proposed to invoke the Deity in the preamble, old Cisneros argued vehemently for a republic of and by the people. Joined by Zayas, he claimed the subject of God had no place in the Cuban constitution. This aroused Llorente, who emotionally testified to the existence of God and the reliance of all people upon Him. Sanguily pointed out that faith was needed to perpetuate civilization and that most persons put their faith in a higher being. The delegates, persuaded either by the arguments from the floor or by their respective backgrounds, decided the question in the affirmative.[36]

After the preamble, the first three titles or articles defined the nation, citizens and rights of foreigners.[37] Following some argument about the nature of immigration regulations, the assembly agreed to a clause which would encourage immigration of foreigners by giving them equal rights with Cubans. The fourth article concerned individual rights such as *habeas corpus,* prompt and legal trials, inviolability of domicile and mail, freedom of speech, petition, patent, assembly and property, and freedom from forced migration.

Llorente and Cisneros were again opposed on the matter of separating church and state. Llorente felt the state could best protect free worship and religion, while Cisneros wanted a free state, unhampered by religious impediments. Giberga joined with Llorente in maintaining that religion helped to provide order by forming a moral base for society, but he suggested the convention leave the issue to the future. Sanguily's argument, advocating

liberal, hard to amend, codified, protective of property and individual liberty through separation of powers, *habeas corpus* and judicial review, 332-42.

[34] Portell Vilá, *Historia de Cuba,* IV, 161, who maintains that the 1901 constitution reflected the will of the people and was thought out with patriotism, serenity and judgment; Martínez Ortiz, I, 192-93 of *Los primeros años de independencia,* said that the United States Constitution, separation of powers and the principles of Montesquieu appealed most to Cubans.

[35] Méndez Capote, *Trabajos,* I, 127-28, e.g., defining territory of Cuba, citizenship, immunity of congressmen, individual rights, universal suffrage, suspension of civil liberties in time of war.

[36] BIA Library, Box 205 A, III, 16-20, Jan. 25 to Jan. 30, 1901.

[37] DIA 1947-25, the official translation of the proposed constitution of the Republic of Cuba, Feb. 21, 1901. Copies are also printed in the reports of the Secretary of War and of the Military Governor of Cuba for 1901.

separation of the two as the modern way, convinced the delegates. The vote was 24 to 4 in favor of separating church and state.[38]

The debate turned next to the relationship of the state to education. After a long discussion of American education, with its many independent schools, the delegates voted 18 to 11 in favor of state control over all levels of education. These men believed that only the state could bring culture to its people and feared that private higher education would lead to license and abnormalities uncontrollable by the state. Schools were to be open to anyone of the proper age. Primary education was to be free and a direct function of the municipality, supervised by the state.[39]

No one in the convention objected to universal suffrage for men, which the Cubans had enjoyed in Oriente during the Revolution. Sanguily caustically observed that the Cuban aristocracy was neither numerous nor distinguished, the middle class numbered no more than one hundred persons, and "none of us know any more about picking a good *alcalde* than do the masses." Although Berriel and Gener agreed that this was a matter for statute, which could be altered more easily than the constitution, the delegates granted suffrage to all Cuban males over the age of twenty-one, with the exception of idiots, criminals and military or naval personnel on active duty. They wanted no discrimination over the franchise, yet balked at women's suffrage; this was too modern.[40]

Article V vested sovereignty in the people of Cuba. Yet government was centralized. The provinces of Cuba, differing but little in terrain, dialect, economy and beliefs, were administrative units established gradually by Spain and continued by the United States and the Cuban Republic. Although Giberga and Sanguily argued cogently for certain sovereign powers in the provinces, Zayas and others countered that this type of federalism would not serve Cuba's interests. While the delegates deplored the centralized oppression of the provinces that had emanated from Spanish controlled Havana, they feared even more the chaos which could come without a central insular authority. They chose the type of federalism which wrote into the constitution certain duties of cities and provinces, continuing past practice.[41]

Article VI discussed the legislative powers of the senate and house of representatives. The senate was to be composed of four senators from each province, elected for eight-year terms (one-half each four years) and chosen by double the number of electors composed of the highest taxpayers and

[38] BIA Library, "Record of Sessions," Box 205 A, Jan. 27, 1901.
[39] *Ibid.,* Jan. 28, 1901.
[40] *Ibid.,* Jan. 30, 1901, February 9, 1901. The vote against women's suffrage was 17-9.
[41] *Ibid.,* Feb. 5, 1901, Feb. 6, 1901. During January and February, they were holding two sessions a day as they debated the proposed clauses.

provincial council. A senator had to be thirty-five years of age, born in Cuba and in possession of his civil rights.[42]

The delegates wished to give the president enough power for control, yet avoid the example of generals who became dictators in Latin America.[43] After intensive debate, they provided that the president could be impeached and tried by the senate. The senate could also try cabinet ministers and governors if they were accused by the house of representatives of violating the constitution. The chief justice of the supreme court presided over the senate sitting as a court of justice; as such, the senate could impose removal from office and debar from another. The senate was also to confirm executive appointments and treaties.

The house was to be composed of one representative for each 25,000 Cubans, elected by universal manhood suffrage for a two-year term. A candidate had to be twenty-five years old and eight years a resident of Cuba. Congressmen could hold no other government positions except professorships. They were granted legal immunity and made their own rules of procedure. The two houses had the usual powers of legislation, except for the power to introduce legislation on appropriations. Only the executive could propose the budget, and this specifically had to be on an annual basis. Congress could contract loans, coin money, prepare laws, regulate commerce, give amnesty, grant citizenship and levy taxes and duties; but it was specifically prohibited from using budget laws to reduce revenue or cause administrative changes. While the president could veto legislation or give it a pocket veto, congress could override a veto with a two-thirds vote.

Article VII covered the powers of the executive. The president had to be at least forty years old and native born, or if naturalized, a ten-year veteran of the Cuban army. (This allowed Máximo Gómez to run.) The president elected in the same manner as a senator and confirmed by a congressional electoral college, served a four-year term and could be re-elected only three times. His duties were to sanction, promulgate, execute and enforce laws and executive orders, convene special sessions and adjourn congress if the two houses disagreed on an adjournment date. He had to present an annual message, budget and matters requested from him by Congress unless they were of a secret nature. He also suspended and pardoned provincial governors and suspended the resolutions of municipal and provincial councils. By a vote of 21 to 6, the *convencionales* provided for presidential suspension of civil liberties in times of national danger. Ironically enough, the men who

---

[42] *Ibid.,* Jan. 30, 1901. The convention voted 15-10, to allow minority representation on *ayuntamientos,* provisional councils and in House of Representatives.

[43] *Ibid.,* Jan. 30, 1901; Box 205 A3, vol. V, sessions 28-35, Feb. 12, 1901.

hated the iron hand of Spain found it necessary to include such a clause in their constitution because they feared the explosiveness of their people.

Article VIII explained the duties of the vice-president. Article IX contained the extraordinary requirement that all decrees and orders of the president must have cabinet approval of the appropriate secretary to be enforceable. The secretaries were held responsible to congress in a quasi-parliamentary way, which handicapped the executive and violated the principle of separation of powers which the *convencionales* sought to follow.[44]

Article X explained the exercise of judicial powers. Justice was to be gratuitously administered, which meant that judges charged no fees as they had under Spain. A supreme court justice had to be a Cuban, thirty-five years old, with ten years of practice as a lawyer or professor. The three *salas*, or chambers – civil, criminal and administrative – were to be continued. The highest court heard appeals, decided upon jurisdiction and constitutionality. Extra courts and commissions were forbidden. Justices were removable only for crime, not for political views or judicial decisions.

Article XI required that provincial governors were to be elected directly by the people and that their duties were those not specifically detailed to the state or municipality. Governors could suspend any municipal resolution. Article XII included the municipalities in the constitution, and Article XIII directed that all property not belonging to the province, municipality, individual or group belonged to the state. The constitution provided for duties and payment of provinces and municipalities.

Some of the detailed clauses in the constitution would not have been found in that of a more stable society. Because of their own and the American fear of their incurring debts which they could not repay, the delegates included a clause which required that any proposal for a loan must also explain the means by which it was to be repaid; furthermore, two-thirds of the total membership of congress had to approve such a loan. The rules on loans for the state applied to provinces and municipalities as well.

Finally, the constitution provided for amendments and transitory rules, such as continuing previous laws in force until revoked. Amendments were achieved by a two-thirds vote of each house. Six months after an agreement to amend, a constitutional convention would convene to approve or reject the amendment.

At 4:50 P.M. on February 21, 1901, the delegates reassembled in the *Teatro Martí* to sign two copies of the finished constitution as corrected by the committee on style. One copy was sent to the archives and the other to General Wood. At that time neither Llorente nor Cisneros would sign the

44 *Ibid., New York Times*, Jan. 27, 1901.

constitution because of objections to certain clauses, but they relented later in the spring. During the twenty-five minute ceremony Méndez Capote delivered these remarks:

We have worked with the good wishes and purposes of which we are capable and have contributed all of our intelligence, will and faculties. We are not the judges of our conduct. We hope that good fortune crowns our desire for its success and the stable basis of a prosperous, free and happy Cuban Republic.

The stenographers recorded great and prolonged applause and cries for *Cuba Libre*.[45] The delegates had two missions left: determining relations between the United States and Cuba and framing an electoral law.

As early as 1850, José Antonio Saco, the Cuban patriot and poet, had claimed that Cuba's revolt against Spain, United States intervention and Spain's defeat were inevitable, but that Cuba would be ruined as a sovereign nation because of America's strength.[46] The high hopes of the delegates for *"Cuba Libre"* waned as they faced the grim reality of determining Cuban-American relations. The Cubans delayed any consideration of these relations throughout the fall of 1900 and most of the first two months of 1901 in hope of avoiding the subject they found so disagreeable until they were independent. They all wanted close ties, especially military and economic, to the United States, but in the form of a treaty between two equal nations.

As the delegates concentrated upon the framing of their constitution, the press and periodicals of both countries erupted in varying predictions. These predictions indicated that the McKinley administration pursued a moderate course. The *New York Evening Post,* ordinarily hostile to the administration's Cuban policies, contended that whatever Cuba's internal government, the United States would have some control of her foreign relations. The *Post* justified this view by Cuba's geographical proximity to the United States.[47]

In the *Forum,* "a Cuban" wrote "A Plea for the Annexation of Cuba," claiming that independence could not have been won without American aid and that Cubans could not be independent because they were racially dis-

---

[45] BIA Library, Box 205 A3, vol. V, "Record of Sessions," Feb. 24, 1901; Robinson, *Cuba and the Intervention,* 221, says the hall was fairly filled, but not overcrowded and that it was not a day of national demonstration, but merely another day to Cubans. Many did not know the new constitution was being signed that day, many doubted American good faith and thought the constitution a meaningless act; Fitzgibbon, *Cuba and the United States,* 74, says Cubans were not elated because they thought the constitution would be rejected by Root.

[46] Martínez Ortiz, *Los primeros años de independencia,* I, 269.

[47] Wood papers, Box 253, *New York Evening Post,* Oct. 26, 1900.

united, poor and politically uneducated.[48] In the same magazine, a clergyman with years of Cuban service pointed out that Cuban independence was recognized in the Joint Resolution and should be granted since it was desired by the majority of the public in both nations.[49] The *Nation* blamed McKinley for not rescinding the portions of Order 301 dealing with relations.[50] J. I. Rodríguez, a Cuban conservative, wrote in the *Forum*, "Cuba is properly American, as much as is Long Island, and I believe there can be but one ultimate disposition of it – to be included in the great American sisterhood of states." [51]

Walter Wellman defined the Cuban problem as one of keeping the pledge of the joint Resolution without turning Cuba over to disorder and failure. Praising the work of Leonard Wood and Elihu Root, Wellman explained that the Island of Cuba was to become an independent republic with restricted outward relations. Foreign relations would be controlled so the Cubans did not endanger themselves; domestic affairs, tariff and commerce matters were to be left to the Cubans. Bonded indebtedness was to be avoided. When McKinley signed the constitution of the Cubans, parliamentary and presidential elections would be held and the republic established.[52] While Wellman was wrong in his prediction about foreign relations, his article probably reflected administration thinking during the fall of 1900. Specific points about these "ties of singular intimacy" which were to bind the two nations had changed rapidly during 1900, and it is not surprising that they did so again before the Platt Amendment was framed in February of 1901, although basic policy remained unchanged.

Apart from the speculations of the press, the delegates moved to form the Cuban diplomatic attitude toward the United States. On the previous November 24, the convention had voted to appoint a commission to consider relations after the constitution was finished. Two days later Juan Gualberto Gómez, joined by Cisneros and Lacret, protested that the delegates were not part of the insular government and thus had no authority to treat relations with the United States.[53] On November 28, Villuendas, Quesada and Sanguily reasoned that the convention was not a legislative assembly with

[48] A Cuban, "A Plea for the Annexation of Cuba," *Forum*, XXX (Oct. 1900), 202-214.
[49] C. W. Currier, "Why Cuba Should be Independent," *Forum*, XXX (Oct., 1900), 139-146.
[50] *Nation*, "Distrustful Cuba," LXXI (Oct. 25, 1900), 324.
[51] J. I. Rodríguez, "Can There Ever be a Cuban Republic?" *Forum*, XXX (Dec. 1900), 437-441.
[52] W. Wellman, "The Cuban Republic – Limited," *Review of Reviews* (American), XXII (Dec., 1900), 708-712.
[53] *Mención histórica*, 191-93.

sovereign powers but was convened to perform certain tasks, and an answer to General Wood such as that proposed by Gómez would only lead to increased control by the intervening power. After short and heated debate, it was decided by a vote of twenty-two to four that the convention was not the place to debate their authority to consider relations.[54] In quashing this radical attempt, the convention agreed that it could consider relations, but off the floor, decided to delay consideration until it was absolutely necessary. Not until February 11, 1901 did the delegates resolve that each section should select one man to serve on a committee to draw up the bases for relations with the United States.[55] The next day the names of Diego Tamayo, Quesada, Juan Gualberto Gómez, Villuendas and Silva appeared on the committee.[56] Tamayo could be counted on to appreciate the interests of both countries, as could Quesada, despite his anti-American speeches. Colonel Villuendas, the darling of Cuban politics, was a Hotspur whose position on Cuban-American relations would change during the spring. Gómez and Silva were violently opposed to dealing with the United States in the manner directed.

While the Cubans delayed and the press speculated, Secretary Root and General Wood discussed the terms, outlined the previous July, which they believed the Cubans should be required to meet. Root spent most of November in Cuba, where he and Wood talked with Cuban leaders. Root's biographer states,

His later correspondence with Wood shows that the main outlines of the anticipated agreement on the relations of the two governments had been talked over at this time. No record of the conversation is available, but judging from expressions in subsequent letters between them, they were substantially along the lines ultimately adopted.[57]

This indicates that the Cubans were apprised discreetly of what to expect and that the American executive branch was far ahead of the legislative in the matter.

On December 22, Wood wrote Root that he would proceed with constitutional relations as Root had indicated, but bringing the matter before the people would be difficult. Wood thought the plans would meet with general acceptance if factions such as labor agitators were dealt with firmly.[58]

---

[54] E. Roig de Leuchsenring, *La enmienda Platt*, I, 54-57. Roig devotes many pages to discussing a motion which was defeated. The significant fact is that the convention voted against Gómez and for obeying orders 301 and 455. Gómez was an ex-slave, had been imprisoned in Spain, was very popular in Cuba, one of the leaders closest to Martí. See Roig's edition of *Por Cuba Libre* (La Habana, 1954).

[55] BIA Library, "Record of Sessions", Box 205A3, vol. V, Feb. 12, 1901.

[56] *Mención histórica*, 393.

[57] Jessup, *Root*, I, 308; *New York Times*, Nov. 11, 1900.

[58] Wood papers, Wood to Root, Dec. 22, 1900.

Thirteen days later he reported, "I have seen different representatives of the different 'groups' of the Convention during the past ten days and most of them are willing to accept 'Relations' on the terms discussed by us on our recent trip." [59] At this point, the radicals, led by Convention President Domingo Méndez Capote, wanted the President of the United States to call a special session of Congress to approve the Cuban constitution, or at least obtain authority from Congress to authorize the new constitution to be provisionally in effect for a year. The radical Cuban program called for American troops to remain in Cuba to observe the state of stability of the new government. The United States would recognize this government only as it existed under American control; if the desired stability was manifested, an agreement could be made to hold general elections in December 1901, approve the constitution and depart the island. The conservatives in the convention, according to Wood, would do whatever the United States wanted. He recommended the radical plan with a military governor veto power added, but Root had his own ideas.

In the Root files is an undated, unsigned piece of brown paper with "read to cabinet" penciled at the top left. Typed beneath are four points: (1) Right of the United States to intervene in Cuban affairs, (2) No other government to get sovereignty in Cuba, (3) U.S. naval bases in Cuba, (4) Laws of the military government to remain in force.[60] These were the points which Root and Wood had suggested to the Cubans that the United States would demand.

A letter to Wood dated January 9, defined most of Root's views on the subject.[61] He thought an operating Cuban legislature with a military governor veto power would be unsafe. He wanted to facilitate a clean cut between the military government and the new government; the military governor would

[59] Root papers, Wood to Root, Jan. 4, 1901.

[60] Root papers, Box 130 rough draft, nd. ns. Pencilled changes placed pt. one in the 3rd spot, pt. 2 in one, 3 in 5 and 4 left as it was. A debts clause was added later. Portell Vilá, *Historia de Cuba*, IV 163-64, found an interview by the *Colorado Springs Gazette* of December 3, of Senator Henry M. Teller, in which he called for a free Cuba with responsible institutions of courts and customs, and foreign relations to be limited by Washington, U.S. Army to remain in Cuba for some time, and a constitutional limitation on the Cuban tariff. Portell maintains these points influenced Root. This is doubtful, given the earlier timing of the Root-Wood conversations. What they really indicate is that the father of the Joint Resolution had doubts about Cuba and shared the views of most congressional and administration leaders about safeguards in Cuba.

[61] Wood papers, Root to Wood, Jan. 9, 1901. Portell on pp. 164-65 of vol. IV, *Historia de Cuba*, says that Wood interfered with the Constitutional Convention in December, by telling certain members the Root desires on relations. Yet Méndez Capote had told Wood that he could not have left the convention more alone "if we were on the moon." Wood papers, Wood to Root, Feb. 8, 1901. Wood of course did talk with various *convencionales* from time to time, stressing the time factor and apprising them of the U.S. interests in relations.

transfer the administration and depart, leaving a few troops to keep order as a favor while the new government took hold. When Wood pressed for tariff reduction, Root replied that action was improbable because the President was indisposed with the grippe. (Both McKinley and Hay were sick most of January, throwing the burden of Cuban affairs on Root.) [62] Furthermore:

[Y]ou might as well ask a foot-ball team in full play for their autographs as expect to get legislation on any important new subject from Congress at present; nor do I think that at the present stage of Cuban affairs it is desirable. In the fall of 1899 I was in favor of legislation giving special advantages to Cuba during our occupation, but matters have gone so far now that I think any action on that subject must necessarily wait until after the presentation to Congress of the whole subject of the relations between the two countries, which will come up on the transmittal of the proposed constitution and of such expression as the convention may make on the subject of relations, or upon their refusal to make any expression.[63]

When the time came, Root continued, the McKinley administration might find itself in an untenable position. It could not demand that Cuba rely on America's benevolence and give America special privileges, while it continued to hold her commercially at arm's length. But Root thought the lobbies, uniting the minority Republicans with the Democrats, would defeat any bill for lowering the tariff on Cuban sugar and tobacco. He did not want the question of commercial relations to jeopardize the question of political relations and hoped the convention would not insert any such proposal into its suggestions.[64] It is notable here that Root considered a breach in the American tariff wall a means to play fair with Cuba, not to control her.

Root desired the Cubans to send up their finished constitution as soon as possible. As he told Wood:

I think they should be promptly confronted with the proposition that we desire as soon as possible to be relieved from the burden and annoyance of their government, and the expense of maintaining troops there which must be about a half million dollars a month. . . . It seems to me, moreover, that the people of Cuba will never come to a realizing sense of what is before them, or of what the relations of this country mean, until they are brought face to face with the prospect of being abandoned to their own devices, and I think the sooner we have the round up the better.[65]

[62] Leech, *Days of McKinley,* 566-67, showing the cabinet did not meet from 8 January to 22 January. Cf. Dawes, *Journal of the McKinley years,* 260-61.
[63] Wood papers, Root to Wood, Jan. 9, 1901.
[64] Wood also wrote to Senators, urgently requesting tariff reduction of 50 percent or even of 25 percent. Among the correspondents were H. C. Lodge, O. H. Platt, H. M. Teller, Redfield Proctor. Letters from Wood of Jan. 12, Jan. 12, Jan. 12, Jan. 18 respectively.
[65] Wood papers, Root to Wood, Jan. 9, 1901.

Root also showed irritation with his colleagues in Washington.

I am getting pretty tired of having Congress on the one hand put us under independence of Cuba resolutions, and Foraker franchise resolutions and resolutions of hostile inquiry and criticism, and on the other hand shirk all responsibility; and I do not relish the prospect of having the Cuban constitution and proposals as to our relations just too late for Congress to act, compelling us to go on and govern for another year with the Cubans howling at us to do something and the democratic press abusing us because we do not do something, and with the certainty that we will be met by a denial of our lawful authority if we undertake to do anything, and with a possibility of a change for the worse in Cuban conditions.[66]

The President agreed with Root's idea of placing on Congress the responsibility for quickly deciding the Cuban question.

Root cautioned Wood to take special care not to give anyone with whom he talked the opportunity to say he was making demands or official suggestions.

It seems to me important that the convention shall be required either to take the initiative in stating what they want the relations to be, or to distinctly refuse it.[67]

Root told Wood to disabuse the Cubans of the idea that the United States would protect them no matter what they did. He asserted that in any future conflict Americans would not be as altruistic as they were in 1898.

Despite his vexation, Secretary Root intended the Cubans to consider that by international law, which all other nations recognized, the United States had as a result of the peace treaty the right to protect Cuba. This right, contained in the Treaty of Paris, should be continued by a reservation, with the consent of the Cuban people, when the government was turned over to them. Root held that if the United States handed over the reins of government and then made a special treaty with Cuba, other nations would no longer recognize an American right to interfere in any Cuban quarrels unless such interference was based on the Monroe Doctrine. But the Monroe Doctrine was not part of international law, and Root maintained,

How soon some one of these nations may feel inclined to test the willingness of the United States to make war in support of her assertion of that doctrine, no one can tell. It would be quite unfortunate for Cuba if it should be tested there.[68]

On the basis of this long letter, it may be concluded that Root had no intention of annexing Cuba and heartily wished the Cubans could manage their own affairs. At the same time, he planned to request further congressional

[66] *Ibid.*
[67] *Ibid.*
[68] *Ibid.*

responsibility for the Cuban question. Finally, he was determined that Cuba should never fall prey to a foreign power or endanger American security.

In his reply, Wood agreed that the Cuban matter should be put into the hands of Congress without delay. Wood urged that Congress state its exact intentions and demand proof of stability before withdrawing control. He added that American policy toward Cuba had made it impossible for the business and conservative elements to state frankly what they desired, because they feared being "left in the lurch by our Government's sudden withdrawal." Wood ended,

I believe in establishing a government of and by the people of Cuba and a free government, because we have promised it, but I do not believe in surrendering the present Government to the adventurers who are now in the Convention and in many of the municipalities.[69]

Many elements in Cuba depended upon the United States for protection. In late January, great excitement was caused in Havana by false reports that all American troops would be withdrawn within twenty-four hours. All business stopped, the customs revenues dropped, orders for merchandise were cancelled. The affairs of the city momentarily ceased, as the Military Government was swamped by pleas for verification. Wood thought this reaction showed what a "great stampede" would result when Americans actually did leave, because of the overall lack of confidence in Cuban capacity for self-government.[70]

Realizing that basic distrust still existed among Cuban factions, Root nevertheless continued to plan the future relations between the two countries. On January 11, he had requested the Secretary of State, John Hay, to consider the issues involved in deciding the ultimate relations between the United States and Cuba.[71] Root listed his own thoughts with these points:

69 Wood papers, Wood to Root, Jan. 19, 1901.
70 Wood papers, Wood to Root, Jan. 31, 1901.
71 Wood papers, Root to Hay, Jan. 11, 1901, copy; McKinley papers, Root to Hay, Jan. 11, 1901, showing the President's close attention to the issue. The points read as follows: (1) That in transferring the control of Cuba to the Government established under the new constitution, the United States reserves and retains the right of intervention for the preservation of Cuban independence and the maintenance of a stable government, adequately protecting life, property and individual liberty.
(2) That no government organized under the constitution shall be deemed to have authority to enter into any treaty or engagement with any foreign power which may tend to impair or interfere with the independence of Cuba, or to confer upon such foreign power any special right or privilege without the consent of the United States, and that the United States shall be entitled to be a party, in the first instance, to any negotiations having in view any such provision.
(3) That to facilitate the United States in the performance of such duties as may devolve upon her under the foregoing provisions and for her own defense, the United

right of intervention, prevention of debts which would impair sovereignty, establishment of naval bases and recognition of the validity of the laws of the Military Government. Root's biographer concluded: "So far as the records disclose, this is the first written draft of what ultimately became famous as the Platt Amendment." [72] With two verbal changes, Root's points were the same as the earlier rough draft, pencilled "read to cabinet." Root was taking the initiative in framing a more definite policy for the time when the Cuban Convention would submit its results to Congress.

The convention delegates had been in touch with Wood, and in January, rumors spread in Havana. Reportedly, the pro-United States faction proffered a program abiding by the Monroe Doctrine and accepting naval bases on Cuba's north and south shores, a defensive alliance, American occupation of Cuban forts and most-favored-nation treaty privileges. This faction also agreed to administration of Cuban foreign relations from Washington for two years. The anti-American group was still reluctant to consider any program for relations.[73] In trying to sidestep a disagreeable subject, Cubans wasted time they could have spent framing proposals to the United States, which might have been acceptable to both sides. Their delay forced the United States to take action.

The general ideas of what was to compose the Platt Amendment were in the air from the fall of 1899 onward. As events progressed peacefully in Cuba, the timetable for Cuban independence was compressed. A plan of relations was agreed upon in Washington in July 1900; during November, specific points emerged. In February 1901 the issue of future relations between Cuba and the United States came to a head.

States may acquire and hold the title to land, and maintain naval stations at certain specified points.
(4) That all the acts of the Military Governor, and all rights acquired thereunder, shall be valid and be maintained and protected.

[72] Jessup, *Root,* 1, 310.

[73] *New York World,* Jan. 3, 1901; Robinson, *Cuba and the Intervention,* 227-28; *New York Times* of Feb. 16, 1901 quoting *La Nación* of Feb. 1, 1901.

CHAPTER VII

BIRTH OF THE PLATT AMENDMENT,
FEBRUARY TO MARCH 2, 1901

The United States Congress attached the Platt Amendment to the Army appropriation bill for 1901 when Cubans delayed deliberation of the delicate subject of future Cuban-American relations. The Cuban Convention did not finish the constitution until February 12, and not until February 26 and 27, when the delegates heard the American Senate was considering the question, did they rush through their proposals for relations with the United States. During the month of February the American position became firm; the Cubans took their stand also but were forced that spring to modify it to coincide with United States demands.

General Wood transmitted the first formal notification of McKinley's desires to the Cuban Convention Commission on Relations on February 21. Although the Platt Amendment became law on March 2, 1901, it was not accepted by the Cubans until June 12.

President McKinley's intention to call an extra session of Congress, if need be, to dispose of the Cuban question, caused a strain on Capitol Hill.[1] Congress had contemplated no legislation, and questions now arose about how to release Cuba. How could Congress circumvent the Teller Resolution and limit Cuban independence? What right had Congress to regulate relations or prescribe the form of government for a foreign country? Constitutions could not be treated like bills.[2] Senator Orville H. Platt of Connecticut, chairman of the Senate Committee on Relations with Cuba, attempted to find an escape from the dilemma. In contact with Root and McKinley, the senator began to formulate the points he deemed important to Cuba relations.[3] On January 11, Secretary Root had already set on paper

---

[1] Leech, *Days of McKinley,* 569.

[2] *Ibid.*

[3] Platt papers, "History of the Platt Amendment," by Kathleen Lawler, 13 page manuscript, May 17, 1928; L. A. Coolidge, *Orville H. Platt, An Old Fashioned Senator* (New York, 1910), 338-56. Miss Lawler, Platt's devoted secretary, was responsible for

the points he had Wood suggest informally to the Cuban *convencionales* in December. Platt prepared a preliminary draft of his own ideas on the 30th and called a meeting of the Republican committee members for Sunday, February 3, at the home of Senator William E. Chandler.[4] Present were Senators Aldrich, Spooner, Cullom, McMillan, Chandler and Platt.

Platt first proposed incorporating the conditions to be required by the United States into the body of the Cuban constitution, an idea with which Root and Wood agreed. It was agreed at that time, however, that these conditions could be recited in an ordinance appended to the constitution if the Cubans objected to incorporation within the document.[5] The conferees also wanted continued the sanitary arrangements made by the Military Government to stop the spread of disease. All considered Cuban indebtedness the most serious problem at the time and quickly agreed that Cuba should not be allowed to "run into debt beyond her means to pay." In such an event the money might be borrowed in Europe; in default of payment, European powers could threaten to occupy Cuba. Senator Chandler later noted that, "Every provision that could be thought of as desirable and that was afterwards adopted was discussed." [6] Practical men that they were, these Republican Senators estimated that before drafting a plan, they would have to decide how to secure the assent of the Democratic committee members and the Senate as a whole.[7]

At a second meeting on February 10, the group determined to prepare a set of propositions to test the disposition of the opposition members of the committee.[8]

collecting his papers and presenting them to the Connecticut State Library, and also provided much of the information in Coolidge's book.

[4] *Ibid.* The Republican members of the Cuba Relations Committee were: O. H. Platt, Conn., Nelson Aldrich, Rhode Island, W. E. Chandler, New Hampshire, J. C. Spooner, Wisconsin, C. K. Davis, Minnesota, Jas. MacMillan, Michigan, Shelby M. Cullom, Illinois. H. M. Teller, Silver Republican, Colorado, H. D. Money, Dem., Mississippi, Marion Butler, Populist of North Carolina, J. P. Talliaferro, Democrat of Florida, and W. Allen, Populist, of Nebraska made up the rest of the committee.

[5] William E. Chandler papers, Memorandum, "Senator Platt and the Platt Amendment," April 21, 1906.

[6] *Ibid.*

[7] *Ibid.*

[8] At the first meeting Chandler had proposed that the Cubans issue to the United States one hundred millions of 4 percent fifty years bonds as a partial compensation for the expenses to liberate Cuba from Spain. Spooner objected, and the point was omitted. The Platt papers have several drafts without date or name, but which probably were the thoughts of the various committee members. The first one in the file is the preliminary draft of four points which Platt probably jotted down on January 30, 1901. They read: troops in Cuba for 10 years, two naval bases, no debts to endanger sovereignty, and treaties and commerce to be operated by the United States. The

Its plan of procedure was shown by Platt in a letter of February 5 to Root:

Talking the matter over with the republican members of the Committee on Relations with Cuba, we think that it would be advisable, without much delay, to formulate a resolution authorizing the President to discontinue the military occupation of Cuba whenever certain things shall have been agreed to and incorporated into the constitution of Cuba, making it certain that results which we deem essential are assured. . . .[9]

Although Root took up the issue of relations first, Platt supplied the means of drafting and passing the amendment which bears his name. Platt reasoned that since Congress had authorized the intervention, Congress could end it. He also calculated, with Chandler's help, that the most expeditious manner of passing the bill through Congress would be as a rider to the Army appropriations bill.[10]

After Platt and Root conferred, the Secretary of War instructed Wood to send up the Cuban constitution and proposals on relations as soon as possible, together with his own comments. If Cubans did not submit a constitution with remarks on relations, Wood was to inform Root so the Secretary could issue instructions.[11]

Letters apparently crossed in the mail, for on February 8, Wood wrote to Root:

What we want now is a clean cut, outspoken statement of just what we are going to do. It really does not make much difference what the details of this action are, only let us block it out and stick to it.[12]

To support his statement, Wood informed Root that Máximo Gómez had told him personally that American withdrawal at that time would lead to bloodshed within sixty days. Wood explained, "This would come not from any desire for fighting, but simply because the present leaders suspect each

Lawler memorandum implies that Platt wrote these points after the meeting of the 10th. The second draft in the papers is typed with the pencilled notation at the top by Platt, "Proposal submitted to the president by me" and states: (1) ratification of the acts of the military occupation and the protection of the interests acquired thereunder. (2) The right of intervention to maintain the independence of Cuba, for the protection of life and property therein, its permanent pacification and the stability of its government. (3) naval stations, and a force necessary for their maintenance. (4) supervision of treaties with foreign powers. (5) supervision of bonded debt of the island. These points show Platt was considering a more stringent plan for Cuba than that which was eventually adopted, and for that reason was not the prime author. These points were submitted on February 11th to the President, probably after consideration of the results of the meeting with Root on the 5th. Olcott, *McKinley*, II, 211-12. The Platt papers contain the final draft by Platt and Spooner.

[9] Jessup, *Root*, I, 311.
[10] *Ibid.*, Leech, *Days of McKinley*, 570.
[11] Wood papers, Root to Wood, Feb. 7, 1901; Jessup, *Root*, I, 311.
[12] Wood papers, Wood to Root, Feb. 8, 1901.

other and each one would make a grab for the first place." Working from such a premise Root, Platt and Wood moved toward a definite statement which would oblige Cuba to maintain stability without American occupation. Despite Wood's basic disagreement with the idea of leaving so soon, he added that everything in the island was in shape for any move Root wanted, either a quick departure or otherwise.

On February 9, Root sent Wood a long letter of instructions containing the nucleus of the Platt Amendment.[13] This letter was a policy statement of the executive branch of the government and

expressly conditioned upon the subsequent action of the Congress. Root drafted it himself, read it aloud to McKinley and the Cabinet and left a copy with the President who made a few changes. Root then gave a copy to Senator Platt.[14]

[13] Wood papers, Root to Wood, Feb. 9, 1901; Wood to Tamayo, Feb. 21, 1901; Tamayo to Wood, Feb. 23, 1901; Wood to Root, Feb. 19, 1901.

[14] Jessup, *Root,* I, 212, Root to Jessup, Nov. 19, 1929 and Root to Hagedorn, Jan. 4, 1930, 312 n. The question of the authorship of the Platt Amendment has occasioned much controversy. Platt later wrote to his oldest friend, Jno. H. Flagg, who had asked him about Walter Wellman's article which said Root was the author of the Platt Amendment: "It is not fair for Mr. Root to claim the entire credit for what is called 'the Platt Amendment'; it is not fair for Mr. Wellman to claim it for him, neither would it be fair for me to claim exclusively, the credit for it. It started with an original draft of four propositions by me, submitted to President McKinley and Secretary Root." It was the subject of conversations with them, then with the committee. Spooner and Platt drafted it in its final form. "While these consultations were going on, Secretary Root gave the orders to General Wood, stating what the President insisted upon...." However Platt's ideas differed from Root's on supervision of treaties, commerce and debts, Root's prevailed and were dated earlier. Platt quotation taken from Platt papers, Platt to Jno. H. Flagg, Jan. 18, 1904. See Wood papers, Platt to Wood, April 24, 1901, where Platt said he was scarcely entitled to the credit of having his name attached to the amendment because it was drafted in consultation with the President and Root on lines which had been communicated to Wood.

In 1916 Root told James Brown Scott that he had authored clauses one through four and seven, Wood authored number five and committee numbers six and eight of the Platt Amendment. Root to Scott, Oct. 24, 1916, in J. B. Scott, *The Recommendations of Habana concerning International Organization* (New York, 1917), 11. It appears that Root's ideas had reached paper on January 11, and Platt's on January 30. Their meeting on February 5 probably revealed happily to both that they thought along the same lines.

Some historians, Cuban as well as American, have gone back to General James Harrison Wilson as the source of the Platt Amendment. Wilson had written Root a six point proposal on Cuban relations. Root ignored this letter, Wilson papers, Wilson to Root, Nov. 3, 1899. See Wilson to Robinson, May 9, 1901, where he said all the Platt bill provisions were suggested by him at one time or another. Jessup and Fitzgibbon point out that the main difference between the Wilson and Root proposals is that Wilson wanted these points to be drafted between two independent governments, after Cuba had been set free. Also Wilson wanted to annex Cuba and Root did not.

Portell argues in *Historia de Cuba,* IV, 170-172, 192, that the amendment's method of passage was sneaked through against the wishes of the majority of Americans, that

After quoting from the Joint Resolution and the Treaty of Paris, Root said:

It is plain that the government to which we were thus to transfer our temporary obligations should be a government based upon the peaceful suffrages of the people of Cuba, representing the entire people and holding their power from the people, and subject to the limitations and safeguards which the experience of constitutional government has shown to be necessary to the preservation of individual rights. This is plain as a duty to the people of Cuba under the resolution of April 20, 1898; and it is plain as an obligation of good faith under the Treaty of Paris. Such a government we have been persistently, and with all practicable speed, building up in Cuba, and we hope to see it established and assume control under the provisions which shall be adopted by the present Convention. It seems to me that no one familiar with the traditional and established policy of this country in respect to Cuba can find cause for doubt as to our remaining duty. It would be hard to find any single statement of public policy, which has been so often officially declared by so great an array of distinguished Americans authorized to speak for the Government of the United States, as the proposition stated, in varying but always uncompromising and unmistakable terms, that the United States should not under any circumstances permit any foreign power other than Spain to acquire possession of the Island of Cuba. Jefferson and Monroe and John Quincy Adams and Jackson and Van Buren and Grant and Clay and Webster and Buchanan and Everett have all agreed in regarding this as essential to the interests and the protection of the United States. The United States has, and will always have, the most vital interest in the preservation of the independence which she has secured for Cuba, and in preserving the people of that Island from the domination and control of any foreign power whatever. The preservation of that independence by a country so small as Cuba, so incapable, as she must always be, to contend by force against the great powers of the world, must depend upon her strict performance of international obligations, upon her giving due protection to the lives and property of the citizens of all other countries within her borders, and upon her never contracting any public debt which in the hands of the citizens or foreign powers shall constitute an obligation she is unable to meet. . . .[15]

Root quoted at length from McKinley's message of December 5, 1899, which stressed American responsibility to form a lasting Cuban government and the need of ties of singular intimacy between the two nations. Finally, he listed the points that the people of Cuba should incorporate in their fundamental law:

1. That no Government organized under the constitution shall be deemed to have authority to enter into any treaty or engagement with any foreign power which may tend to impair or interfere with the independence of Cuba, or to

the U. S. ignored Cuban proposals and that Root's premises in the letter of February 9 were false because the Treaty of Paris obliged the United States to counsel and suggest, not rule and control.

[15] Wood papers, Root to Wood, Feb. 9, 1901.

confer upon such foreign power any special right or privilege without the consent of the United States.

2. That no Government organized under the constitution shall have authority to assume or contract any public debt in excess of the capacity of the ordinary revenues of the island after defraying the current expenses of Government to pay the interest.

3. That upon the transfer of the control of Cuba to the Government established under the new constitution Cuba consents that the United States reserve and retain the right of intervention for the preservation of Cuban independence and the maintenance of a stable Government, adequately protecting life, property and individual liberty, and discharging the obligations with respect to Cuba imposed by the Treaty of Paris on the United States and now assumed and undertaken by the Government of Cuba.

4. That all the acts of the Military Government, and all rights acquired thereunder, shall be valid and shall be maintained and protected.

5. That to facilitate the United States in the performance of such duties as may devolve upon her under the foregoing provisions and for her own defenses, the United States may acquire and hold the title to land for naval stations, and maintain the same at certain specified points.[16]

Thus Root enunciated those propositions the United States Government considered essential to preserve its own security and Cuba's independence.

On February 12, Wood wrote to Root that he was doing his best to hurry matters along but had to go slowly because the *convencionales* were inexperienced and sensitive. He had told Méndez Capote of Root's desire that the constitution and resolutions on relations go to Washington together. Root's long letter of instructions, which had been delayed in the mail, arrived on the 15th. Wood, who was about to depart for a crocodile hunt in the Zapata swamp, asked the members of the Convention Commission on Relations to accompany him on the train to Batabanó. After a state banquet there, Wood invited his guests aboard the yacht *Kanawha*, which was provided by the United States Government for his travels around the island. There he informed the Cubans of Root's letter, treating the contents as suggestions. The entire affair passed amicably, and by midnight the Cubans were on the train for Havana. When he returned to the capital two days later, he found an uproar over his interference in convention affairs. His manner of delivering the suggestions was considered an insult and the points themselves were decreed contrary to the idea of a free Cuba. Wood suspected the Cubans of taking offense to avoid the public appearance of acquiescence.[17]

[16] *Ibid.*

[17] Wood papers, Wood to Root, Feb. 12, Feb. 19, 1901. *New York Times,* Feb. 9, Feb. 11, Feb. 16, Feb. 17, 1901; Hagedorn, *Wood,* I, 350; Fitzgibbon, *Cuba and the U.S.,* 76; J. K. Bangs, *Harper's Weekly,* XLV (March 30, 1901), 334. Bangs was one of Wood's hunting guests. Portell, *Historia de Cuba* VI, 178, thought that the Batabanó

As soon as Wood returned to Havana, he acknowledged Root's February 9 letter, reporting that the convention commission's chief objections were to the points on coaling stations and intervention. In his own opinion, the demands were,

liberal, equitable and just and should be insisted upon throughout. It is very probable that we shall have to exercise directly the intervention provided for under the third article, and it is certain that we should were it not known in Cuba that in case of lack of stability and failure to observe the provisions imposed by the Treaty of Paris the United States would promptly intervene. Such knowledge will probably act as a check on the government to come.

Wood suggested the addition of a clause concerning sanitation. While Root thought it might interfere with the Foraker Act, he promised to refer the suggestion to the Cuba Relations Committee. As it turned out, the committee had already considered such a clause and included it in the final draft when Wood encouraged it.[18]

On the 21st, Wood officially communicated the executive terms to Diego Tamayo, who presented them to the Commission on Relations.[19] Despite the politically designed uproar of the *convencionales,* Wood's method of informally suggesting proposals, followed by official transmission to the Commission on Relations was effective in preparing the convention for eventual acceptance.

Back in Washington, the President's hand was evident in the shaping of the Platt bill. On February 23, Charles Gates Dawes, McKinley's youthful comptroller of the currency, called at the White House to discuss Illinois matters. He later recorded in his diary that

The Cuban constitution and its treatment at the hands of the United States is the all-absorbing problem at the White House. The President insists that in the settlement of the relations between the two countries the Congress shall bear its proper part of the responsibility. . . .
Senators Spooner of Wisconsin and Platt of Connecticut have been in consultation with the President. He has furnished them privately with his instructions to General Wood and has guided them in large part in their deliberations.[20]

The President had desired a resolution of the Cuban question from 1898 to 1901, and gladly accepted the proposal of Root and Platt. He modified

affair was another attempt to split the delegates. Bravo Correoso said as a result of Batabanó, a great dread rose in their hearts: See *Como se hizo la constitución de Cuba* (La Habana, 1928), 83.

[18] Wood papers, Wood to Root, Feb. 19, Feb. 21, 1901.

[19] CDDC 3051, Wood to Tamayo, Feb. 21, 1901; Tamayo to Wood, Feb. 23, 1901; *Mención histórica,* 523.

[20] Dawes, *Journal of the McKinley Years,* 263. "His instructions" meant his endorsement of the Root proposals with modifications, in the cabinet.

Root's letter of February 9 before approving it; he asked Platt, whose ability and influence he respected, to assist in incorporating in the statutes of the United States a definite statement of the future policy of the government toward Cuba.[21] George B. Cortelyou, the President's able secretary, even believed that the Platt Amendment was the President's plan. Many men, among them Root, Mark Hanna, John Bassett Moore, Dawes and Paul Cambon, testified to McKinley's leadership. Of cabinet meetings, Root said: "McKinley always had his way." [22]

Late on the night of February 23rd, with the aid of endless hands of solitaire and his omnipresent "Bobby Burns" cigars, Platt wrote out the first full draft of his amendment.[23] Struck with the grippe on the 24th, he asked John Coit Spooner to give the draft the benefit of his expert phraseology. When Spooner finished the next morning, he and Platt showed it to McKinley and sent a copy to Root. Both men approved. The opposition members made little objection, and it was reported to the Senate as an amendment to the Army appropriations bill. On February 27, it was moved by Senator Platt and discussed on the floor.[24]

On February 23, Root reassured Wood about recent events and explained his elicitation of public support:

My Dear General:
Do not think because I do not answer your letters specifically that they are not satisfactory and comforting. The President and I both feel that matters are going just as well as they possibly could and that you are handling the situation admirably.

Root continued by saying that through public discussion opinion was beginning to form behind the administration and with this support, the Congress would have to act and the United States could stand firm with its Cuban policy.[25]

Root enclosed a letter to Albert Shaw, his friend and editor of the *Review of Reviews*, which indicated a strategic security motivation for Cuban-American intimacy.[26] Shaw, who intended to publish an article on Cuban relations, had asked Root to check the advance sheets. Root suggested that the *Review*

[21] Olcott, *McKinley*, II, 211-212, 334-375. The Platt memo and the draft of Feb. 25 are in the G. B. Cortelyou papers with McKinley's notations in margins.
[22] *Ibid.*, 345-346. Leech, *Days of McKinley*, 667, notes. Dawes called the Platt Amendment the President's plan.
[23] Platt papers, Lawler memo.
[24] Chandler papers, Chandler memo.
[25] Wood papers, Root to Wood, Feb. 23, 1901. Wood, promoted to Brigadier General in the regular establishment at this time, jumped some 700 numbers. Yet General Bell jumped more numbers than did Wood at the same time.
[26] Wood papers, Root to Albert Shaw, Feb. 23, 1901.

of Reviews had not considered the problem of interpreting the Teller Resolution, which completely ignored special relations. According to Root, both Cubans and Americans seemed to think axiomatic America's legal right and duty to allow Cuba to establish a lawful government under any reasonable constitution and get out. Such a course, Root contended, would leave United States interests in a worse position than before the war and also abandon the safety of Cuba. Foresight demanded constitutional limitations upon the Cubans. Since Congress had tied the President's hands with the Teller Resolution, unless Cubans could be induced to cooperate voluntarily, the President had either to foresake American interests by literal interpretation of the Teller Resolution or to engage in controversy with the Cubans, in which they would hide under the wing of Congress. This would split the solid front of the United States Government. Root believed the solution was a congressional statement either abandoning American rights in regard to Cuba or requesting negotiations for Cuban and American rights as part of or an addition to the pacification which then stood as the sole object of American occupation. Root would resolve the dilemma by legalizing America's right to support Cuban independence and placing the responsibility for such action where it belonged, in the United States Congress.

On February 25, Root advised Wood that the Cuba Relations Committee was sending the Platt Amendment to the Senate with seven points agreed upon.[27] He had told Wood on the 21st that he realized the constitution could not reach Washington before the end of the session, so at this point it did not matter when the Cubans acted. Root said the President wanted the Cubans to take their time and forward provisions in regard to relations along with the constitution.[28] Root had decided to draw the United States policy line regardless of Cuban action; from this point onward, the United States Government assumed the initiative the Cubans had failed to seize.

The General pointed out to Root that the Cuban politicians believed they would lose popularity by initiating cooperative proposals. Willing to soothe the Cuban *amor propio*, Wood recommended that the provisions being drafted in Washington be sent to Havana in the form of a request instead of a suggestion.[29] The Cubans were forcing Root's hand, by showing opposition, then appearing to be coerced.

On the afternoon of the 25th, Root cabled to Wood the text of the Platt Amendment as reported to the Senate by the committee. He asked Wood to advise him of its reception by the Convention Commission on Relations.

[27] Wood papers, Root to Wood, Feb. 25, 1901.
[28] *Ibid.,* Root to Wood, Feb. 21, 1901.
[29] Root papers, Wood to Root, Feb. 25, 1901, cable.

At 8:07 P.M. Wood reported the attitude friendly as far as could be learned.[30]

Diego Tamayo told the convention in secret session the next day that the Platt Amendment had been introduced to the United States Senate. This instigated a rush to complete a set of proposals and they were finished at 2:00 A.M. the next day. Wood contended the proposals were rushed through to embarrass him and the United States. The *convencionales* believed their program would satisfy the United States Government and ward off the stringent American requirements. Perhaps they hoped their show of resistance would divide American opinion and delay American action until Congress adjourned. While their suggestions failed, the Cubans avoided acceptance of the American proposals until June.[31]

Various delegates, including Morúa, Portuondo, Núñez and Giberga, had prepared projects on relations dating back to February 12 but shelved them in favor of immediate action upon Wood's announcement. After some disagreement it was decided to treat Wood's communication as secret, as he desired, and to limit debate on the proposals to be framed by the commission.[32]

The commission submitted a preamble and five clauses in some ten pages. After mentioning civil orders 301 and 455, the preamble declared that rendering an opinion would be both easy and brief, considering the gratitude Cubans felt toward America. The delegates understood, stated the preamble, that Root's letter of February 9, signified only the opinion of the American executive and such proposals might not be approved by Congress. They deemed the communication so important that they wished to render judgment upon the question of relations between Cuba and the United States. They had carefully considered the expressions forwarded through the Military Governor and understood the United States did not want Cuba to create "danger that might be occasioned by the instability of our future institutions, disorder of our finance, or the noncompliance on our part with international duties." The Cubans found some of the American proposals, while intended to guarantee Cuban independence, unacceptable because they violated Cuba's independence and sovereignty. The delegates further averred:

[30] Wood papers, Root to Wood, Feb. 25, 1901, cable copy; Wood to Root, Feb. 25, 1901, cable. It took four minutes for one man to transmit to the other by direct cable. *New York Times,* Feb. 27, 1901.

[31] *Diario de la Marina,* Feb. 26, 1901. *Mención histórica,* 522-523; Martínez Ortiz, *Los primeros años,* I, 278-79. The delegates knew the main U.S. concern was to avoid a threat from outside the hemisphere.

[32] *Mención histórica,* 524-527.

Our duty is to make Cuba independent of any other nation, including the great and noble American nation; and if we should bind ourselves to request the consent of the United States government to our international agreements; if we should admit that they reserve and retain the right to intervene in our country in order to maintain or overthrow situations, and to fulfill duties which pertain only to Cuban governments; if, lastly, we should concede to them the power to acquire and preserve title to lands for naval stations, and to maintain them at certain places on our coast, it is clear that we might appear independent of the rest of the world, although in reality we might not be, but we never would be independent in relation to the United States.[33]

The plea stressed the care the delegates had exercised in laying the groundwork for independence in their constitution. They had resolved upon a balanced representative government and had detailed special clauses to safeguard foreigners and prevent excessive debt.[34]

When the delegates had agreed to the preamble, Zayas read the first clause, stipulating that Cuba would never enter into a treaty compromising to her sovereignty or allow foreign military forces on the island. This provoked numerous objections: the convention did not possess the power to agree to this, it should be left to the future congress of the Cuban republic, it impaired Cuba's sovereignty, Cuban agreement to the Monroe Doctrine would suffice. Giberga rose to advocate acceptance of the American executive proposals and a treaty between the two countries. Ríus Rivera countered by claiming the Congress might reject the executive proposals, hoping that the Congress might be more favorably disposed toward the Cuban proposals.

After recess the night session began. The first clause was accepted, with a second added by Sanguily and Giberga, that Cuba would never allow her territory to be used as a base for military operations against the United States or any other foreign nation. In the third clause, unopposed, the Cuban government accepted the obligation to preserve life and property under the Treaty of Paris, which had been observed by the United States. The fourth stipulation recognized the acts of the Military Government, including the Foraker act, as legally valid. After debate, Sanguily's amendment to include the Joint Resolution of April 1898 as insurance in the clause won enough adherents for passage. The fifth clause suggested a reciprocal trade agreement. After some arguments for free trade, the convention agreed that reci-

---

[33] *Ibid.,* 416.
[34] *Ibid.,* 413-422; Root papers, "Report on the Relations which ought to exist between Cuba and the United States . . ." translation of *Mención histórica* made by the Carnegie Foundation at Root's request in 1918; Geo. A. Finch to Root, May 21, 1919, letter of transmittal of documents 63 and 64 from *Mención histórica* by Secretary of Carnegie Endowment for International Peace. Wood papers, Feb. 28, 1901, 7 page certificate, Méndez Capote to Wood.

procity was more appropriate to their situation, indicating that the United States was by far their largest market. Among the other clauses debated and rejected were clauses for arbitration and sanitation: the former because it would bind future Cuban foreign policy and the latter because it was deemed an insult.[35]

The Cuban proposals of the 27th attempted to assume the initiative for providing safeguards without entering into the necessary contract with the United States. These indefinite propositions attempted to protect Cuban sovereignty from the United States, but managed to avoid all responsibility. Articles were not put into a form binding to the future Cuban government but were merely approved by the convention, with repeated assurances that Cuba would never cause the United States anxiety. Points concerning intervention, coaling stations and sanitation were virtually rejected. The *New York Times* pointed out the practical difference between the Cuban and American plans: the former granted Cuba a free hand over debts and treaties, where trouble could arise, while the American plan could prevent such danger to both countries.[36]

By early morning of the 27th, it was clear that the convention, using the American executive proposals as a guideline, was trying to weaken its strands, forgetting that the guideline was also their only lifeline. All the delegates were opposed to coercion by the American government, and a few objected to any dealing with the question of relations. Most realized some relations were necessary and hoped they could render an opinion and salvage independence. Their next task was presentation of the project to the Military Governor.

Diego Tamayo informed the convention that Wood desired the clauses to be transmitted in confidence. Giberga agreed to this plan, as did Méndez Capote, despite the charge (actually untrue) that Wood had made public the previous communications. Recalling the friction caused by the secrecy of the Batabanó meeting, Sanguily and Zayas wanted to make the clauses public. Villuendas thought Wood's confidence should be respected but said his conscience made him wish to report to the people of Cuba. This began to swing the delegates toward public announcement of the plea. With only Quílez and Giberga in opposition, the other nineteen delegates present voted to make the proposals public.[37] In open session on the 27th, the project as approved was read and given to the press, with cheers and applause from the onlookers.[38]

[35] *Mención histórica*, 527-34.
[36] *New York Times*, Feb. 27, 1901; *New York World*, Feb. 26, 1901, Feb. 27, 1901.
[37] *Mención histórica*, 534-35.
[38] BIA Library, "Record of Sessions," Box 205A3, no. 32, Feb. 27, 1901; *La Discusión*, Feb. 28, 1901. Cubans present realized the project flouted American desires.

Although Wood probably knew the general nature of the convention's deliberations, he did not receive the official transmission from Méndez Capote until the 28th.[39]

This disregard for his counsel irritated Wood; he knew the Cuban action would be overridden by the coming Platt Amendment and that negotiations would become increasingly difficult if the Cubans had to back down. Wood had cabled Washington the previous afternoon that the convention expected to deliver the results of its work that evening.[40] In a letter written the same day, Wood explained that some resistance by the convention was counseled by American agitators in Havana to cause a division in Congress. He vented his feelings to Root:

The danger which confronts us is the moral cowardice of all these men, even as good ones as Tamayo. They are emotional and hysterical. . . . They will individually assure me that the relations proposed are just, with the possible exception of the naval stations and ought to be accepted without question; collectively they are timid. They are unwilling to be responsible for anything, but say that they are willing to accept pretty much whatever we propose if the United States insists upon it. . . .[41]

Wood maintained the delegates knew full well that 90 percent of their countrymen approved the American resolutions but were silent, while the radical 10 percent were vociferous. To prevent the convention from disclaiming the power to agree on relations with the United States, Wood intended to inform the delegates that they did have that power; that was why they were assembled in the first place. Wood advocated the strong hand of authority as the only device Cuban politicians could understand.

Máximo Gómez had again visited Wood on the 26th claiming that the country would go to pieces if the Americans did not stay. The old general offered the support of the veterans to Estrada Palma for president. Wood and Gómez agreed the new government could not be established in less than a year and a half or two years and that Gómez would meet Estrada Palma in Washington in the near future for discussions. Wood concluded,

These two men swing ten times the influence of the Convention and they should be dealt with accordingly. With these two men supporting our policy we can hold the situation here absolutely without any wavering.[42]

[39] Wood papers, Méndez Capote to Wood, translation, Feb. 28, 1901, Resolution adopted by Constitutional Convention on February 25, 26, 27, on relations with the United States.
[40] Root papers, Wood to Root, Feb. 27, 1901, cable; Wood papers, Wood to Root, Feb. 27, 1901, March 2, 1901; New York Times, March 2, 1901.
[41] Wood papers, Wood to Root, Feb. 27, 1901.
[42] Robinson, Cuba and the Intervention, 244-45; Portell, Historia de Cuba, IV, 180-81. cf. New York Times, March 2, 1901; Wood papers, Wood to Root, Feb. 28, 1901,

Assured the support of Gómez and Estrada Palma, Wood reported to Root on the 28th that the constitution and project on relations were translated and ready to be sent to Washington when desired by the Secretary. He assured Root that no danger existed and that the passage of the amendment to the Army bill would have an excellent effect in Cuba. On the first of March, Root told Wood that both houses were passing the amendment as worded in his February 25 communique and that Wood would be advised as soon as the President signed, so he could inform the convention. On March 2 Wood received the Platt Amendment as passed by Congress from Root, and transmitted it to the convention on the same day.

In Washington, the Senate had passed the Platt Amendment to the annual Army appropriations bill by a strict party alignment vote of 43 to 20.[43] Platt felt indebted to the Democratic, Populist and Silver Republican committee members, who apparently agreed not to organize opposition for reasons of national solidarity. The Republicans had the votes, and opposition was desultory; the floor speeches were heartfelt but lacked organized support.

Senator John Tyler Morgan of Alabama rehearsed the usual opposition points about damage to Cuban pride, the error in legislating for a foreign country and the benefits Cubans would enjoy if they were part of the United States, ignoring the contradictions involved. Opposed to the Platt bill because he was annexationist, Morgan proposed absolute free trade and immediate independence, leaving Cuba to flounder.[44]

Democratic Senator Hernando DeSoto Money of Mississippi spoke for the Platt Amendment. While he believed any people capable of self-government and wanted the United States to leave Cuba, he had the growing feeling that withdrawal would lead to conflicts which would shake the new republic to its foundations. Senator George Frisbie Hoar of Massachusetts, high-principled foe of imperialism, found the Platt Amendment "eminently wise and satisfactory," solving a difficult problem with "wisdom and moderation." [45]

Senator J. K. Jones of Arkansas attempted to delete the bill's intervention clause. Teller rose to explain that he had represented this view in committee and was still not completely satisfied, but the Platt Amendment was more lenient than it might have been.[46] Teller's opposition was due to party considerations, pressure from Colorado silver and beet-sugar interests, and hesitation to wound Cuban sensibilities needlessly. Actually, Teller did not

cable; Root to Wood, March 1, 1901; Root to Wood, March 2, 1901, cable; Wood to Root, March 2, 1901.
  [43] U.S., *Cong. Rec.*, 56th Cong., 2nd Sess., 3151-2, 3331-2.
  [44] U.S., *Cong. Rec.*, 56th Cong., 2nd Sess., 3038-41.
  [45] *Ibid.*, 3132-5.
  [46] *Ibid.*, 3145-52.

claim that the Platt Amendment was wholly inconsistent with his resolution of 1898. The Platt Amendment allowed Cuba more independence than Teller had intended by his resolution; he never desired much more than local self-government for Cuba. Later, when the Senate congratulated him on his role in the Cuban question, Teller said he had not thought any promise necessary to make the American government give Cuba independence but had offered his resolution to ward off European intervention. He felt the Platt Amendment did not impair Cuba's sovereignty, because she could always amend her constitution.[47]

"Pitchfork Ben" Tillman turned his invective on the Republicans, claiming the Platt Amendment superseded the Joint Resolution, and men who had voted for war in 1898 were voting for the amendment to fulfill their predatory and economic inclinations. Hale of Maine countered that the Platt bill would allow the Cubans to work out their own government.[48] After Foraker failed to amend the intervention article by authorizing intervention only when there was no government capable of preserving life, liberty and property, the vote was taken and the amendment passed.[49]

In the House, John Dalzell of Pennsylvania assumed responsibility for steering the Platt bill to passage. A House Rule allowed taking the Army appropriation bill from the table, without intervening motion, to concur in the Senate amendments thereto in gross; after two hours of debate the previous question was considered as ordered and the vote taken. The Republicans had the votes and forced the House to a two-hour debate on a question already decided. Opposition members protested the infringement upon Cuba's sovereignty; others criticized McKinley's imperialism and the Republican attempt to railroad the Platt bill. Republicans countered by pointing out past Democratic administration attempts to annex Cuba and criticizing Democratic delaying tactics. Some argued for the amendment because it avoided mixing Anglo-Saxon with Latin blood, while others approved its continuation of American sovereignty over Cuba, thereby ensuring liberty for the individual Cuban. Democrats tried to arouse votes by pointing to the increased cost of the Army and Navy since the days of Grover Cleveland. Republicans retorted that no one would stand for yellow fever any more than for a pirates' nest. The debate was complicated by simultaneous consideration of the controversial Spooner Amendment on government for the Philippines. Some Republicans tried to gloss this over by ungraciously

[47] E. Ellis, *Henry Moore Teller* (Caldwell, 1941), 311-12, 343.
[48] U.S., *Cong. Rec.,* 56th Cong., 2nd Sess., 3146-7, 3150-1.
[49] U.S., *Cong. Rec.,* 56th Cong., 2nd Sess., 3151-2. See Foraker, *Notes on a Busy Life,* II, 52-5, where he predicted that the 3rd clause would be used by the Cubans as an excuse for political irresponsibility and a whipping post in their elections.

wondering aloud why their southern colleagues cared more for the freedom of Cubans and Filipinos than for the freedom of Negroes. Actually, the votes were set, and when Dalzell called for the question, the Platt bill passed by a partisan vote of 159 to 134.[50]

The significance of the congressional debate on the Platt Amendment was the extent of agreement regarding the Cuban question. Most senators and congressmen accepted the decision that despite respect for Cuban pride and the principle of self-determination, Cuban attempts at self-government should be guaranteed by the United States.[51] The reasons for the method of passing the bill were shortness of time and desire to avoid minority delaying tactics. The Platt Amendment reflected the majority opinion in the United States about Cuban-American relations.

The motives of the authors, Root and Platt, indicated their desire for an independent Cuba. Platt initially preferred to work on the Philippine question. When McKinley asked him to head the Cuba Relations Committee, however, he conscientiously made himself an expert on Cuban affairs. Platt was not impressed by the Cuban desire for freedom. Dreading American annexationist sentiment, he visualized Cubans as wards until they proved their self-control; but he did not believe they should or could be assimilated into the United States, because of their race, culture and religion.[52] He had no doubts about the beneficial influence protestant republicanism could have upon Cubans and Filipinos. He thought the Joint Resolution hampered the free action of the United States in future, unforeseen circumstances. Actually he favored closer control of Cuba's foreign relations and finances as well as a longer occupation. From Platt's point of view, despite his protective attitude, his amendment could in no way be construed as an attempt to annex Cuba.

Root, who "took the government as his client" when he became Secretary of War, always worked for Cuban nationhood. Fundamentally, he wanted to prevent foreign intervention in Cuba and attached great importance to a solid legal basis for keeping foreign interests out of Cuba. Because he en-

---

[50] U.S., *Cong. Rec.*, 56th Cong., 2nd Sess., 3331-3384. Some of the American papers opposed to the Platt Amendment were: *Boston Herald, Detroit Frees Press, Buffalo Express, Rochester Union and Advertiser, Boston Post, Philadelphia Ledger, Cincinnatti Inquirer, New York World*, March 1, 1901; Also listed by Portell, *Historia de Cuba*, IV, 202: *Baltimore American, Chicago Journal, State Diary of Columbia, S.C.*

[51] Coolidge, *Platt*, 314.

[52] *Ibid.*, Platt papers, *passim.* A strong Congregationalist, Platt's forebears arrived in the New World in 1638. If any motive is most basic in Platt's conduct at the turn of the century, it is missionary-republican. Jno. H. Flagg to Platt, April 24, 1898; Platt to Reverend George Fisher, August 19, 1898. Miss Lawler was convinced that Platt wanted Cuba to be free.

visaged that Cubans might cede the island or a part of it to a foreign power, he wanted to extend the Monroe Doctrine by fitting the Platt Amendment into the Cuban constitution, United States statute law and a treaty between the two nations. To Philip Jessup, the Secretary was even more deeply concerned about Cuban independence than might be thought:

Root also felt that it was desirable to guard against the possibility that the United States itself might try to annex Cuba through some foreclosure procedure. He was steadfastly opposed to such annexation at the time or in the future.[53]

The final possibility Root wished to avoid was that the Cuban government might become too impotent to fulfill its international obligations to protect foreign lives and property and that this condition would lead to interference by a foreign power. This concern was accentuated by the experience of the Boxer Rebellion in China at the time; he wished to avoid such an instance in the Caribbean. Root had little fear of interference with American property after termination of the occupation but believed he had a duty under the Treaty of Paris to protect the Spanish residents against reprisals.[54]

Neither Root nor Platt considered definite measures for protecting Cuba from the United States, probably because they neither favored nor expected annexation. In a day when European nations carved colonies out of Africa and concessions out of China, the Platt Amendment was not merely a clever way to establish a protectorate; the men who framed it expected Cuba to become a free, independent republic which would not cause the United States serious anxiety.

In fact, Cuba and America agreed on most points. The preamble to the Platt Amendment cited the Joint Resolution, stating the Amendment fulfilled the Resolution by directing the President to "leave the government and control of the island of Cuba to its people," when the island was pacified, adding,

so soon as a government shall have been established in said island under a constitution which, either as a part thereof or in an ordinance appended thereto, shall define the future relations of the United States with Cuba, substantially as follows:

On this definition of pacification and the duration involved centered the disagreement among American government officials and in the press. The opponents of the administration argued that Cuba was pacified as soon as the Spaniards left. Administration adherents countered that further precautions were necessary to make pacification permanent. The administration was bound to utilize a broad interpretation of Teller's clause.

The first article of the Platt Amendment read:

[53] Jessup, *Root*, I, 315, 318n. Root to Jessup, Nov. 1, 1930.
[54] *Ibid.*, 313-314.

That the government of Cuba shall never enter into any treaty or other compact with any foreign power or powers which will impair or tend to impair the independence of Cuba, nor in any manner authorize or permit any foreign power or powers to obtain by colonization or for military or naval purposes or otherwise, lodgment in or control over any portion of said island.

Aside from a few doctrinaire radicals of the convention, the delegates agreed in substance with this point. They wished to place such a stipulation in a treaty between two sovereign nations, however, instead of having it imposed upon them and placed in their constitution.

The second article said:

That said government shall not assume or contract any public debt, to pay the interest upon which, and to make reasonable sinking fund provision for the ultimate discharge of which, the ordinary revenues of the island, after defraying the current expenses of government shall be inadequate.

Most of the delegates thought some provision on this topic appropriate but believed they met American requirements by inclusion of a specific article covering the problem in their constitution. The United States considered this inadequate; it wanted authority for controlling this situation in its own statutes and in a recognized treaty.

The third and most controversial article read:

That the government of Cuba consents that the United States may exercise the right to intervene for the preservation of Cuban independence, the maintenance of a government adequate for the protection of life, property and individual liberty, and for discharging the obligations with respect to Cuba imposed by the treaty of Paris on the United States, now to be assumed and undertaken by the government of Cuba.

The Cuban Convention tried to avoid the intervention provision in its own proposal by declaring Cuba would assume the obligations under the treaty of Paris and would allow no foreign country to use Cuban territory as a base for operations. This was the most important article to the American government in its attempt to stabilize Cuba. Root's original draft contained the phrase that the United States would "reserve and retain the right of intervention," and a government "adequately protecting" life, property and individual liberty. His wording would have given greater weight to a right, legally grounded, by carrying it over from the Treaty of Paris.[55] Platt's wording, that Cuba "consents that the United States may exercise the right to intervene," made it easier both for the Cubans to accept and for it to pass Congress; but such a statement could have been interpreted to mean that the

[55] *Ibid.*, 312; National Archives, Diplomatic and Legal Branch, P. C. Jessup, "Memorandum on the Platt Amendment," confidential, 711.37/142, Oct. 13, 1930.

Cubans granted this right to the United States.[56] Platt did not intend this, and the whole amendment was worded to force the Cubans to consent.

The fourth article said:

That all Acts of the United States in Cuba during its military occupation thereof are ratified and validated, and all lawful rights acquired thereunder shall be maintained and protected.

This standard procedure in the peaceful change of governments was agreed to by the Cubans in their own fourth clause. The United States Government had in mind the protection of the rights of groups who had received such rights from the Military Government, as well as preservation of the many modifications in law and procedures.

The fifth article read:

That the government of Cuba will execute, and as far as necessary extend, the plans already devised or other plans to be mutually agreed upon, for the sanitation of the cities of the island, to the end that a recurrence of epidemic and infectious diseases may be prevented, thereby assuring protection to the people and commerce of Cuba, as well as to the commerce of the southern ports of the United States and the people residing therein.

Wood's interest in preserving the invaluable work of sanitation and eradicating yellow fever is understandable. The objections that enforcing contracts under this article might violate the Foraker Act were overridden by the Cuba Relations Committee on the premise that such an article would merely be permissible even with Cuban agreement. But the Cubans wished to negotiate upon this subject after they were released by the United States. They felt that this subject might be fit for a treaty, but not for their constitution.

The sixth article read: "That the Isle of Pines shall be omitted from the proposed constitutional boundaries of Cuba, the title thereto being left to future adjustment by treaty."

Articles I and II of the treaty of Paris were interpreted in opposite ways. Root always contended the Isle was Cuban, but the antecedents were sufficiently vague to warrant the clause. Furthermore, many Americans coveted the Isle, and others figured it became American as a result of the war. Although the Cubans quickly ratified the subsequent treaty, it took the United States Senate until 1925 to do so, thereby releasing the Isle of Pines to full Cuban sovereignty.[57]

---

[56] *Ibid.*
[57] Fitzgibbon, *Cuba and the United States,* 94-103.

The seventh article read:

That to enable the United States to maintain the independence of Cuba, and to protect the people thereof, as well as for its own defense, the government of Cuba will sell or lease to the United States lands necessary for coaling or naval stations at certain specified points, to be agreed upon with the President of the United States.

This was the second most objectionable article. At Wood's behest, McKinley relented to the placing of "or lease" in the article, to make it more palatable to the Cubans. The motivation of the United States was less ominous than the wording of the article. The United States did not want Cuba; it desired only to protect the isthmus and the Caribbean. However, it was apparent to both American and Cuban onlookers that the bases in Cuba were intended to stabilize the society there.

The eighth article provided, by way of further assurance, that the Cuban government would embody the foregoing provisions in a permanent treaty with the United States. This article came at the last minute from the Cuba Relations Committee, probably from Platt or Spooner. This treaty was signed on May 22, 1903.

What would the Cubans have proposed had the United States simply held a convention and established the republic after delegates formed a constitution and electoral procedure? Probably they would have initiated negotiations for a treaty with the United States which would embody reciprocity, a defensive alliance and ratification of the acts of the Military Government until superseded or revoked.

The Platt Amendment became law and was intended to underwrite Cuban independence with safeguards. Because of doubt of Cuban capacity for responsible self-government, the American desire to ensure strategic security in the Caribbean was not quite balanced by the heritage of republican self-determination. Cuban delay forced the United States to take the initiative in the proceedings. The tardy Cuban proposals were ignored, and negotiations for the acceptance of the Platt Amendment by Cuba began.

CHAPTER VIII

NEGOTIATING THE PLATT AMENDMENT,
MARCH THROUGH APRIL 15, 1901

If February was the month of proposal and counterproposal, when policy lines were drawn by the two countries, in March and April the McKinley administration bided its time, making a few interpretations to ease the burden of consent, and the Cuban Convention gradually agreed upon a *modus vivendi* that would lead to eventual acceptance of the Platt Amendment. The *Times of London* maintained that the "essential security for American interests will be secured," and the Platt Amendment eventually accepted.[1] The British newspaper understood the United States' fear of foreign incursion into Cuba and stated that unless Cubans submitted to the Platt Amendment, American troops would remain until there was a guarantee that the United States' policy would prevail. The next few months would confirm this statement.

At the Governor's Palace in Havana, Domingo Méndez Capote announced to Wood that because the congressional enactment of the Platt bill embarrassed the Cuban Constitutional Convention, the delegates were undecided whether to dissolve or continue. Wood urged them to continue in session by working on the electoral law.[2] Then, on March 2, Wood transmitted the Platt Amendment to Méndez Capote for the "consideration and action" of the convention.[3] Two days later the General told the Commission on Relations that the bill had become law with the signature of the President.[4] Finally a

---

[1] *London Times,* March 2, 1901.

[2] *New York Times,* March 2, 1901.

[3] CDDC 3051, Wood to Méndez Capote, March 2, 1901.

[4] Wood papers, Wood to Root, March 4, 1901; Root papers, Wood to Tamayo, March 2, 1901. March 2 was a Saturday, Wood gave the information to the Commission on Relations in person on March 4 at 5:00 p.m. The same afternoon Wood delivered a letter containing the provisions of the Platt bill as passed by Congress to the President of the Convention. The Platt Amendment was now the object of attention and the United States never considered the Cuban proposals of February although they were sent to Root by Wood officially. Wood papers, Root to Wood, April 15, 1901.

group made up of Juan Gualberto Gómez, Alfredo Zayas, Enrique Villuendas, Pedro Betancourt and José de J. Monteagudo requested that the Platt Amendment be considered in secret session, and it was so agreed. This was scheduled for the seventh, the only session held in March.[5]

When Wood told Root that the delegates were avoiding the American terms the Secretary of War replied strongly that the convention had been called to agree to the American terms, and if they failed to do so, another convention would be called. Talk of not agreeing or not having the power to agree was "childish nonsense."

In brief, there is only one possible way for them to bring about the termination of the military government and make either constitutional or electoral law effective; that is to do the whole duty they were elected for.

The Secretary ignored the principle of allowing duly elected representatives to reach a free decision; he wanted these representatives to volunteer a set of proposals which he hesitated to press himself. Now this seemed impossible. For the first time Root seemed ruffled, and he was willing to consider a recess of the convention until matters were explained.[6] On March 4, Wood informed the Secretary of War that conferences held during the previous three days with members of all the political groupings in the convention indicated "that they all want time to think over the relations as set forth" in the Platt Amendment.[7]

Root also learned from Wood and the press that on March 3, a parade of five to six thousand Cubans in Havana protested the Platt Amendment. This group was reviewed by members of the convention at the Martí Theater. The demonstrators then marched to the palace, where they presented Wood with a petition for independence, and marched away, cheering for the United States. Cubans loved parades, and Wood considered the demonstration to have been in good temper and of little significance. The parade was no spontaneous affair, but had been called by the politicians of Havana who opposed the Platt Amendment. Wood transmitted the petition to Root. Later he talked with Méndez Capote of the Republican party, Tamayo of the *Nacionalistas* and Quílez, a conservative, to find they thought that their government needed one and one-half to two years to reach stability and that municipal governments still needed supervision. Méndez Capote had declared on another occasion that time was immaterial just so long as a definite program could be agreed upon for independence.[8]

---

[5] *Mención histórica*, 538, 423.

[6] Root papers, Wood to Root, cable, March 2, 1901; Wood papers, Root to Wood, March 2, 1901.

[7] Wood papers, Wood to Root, March 4, 1901.

[8] Wood papers, Wood to Root, March 4, 1901; *New York World*, March 4, 1901; Wood to Root, Feb. 8, 1901, cited in Hagedorn, *Wood*, I, 347.

NEGOTIATING THE PLATT AMENDMENT

While public order on the island remained excellent, many municipalities and associations protested to Wood against the Platt Amendment. The General received a total of fifty-four cables and letters in support of the convention proposals against the bill (to Root he reported thirty-one telegrams).[9] The number is less significant than the fact that anti-amendment sentiment was unmarked by disorder and violence. Allowing for repetitions from some groups, around one-half of the eighty-three municipalities sent in protests. Some of these were triggered by agitators, others were spontaneous; whether they represented the majority feeling of the people in the localities is impossible to say. It is certain, however, that the Platt law was unpopular.

The General tried to dissuade Cuban hopes for another session of the United States Congress, denying that he had ever promised another session. His private suggestions that some of Root's demands might perhaps be modified had been intended to soothe Cuban feelings, not to make a real alteration. Unfortunately, Wood's softening suggestions were seized upon and magnified by the desperate Cubans, thus making it even harder for them to acquiesce.[10]

In secret session on the 7th of March, the delegates received communication of the Platt Amendment from General Wood and debated what their reply, if any, should be. After discussion, the delegates decided by ordinary voice vote to select a commission to reply to General Wood's communication of the Platt Amendment. Following recess, the members of the Commission on Relations were selected: Manuel Silva, J. G. Gómez, Diego Tamayo, Gonzalo de Quesada, and Enrique Villuendas.[11]

At the March 7 session the convention was uncertain of its course, and the delegates resorted to the familiar outlet of a committee to work out a plan of action. While neither rebellion nor capitulation was contemplated, the former was a much more remote possibility than the latter. The convention debate centered on the somewhat irrelevant question of its power to consider relations with the United States, something the delegates had been instructed to do and which they had agreed they could do the previous November. Men like Giberga, Sanguily and Juan G. Gómez changed their positions; others hesitated. There were no more convention sessions until the

[9] CDDC 3051, file of telegrams and letters on the Constitutional Convention.
[10] Martínez Ortiz, *Los primeros años*, I, 286; *Diario de la Marina*, March 6, 1901; Wood papers, Wood to Root, March 6, 1901, March 7, 1901, Root to Wood, March 7, 1901, cable; CDDC 3051, Tamayo to Wood, March 9, 1901, transmitting protest against Platt Amendment by Máximo Gómez. Wood explained to Root that Gómez protested only to retain his hold on the radicals and that Gómez assured Wood there would be no trouble in Cuba, Wood papers, Wood to Root, March 13, 1901.
[11] *Mención histórica*, 538-39.

first of April. During the remainder of March, the commission met to work out a proposal which would satisfy both Cubans and Americans.[12] The secret session of March 7 was a victory for Cuban moderates and conservatives, because the convention voted to continue meeting and to refer the Platt Amendment to a commission for study and report. The crisis was past and the Cubans less bitter; conditions presaged eventual acceptance of the Platt Amendment.[13]

On March 12, as a result of the debate in convention, Wood wrote to Méndez Capote in an attempt to alleviate some impressions held by the delegates and eliminate some of their arguments.

During recent interviews with members of the Constitutional Convention I have been informed that members of the Convention were of the opinion that the Convention had not the authority to agree with the government of the United States upon the relations to exist between that government and the government of Cuba.

I have the honor to inform you that no orders have been issued by the Military Government which in any way curtail or limit in this particular the authority conferred by the people upon their representatives, elected in accordance with the terms of Orders No. 301, July 25, 1900, from these Headquarters, therefore the Constitutional Convention is fully empowered to act in this matter.[14]

It was becoming more difficult for the men of the Cuban Convention to avoid the issue of relations with the United States.

Meanwhile, Estrada Palma, who had been running a boys' school in Central Valley, New York, since the war, signified his approval of the new constitution because it paralleled the modern doctrine on republics, although he worried that factions might tear apart the government. Estrada Palma explained that he had never agreed with McKinley's policy but had not wanted to cause trouble between the two countries. The Platt Amendment offended him, but he understood the strategic importance of Cuba to the United States. Furthermore, Cuba depended on the United States for "political existence" and a market to sell Cuban produce. Estrada Palma feared the convention would endanger reasonable and harmonious relations with the United States that were possible.[15]

In Havana, rumors of rejection filled the air. On March 20 Wood reported to Root that the more conservative delegates, according to Diego Tamayo, feared that the radicals, led by Juan Gualberto Gómez and Quesada, would induce the convention to reject the Platt Amendment, in hope that the United

[12] *Ibid.*, 539-40.
[13] *New York Times,* March 8, 1901.
[14] Wood papers, Wood to Méndez Capote, March 12, 1901.
[15] *Epistolario,* I, 149, Estrada Palma to Quesada, March 14, 1901.

States Congress would modify it in the next session. On the other hand, Wood assured his superior that all the real leaders during the revolution were quietly at work on the project of Cuban self-government.[16]

Yet Wood wanted to prepare for emergencies. He asked Root what action should be taken in case the convention refused to accept the American terms. The General thought they should be ready, if necessary, to dissolve the convention and announce the election of a new one at the municipal elections on June 1. He believed the proper course was to convince the opposition that American policy was fixed and that it confronted a serious responsibility. Again he noted that the "best elements are with us." [17]

The same evening, Root approved Wood's ideas. In strong language he warned the Cubans, through Wood, that:

The Platt Amendment is of course final and the members of the Convention who may be responsible for refusing to establish relations on that basis will injure only themselves and their own country. If the Convention takes such a course it will have failed to perform the duty for which it was elected and the duty must be performed by others.[18]

During the second and third week in March, General Nelson A. Miles and Senators Redfield Proctor (Rep., Vermont) and F. M. Cockrell (Dem., Missouri) visited Cuba. The Cubans had hoped in vain to see congressional disagreement with McKinley. The senators counseled the Cubans to end their delay. When questioned on the possibility of the convention rejecting the Platt Amendment, Cockrell stated that the President could change nothing in the bill and would not call another session. Cockrell added that Cuba was losing time and had better decide soon.[19] The respected Missouri Democrat, with a reputation for dedication to the public service, had voted against the Platt Amendment.

As a result of the united American front, by the 25th, changes began appearing in the Cuban opposition. The Republican party of Santiago had endorsed the amendment and instructed its delegates to vote for it, although they disregarded the instructions. The mayor of Cienfuegos, a town staunchly opposed to the Military Government, in a public letter advised acceptance of the Platt Amendment. The major surprise, however, came when Manuel Sanguily, one of Cuba's most respected and influential men, publicly declared the amendment must be accepted. The motives for this change are

[16] Wood papers, Wood to Root, March 20, 1901.
[17] *Ibid.*
[18] Root papers, Root to Wood, March 20, 1901; Wood papers, Wood to Root, March 20, 1901, both cables.
[19] *La Discusión,* March 27, 1901; Wood papers, Wood to Root, March 23, 1901.

not revealed in the records. It is doubtful if Wood persuaded him, for Sanguily was too caustic and fiery to listen. He cared nothing for party pressure; in fact, he resigned from the Republican party over the issue. It is probable that he thought the matter out in solitude and succumbed with fatalism to a larger power. Chances for acceptance of the Platt Amendment were improving.[20]

The Secretary of War continued his firm line, in hope that Wood had disabused the convention of its fears about American meddling in Cuban affairs. The Platt Amendment gave the United States no rights she did not already possess. It did give to the United States, for the benefit of Cuba, a standing between Cuba and foreign nations which might be of immense value in enabling the United States to protect Cuba's independence. In answer to inquiries about the phrase "lease or sell naval bases," Root said it was unchangeable but that the method in which that amendment should be complied with in regard to stations could be subject for negotiation.[21]

By the end of the month, the *convencionales* still appeared to disagree. The newspapers carried the proposals of various delegates, among them Giberga, Diego Tamayo and Joaquin Quílez. Juan Gualberto Gómez had also prepared an analysis of the problem of relations, and it was reported that Villuendas and Silva had signed it, giving the radicals a commission majority against Tamayo and Quesada. If Gómez' proposal reached the floor of convention and was adopted, relations with the United States might worsen. Also, the convention was warring over local matters; delegates had been repudiated by their parties in Santiago and Santa Clara, yet still held their seats, and members of the same party held opposing views.[22]

In a long exposition of his views in *La Discusión,* Tamayo reasoned that in spite of American intentions, their defense requirements and the good the amendment might do Cuba, it was irreconcilable with Cuba's sovereignty and independence. He proposed a nine-point substitution that accepted most of the Platt Amendment and added military alliance and reciprocity.[23]

By the first of April, eight plans were ready for the consideration of the convention. The large number indicated that the *convencionales* were still

[20] *New York Times,* March 25, 1901, March 28, 1901, March 26, 1901; Wood papers, Wood to Root, April 4, 1901; *Diario de la Marina,* March 25, 1901, Feb. 26, 1901, reporting a majority of the convention disposed to accept the Platt Law; *La Discusión,* March 27, 1901.

[21] Wood papers, Root to Wood, March 29, 1901; *Mención histórica,* 549, 457.

[22] *New York Times,* March 30, 1901; *Diario de la Marina,* March 29, 1901, March 30, 1901; *Mención histórica,* 425-26.

[23] *La Discusión,* March 27, 1901; CDDC 3051, Tamayo to Wood, April 4, 1901, showing Tamayo sent proposals to Wood for his consideration.

not ready to agree on a course of action. The plans of Quílez and Giberga, which had been published by the *Diario de la Marina* and other papers on the 29th and 30th, respectively, were little more than wordy repetitions of the Platt Amendment.[24]

The proposal of Juan Gualberto Gómez represented the majority opinion of the five-man commission appointed to decide how to reply to Wood's transmittal of the Platt Amendment. It was read in the secret session of April 1, along with the plans of Diego Tamayo, Quesada, Núñez, Giberga, Quílez, Alemán, Fernández de Castro and Portuondo. J. G. Gómez wanted to prove that the convention could not remain true to *Cuba Libre* and follow the lines set out for them by the United States. He asserted that the Platt Amendment violated the Treaty of Paris, made vassals out of Cubans and threatened them with continued military government. He stated that the convention rendered its opinion in February, but the commission was fulfilling the injunction of March 7 by advocating acceptance of Articles 1, 2, 4 and 5 and rejection of Articles 3, 6, 7 and 8. He argued that any government had to protect life, liberty and property; if the Cubans could not do this, intervention would come with or without permission. But Gómez thought determining the proper time to intervene would be impossible. Gómez demanded that the United States leave Cuba immediately, to fulfill the terms of the Joint Resolution. In closing, the Gómez proposals recommended consideration of a treaty between sovereign powers.[25] They were tabled without action.

The proposals of Giberga and Gómez represented two extremes. Only Quílez was as conservative as Giberga, and only Silva, Cisneros, Lacret and Portuondo were as radical as Juan Gómez. After these two plans were tabled, Fernández de Castro presented a plan formulated by himself, Ferrer, Monteagudo, Núñez and Robau. Stressing their realization of the importance to Cuba's future of the decision confronting the convention, and the possibility that any clause could be good or bad according to its interpretation, they proposed selecting a commission of five men to visit Washington to learn the limits of McKinley's intentions regarding the usage of the Platt Amendment. This commission would have plenipotentiary powers to define the terms and time of any intervention and to frame a treaty with the United States embodying these points: recognition that debts were prevented by the Cuban constitution, intervention only when Cuba requested it or was in

[24] *Diario de la Marina*, March 29, 1901, March 30, 1901; *Mención histórica*, 422-50, Quílez' proposal was not even printed and p. 542 shows omissions in the minutes made by the secretaries.
[25] *Mención histórica*, 427-40. Portell, *Historia de Cuba*, IV, 214-215, maintains that with Gómez' report most delegates opposed the Platt Law.

danger, and then only for a certain time and until constitutional government was reestablished. After argument about the propriety of considering such a proposal, the motion was defeated 13 to 12.[26] However, the proposal of sending a commission and recessing to meet at Méndez Capote's call continued to be the most prevalent idea discussed. After the vote, the president adjourned the session.

Meeting the next day at the usual time of 2:30 P.M., Llorente took the chair in Méndez Capote's absence. During the customary refusal of Cisneros' repeated demands that the sessions be made public, they found themselves in a full scale debate on the issue and used up the afternoon deciding that they would continue to hold secret sessions. Those arguing for public sessions claimed that the people should be informed of what was taking place, while the proponents of secret sessions claimed these matters were too delicate and that delegates too often played to the galleries.[27]

They met again on the third of April, and the moderates seemed to be losing. After brief discussion, Tamayo's opinion was defeated 20 to 6; shortly thereafter Quesada's went down 23 to 3. At this point Giberga asked for a suspension of debate to pass General Wood's most recent letter, which lay on the table, to the Commission on Relations. This touched off a wave of criticism from Morúa, Lacret and Cisneros, who demanded that the visits of the commission with Wood be discussed with the convention. Sanguily retorted that such suspicion insulted the honor of the commission members. The incident illustrates the mutual suspicion among the delegates. After further dispute, Giberga's motion was defeated 18 to 9, and the letter from Wood, with accompanying documents, was read.[28]

On April 2, Wood had cabled Root for an official statement of his letter of March 29 which interpreted intervention. With assurance that the United States would not intervene for trifling reasons, Wood thought he could persuade the delegates to accept the Platt Amendment into their constitution. Root cabled back at 7:00 P.M. the same day, authorizing the General to explain the third clause of the Platt Amendment:

You are authorized to state officially that in the view of the President the intervention described in the third clause of the Platt Amendment is not synonymous with intermeddling or interference with the affairs of the Cuban Government, but the formal action of the Government of the United States, based upon just and substantial grounds, for the preservation of Cuban independence and the maintenance of a government adequate for the protection of life, property and

[26] *Mención histórica*, 451-54, 542-44. The commission idea first appeared in March.
[27] *Ibid.*, 545-46.
[28] *Ibid.*, 547-49.

individual liberty and for discharging the obligations with respect to Cuba imposed by the Treaty of Paris on the United States.[29]

Wood felt that the mood of the country was shifting toward acceptance of the Platt Amendment, but the convention was rejecting the conservative and moderate proposals. At the next secret session of the convention, held on April 6, the delegates defeated the Quílez proposal 22 to 2, and rejected Giberga's plan 21 to 4, showing contempt for the conservative course.[30] Only J. G. Gómez' plan remained on the table, and it seemed that the forces of conciliation were in retreat.

On Good Friday, *La Discusión* printed a cartoon depicting the figure of the Cuban people being crucified between two thieves, McKinley and Wood, with Platt as the centurion, offering up a sponge entitled "Platt Amendment." Wood, who usually ignored the most pointed insults of the press, jailed both editor and artist and turned the matter over to the courts. He explained to Root that it mattered nothing to him personally, but

when it comes to taking this attitude against the President, it is a serious matter, especially among a Latin people, where respect is in proportion to the amount of energy which the government displays in defending itself, and trouble may easily arise unless matters of this kind are dealt with summarily.

Méndez Capote expressed his disapproval of the cartoon and said most members of the convention felt it was a radical attempt to stir up some popular demonstration. The cartoon, calculated to gouge Wood into action, failed to injure him or the United States Government. When the editor and artist were released the next day, they found their scheme had backfired.[31]

The convention did not meet again until the ninth of April. They stood irresolute before the choices of adopting the Gómez proposals, which would either be ignored by the United States or break up the convention, and accepting the Platt Amendment verbatim. They wanted neither and were searching for some means to settle honorably the question of relations. While they searched, the delegates drifted toward acceptance of the Platt Amendment. Cubans did not fear aggression or annexation by the United States,

[29] Wood papers, Wood to Root, cable, April 2, 1901; Root to Wood, April 2, 1901, cable; Wood to Méndez Capote, April 3, 1901; Wood to Root, April 3, 1901; Root to Wood, April 3, 1901; Wood to Root, April 4, 1901; *New York Times,* April 4, 1901, showing Portuondo, Alemán, J. G. Gómez, Manduley met with Wood and received assurances about clause 3. At the behest of various Cuban leaders, Wood obtained this statement from Root.

[30] *Mención histórica,* 550-51.

[31] Wood papers, Wood to Root, April 6, 1901; Portell, *Historia de Cuba,* IV, 228-29 claimed that Wood wantonly abridged the freedom of the press.

but they did resent being treated as if they were incapable of running their own affairs.[32]

Sovereignty was the key word to the delegates. A *New York Times* correspondent told of discussing the Platt Amendment with the delegates in the Martí Theater, after the day's deliberations. Sanguily, perched on a table, pulled from the breast pocket of his coat a copy of the Teller Resolution and

read it as unemotionally as a schoolboy at his reading book until he came to the word 'sovereignty.' Then his voice rose to a pitch and volume that awoke the echoes of the empty galleries.[33]

Sanguily's cry may well have been the cry of Cuba. Despite all America's good intentions, the Cubans, however lacking in initiative, still suffered a great wound from the Platt Amendment. To them, the Joint Resolution had been broken, and they were doubly bitter because they had not the power to resist.

On the ninth of April, the delegates met again in secret session. They heard a proposal from Berriel, Núñez, Llorente, Ferrer and Monteagudo who wanted to send a commission to Washington to learn the views and proposals of the United States Government with respect to the establishment of a definite order of relations with Cuba. Diego Tamayo asked that the proposal be tabled for twenty-four hours, and it was so agreed.[34]

Meeting again on April 10, the convention displayed its preparations for a skirmish by discussing the Berriel motion and voting to extend the session by an hour, but Méndez Capote had to adjourn the session due to lack of quorum. Absenteeism afflicted the sessions during this period and was a tactic of both sides, as well as an indication of the lack of desire to reach an accord.[35]

The next day the assembly continued into an evening session.[36] Llorente read an amendment to the Berriel motion, proposed by Portuondo, Alemán, Morúa, E. Tamayo and Fortún, which would require any commission going to Washington to state opposition to the Platt Amendment. Juan Gualberto Gómez also wanted to add the stipulation that the commission should contact the Military Governor about the means to carry out its mission. Giberga obtained the floor and moved that the Portuondo motion could not be heard in the session, because it tied the hands of the commission, being calculated

[32] *New York Times,* April 8, 1901.
[33] *Ibid.*
[34] *Mención histórica,* 552. Martin Morúa Delgado submitted a moderate plan, but it lacked support; *Ibid.,* 458-64; J. González, *Martin Morúa Delgado, Impresiones sobre su ultima novela y su gestion en la Constituyente de Cuba* (La Habana, 1902).
[35] *Mención histórica,* 553-54.
[36] *Ibid.,* 555-56.

to promote discord on the Platt Amendment rather than accord. After Alemán spoke in opposition, the convention rejected Giberga's motion, 19 to 7.[37]

On the 12th, the convention at last seemed to take a stand. It voted 18 to 10, after hot debate, to pass the Portuondo amendment and bind the committee headed to Washington, D.C. When Cisneros approvingly exclaimed that now the general feeling of the assembly had rendered a particular instruction meaningful, Núñez rejoined that the vote destroyed the effect of sending a commission at all. Manduley favored the vote, because it rejected the Platt Amendment; Villuendas opposed it because it would dissolve the convention. Zayas thought it would tie the hands of the committee and was unnecessary after the opposing stand the delegates had taken. Still, by this action, the convention members did not consider that they had rejected the Platt Amendment.[38]

The main motion (Berriel's) to send the commission to Washington was then heard. Berriel and his co-signers had phrased their motion carefully. Since the opinion in the convention about the Platt Amendment was already determined, and esteeming it necessary to formulate some answers to Wood's communication of March 3, they proposed to the convention the following resolution: to nominate a commission of five of the delegates which would contact the Military Governor and the United States Government, to learn the views and proposals of that government about the numerous particulars relative to the establishment of a definite order of relations in politics and economics between Cuba and the United States.[39]

Convening again on the 13th, the delegates voted 25 to 0 to treat with Washington but to coordinate with Wood about the trip. The unanimity stemmed from varied reasons, but all wanted to support the commission idea. At this point, José Miguel Gómez, Monteagudo, Morúa and Ferrer proposed

---

[37] *Ibid.*, 557.

[38] *Ibid.*, 558. Yeas: Alemán, J. M. Gómez, Robau, Fortún, Cisneros, Silva, Betancourt, Llorente, Quesada, Berriel, Lacret, Portuondo, Fernández de Castro, Ferrer, J. G. Gómez, E. Tamayo, Manduley, Méndez Capote. Nays: Monteagudo, Morúa, Giberga, D. Tamayo, Sanguily, Gener, Núñez, Quílez, Zayas, Villuendas. *New York Times*, April 13, 1901, April 14, 1901; *Diario de la Marina*, April 12, 1901; *La Discusión*, April 13, 1901. *Diario* of April 13 quoted *Patria* statement of J. G. Gómez as saying the Platt Amendment was not rejected. Radicals did not want to break relations with the U.S. *Patria* on April 9 said that the Platt Amendment had been practically rejected because the proposals of Diego Tamayo, Giberga, Quesada and Quílez could not obtain any votes. On April 13, *La Discusión* said that the assembly declined to maintain further political relations with the American government through the Military Governor whose "failure is now recognized." Cf. Robinson, *Cuba and the Intervention,"* 260-63.

[39] *Mención histórica*, 559.

an addition to the Berriel motion: in negotiating with the United States, any bases of accord should be submitted to the convention for its definite resolution. After discussion, this was approved, 24 to 2. By this time the wording of the main motion was uncertain, and the moderates were anxious to negate the Portuondo amendment. Juan Gualberto Gómez, Berriel and Sanguily were appointed to draw up an integral motion, and the session was declared extended.[40]

Reconvening after a fifteen minute recess, the delegates heard Villuendas read the new motion. It was similar to Berriel's original, but added at the end the J. M. Gómez and J. G. Gómez motions, to refer accords to the convention and to coordinate with Wood. The Portuondo motion, which had bound the commission to oppose the Platt Amendment, was omitted from the integral motion.[41] The integral motion was passed, 16 to 6, with only the hard shell radicals (Cisneros, Betancourt, Lacret, Portuondo, Juan Gualberto Gómez and Manduley) in opposition.[42]

Through parliamentary tactics, the moderates and conservatives had managed to outmaneuver and outvote the radicals. The *modus vivendi* was achieved. The Cubans had found a device which would allow them to preserve their honor while continuing negotiations with the United States Government. They genuinely hoped to negotiate new agreements in Washington, but probably realized that at best the trip would allow them to utilize the American explanations as a way of accepting the Platt Amendment.[43] A compromise was reached, and a split among radicals was avoided by agreeing

[40] *Ibid.*, 560-62.

[41] *Ibid.*, 562. Here part of the minutes are deleted. Martínez Ortiz, *Los primeros años*, I, 291, said the commission was ordered to follow the declaration of Portuondo, that the commission was to inform McKinley that the convention opposed the Platt Amendment. But the integral motion as it appears in *Mención histórica* omits Portuondo's motion. Martínez Ortiz agreed that the convention decision was not intended to break negotiations, rather to express a general opinion about the issue in order to obtain some concession from Washington. Opinion in the convention wanted to show non-acceptance, not rejection. Portell Vilá, *Historia de Cuba*, IV, 214-15, said that the commission intended to state opposition to the Platt law and obtain concrete interpretations and reciprocity. The commission did not go, Portell maintained, to accept the Platt law.

[42] *Mención histórica*, 562-63. This vote was probably closer to real feeling in the convention than the 18-10 vote on the Portuondo amendment. Absent were Fortún, Ríus Rivera, Gener, Bravo. Abstaining were E. Tamayo, Alemán, Robau, Silva, Quesada. All of these men were radicals, except Quesada. In some cases their failure to appear or vote indicated they were not as hostile to the Platt law as they said; they wished to avoid responsibility.

[43] *New York Times*, April 14, 1901. Martínez Ortiz, who was there, said that the commission was to take the pulse of the government in Washington and measure its intent, to examine how far they could go on the road of intransigence. *Los primeros años*, I, 288.

not to express themselves for or against the amendment until the commission returned.

On April 15, the convention met to choose the delegates who would make the trip to Washington. Méndez Capote received 22 votes, Portuondo 20, Berriel 19, and Diego Tamayo 15; after a revote, Llorente, the fifth member, was chosen. Berriel withdrew because of age and health and was replaced by Betancourt. Of the five, only Tamayo could be said to have been a solid supporter of the Platt Amendment. Llorente and Méndez Capote, although radicals, were amenable. Betancourt was radical but later changed his mind; Portuondo was dead set against the Platt Amendment.[44]

Wood supplied a more accurate explanation for sending the commission to Washington. On the 15th he sent Root a confidential cablegram:

Committee of Convention will be nominated to-day to come and see me about going to Washington. Men nominated are good representative men. Purpose of this visit is in reality to accept Platt amendment but this must not be even intimated. That such is the fact I know from the men themselves. Everything depends upon this being unknown. Gradual reaction throughout the country in favor of the Platt amendment. Please answer at once as I want to inform President of Committee who is also President of Convention in order that they may be assured that after committee is named there will be no doubt of its going. Apparent purposes here will be to obtain information on certain of the articles of the amendment which they do not quite understand. Information received will remove doubt and the amendment will be accepted. This is latin method but we are after results. I strongly recommend their going. I desire to accompany this committee and will leave in a few days. . . . Everything in the country is absolutely quiet.

Root replied the same day:

The President will be pleased to receive a committee of the convention. It is desirable that you should be here at the same time. The President will be absent from Washington on a journey to the Pacific Coast from April twenty-eighth to June fifteenth.[45]

To the Cubans, Root's acceptance of the idea meant that he would consider concessions.[46] The convention recessed from April 15 until early in May, when the commission would report upon its mission. As the representatives of both sides looked forward to the coming meeting in Washington, the moderates and conservatives of the convention considered the trip to be a means through which they could accept the Platt Amendment with honor and without losing the radicals. The radicals hoped to find new bases of

[44] *Mención histórica,* 564, 566-67.
[45] Wood papers, Wood to Root, April 15, 1901, Root to Wood, April 15, 1901.
[46] Martínez Ortiz, *Los primeros años,* I, 291.

accord. The negotiations had at last taken a positive step forward. In March the mood to reject the Platt Amendment had been highest; in April the factions in the convention, realizing their position was becoming less and less tenable, reached an agreement to agree.

Wood aided this development by keeping his hands off the convention. Had he meddled, Wood could have upset matters and given the radicals a target.[47] He maintained contact, and offered suggestions, but did not, at this point, dictate to the *convencionales*.

---

[47] Bravo Correoso accused Wood: *Como se hizo la constitución de Cuba,* 78-80.

CHAPTER IX

THE CUBANS GO TO WASHINGTON:
AN EXEGESIS OF THE PLATT AMENDMENT

As the Cuban commissioners travelled to Washington, the press conjectured about the significance of their visit.[1] While the commissioners sought to obtain new bases for agreement, they actually were questioning a law McKinley could not alter. The time spent and the views learned in Washington would assist the Cubans to accept the Platt Amendment after a further show of resistance.

When the commission landed at Jacksonville, Portuondo was quoted as saying that ninety percent of the Cubans wanted immediate and absolute independence; only the Spaniards, although they hated the United States, wanted American protection to guarantee their property. Portuondo claimed peace between the two countries was impossible until the military occupation was ended and Cuban independence was achieved.[2]

The five commissioners arrived in Washington at 8:00 A.M. on April 24, accompanied by their interpreter and representatives of the Havana press. The commission, received not as distinguished citizens but as an official body delegated by the Constitutional Convention, was met by Assistant Secretary of State David J. Hill, Assistant Secretary of War William Cary Sanger, and Captain Sawtelle and Lieutenant Overton, army officers assigned as escorts to the delegation. General Wood, who had arrived separately, called at the War Department to brief Root, Sanger, Platt and Admiral Bradford (Chief

---

[1] *New York Times*, April 18, 1901; for an example of press opposition, see A. G. Robinson in the *New York Evening Post*, April 17, 1901, "The Failure of General Wood."

Roosevelt waxed apoplectic about the *New York Evening Post* and *New York Journal*. "The Villards, Godkins and their like are simply unhung traitors, and are liars, slanderers and scandal mongers to boot. It is bad enough when they exercise these traits in home matters, but when they deliberately try to nullify and undo work such as that you are doing, in which the national interests are vitally concerned, their conduct becomes absolutely infamous." He used *Harper's Weekly* and the *Commercial Advertiser* to counter the *Post*. Wood papers, Roosevelt to Wood, April 17, 1901.

[2] *New York Times*, April 24, 1901.

of the Bureau of Naval Equipment) on the Cuban situation. He stressed reduction in the sugar and tobacco tariffs, followed by revision of articles three and seven of the Platt Amendment, as the most important items for the discussion with the Cubans. Wood and Root lunched together after a three-hour talk.[3]

The commission's requested audiences with the President and the Secretary of War were scheduled for the following day. On the 24th the delegates held a four-hour briefing at which they decided that they would analyze the Platt Amendment when they met Root, emphasizing its defects and inconveniences. They decided first to obtain information concerning the United States purpose regarding these matters, to search for principles other than those found in clauses three, six and seven of the Platt Amendment, and to negotiate an agreement the convention could ratify. If this proved impossible, the mission would be limited to obtaining extensive information so the convention could finally agree upon a reply to General Wood's communication of March 2.[4]

At 11:00 A.M. on April 25, Wood and Sanger introduced the Cubans to Root, who inquired if they wished to make any statements before he introduced them to the President. Present were the five Cubans and their interpreter, Alejandro González (Wood's secretary) and the escorts. Méndez Capote explained that the Platt Amendment had been neither accepted nor rejected by the convention, although the prevailing sentiment opposed acceptance. The chairman gave several reasons for this stand. The amendment

[3] *New York Times*, April 25, 1901; Wood papers, translation from *Mención histó-rica*, no. 72. doc. M, "Report of the Committee appointed to Confer with the Government of the United States, Giving an Account of the Result of its Labors." Hermann Hagedorn evidently obtained a copy of this translation from James Brown Scott who informed him that there was neither a Spanish nor an English copy in the War Dept. files. Root asked the Carnegie Foundation on International Peace to prepare a translation. (Hereafter cited as Commission Report.) The minutes of the commission were kept by Pedro Betancourt and after each session he corroborated his notes with his colleagues. Root kept no notes of the discussions, hence there is no official American record of the meetings. Root later examined the translation from *Mención histórica* and stated that it was substantially correct although the exact phraseology could not be relied upon. "He specifically declined to have a stenographic record made of the conversations because he did not believe that he was authorized to make official interpretations of the Act of Congress and preferred to have the talk retain the character of unofficial and personal conversations." Root to Jessup, Nov. 17, 1930, in Jessup, *Root*, I, 318.

[4] Commission Report. Senator John Tyler Morgan sent the commission a proposal for union of the two countries which repelled the Cubans. J. T. Morgan papers, Morgan to Méndez Capote, April 24, 1901; A. A. Menocal to Morgan, May 29, 1901, Morgan to Root, April 24, 1901; C. C. Pintó to Morgan, April 29, 1901. Wood papers, Daniel E. Sickles to Root, April 22, 1901. Morgan and Sickles favored annexation.

did not fulfill the Treaty of Paris. Cubans knew Cuban-American relations were unique; but despite this, such relations should be rooted in the principle of mutual respect for each other's sovereignty. The Platt Amendment put the situation on a different footing, and now the convention felt the need for clarification of the amendment and a discussion of economic relations ignored in the Platt Amendment. Méndez Capote concluded by stating that the commission had traveled to Washington because Cuba trusted American intentions and had only cordiality for the United States, especially since Americans had shed blood along with the Cubans who had fought fifty years for independence.[5]

The Secretary of War, pleased to hear such sincere and frank declarations, promised to speak in the same way; first, however, he would present the commission to the President, whose express authorization he needed to treat with the commission. The five Cubans exchanged salutations with McKinley who said he would instruct Root to lend his utmost assistance in successive interviews. From 3:00 to 6:00 P.M., the commission met with Root and obtained declarations the members considered important. This meeting took place after the Secretary of War and the President conferred and after a cabinet meeting.[6]

The Secretary of War opened the afternoon interview with a detailed exposition of what he considered to be America's traditional policy respecting Cuba. Regarding the question of relations, he said the Platt Amendment implied fulfillment of the purpose of the Treaty of Paris. Root stressed for three hours the long-standing conviction that the United States could not permit any foreign country to acquire or control Cuba. He emphasized that the American position was based on the Monroe Doctrine. With Spain out of the way, the United States incurred an even closer relationship to Cuba. Aware of this new responsibility, the President had asked Congress for its advice, consequently receiving the Platt Amendment. This law had no other object than preservation of Cuba's independence; and it proposed steps to ensure this. Clause three was a legal extension of the Monroe Doctrine. The United States had no interest in intervening in Cuba; it offered no profit or glory. The third clause, when accepted, would give international force to the Monroe Doctrine and serve notice that any European power would have to contend with the United States if it interfered in Cuba. Furthermore, this clause put any other power in the position of the aggressor and left the United States and Cuba legally in the right. Without granting the United States more rights than it had at the time of the intervention, clause three

[5] *Ibid., New York Times*, April 26, 1901; *Mención histórica*, 466-67.
[6] Commission Report.

did give America better authority to defend Cuba's independence than that derived from the Monroe Doctrine. Root also stated that the coaling station clause and others assisted Cuban independence. He reassured the commissioners that the United States would never consider intervention unless an extreme occasion arose, God granting that it never would.[7]

Méndez Capote then said that the Cubans wanted something more concrete than the wording of the Platt Amendment. The amendment, he pointed out, could be interpreted to mean that Cuba was subject to the suzerainty of the United States; it would be difficult to obtain recognition as a member of the international community. Root explained that the United States intended to recognize Cuba as a fully sovereign and independent nation first, an act which could not but aid Cuba in obtaining full recognition internationally as a sovereign power. Méndez Capote disagreed, saying Cuba would be born without authority and prestige. Root reassured them and then asked if the Cuban people's consent to United States intervention for preservation of their independence could be considered a threat to the independence of Cuba. Méndez Capote countered by asking, if the United States considered it had a right to intervene, why was previous consent necessary in the Cuban constitution? Root denied that the stipulation limited Cuban sovereignty.

Stalemated, Méndez Capote turned to the question of coaling stations. Root said he considered them as essential to the welfare of Cuba as to the United States, because Cuba needed an ally. Root explained that the American government proposed only to obtain strategic military points to defend both countries. This gave the United States no right to intervene in Cuban affairs but facilitated the maintenance of independence. The United States wanted the convention to empower the coming Cuban government to treat with America concerning certain naval or coaling stations, to be agreed upon by the two governments.[8]

Both Méndez Capote and Root agreed that the Isle of Pines issue was open, that Cuba had a right to the Isle. They believed the issue should not impede the sovereignty of Cuba and should be left to the Cuban government to resolve. Then Méndez Capote, Portuondo, Betancourt and Tamayo all spoke of the immediate need for commercial relations based upon reciprocity. Root replied that the reduction on tariff duties could be made in only two ways: with a preferential duty, as in the case of Puerto Rico, the United States would have to exercise sovereignty over the exporting country. Secondly, a reciprocity treaty could be agreed upon only by sovereign powers, and Cuba did not yet possess this status. When Méndez Capote inquired if

---

[7] *Ibid.*; Jessup, *Root,* I, 318-19.
[8] Commission Report; *Mención histórica,* 471.

the Chief Executive could promise favorable economic measures, Root offered his opinion – also speaking in the name of the President – that when the Cuban government was established and sent representatives to propose a commercial treaty, the United States would respond favorably. At the close of the meeting, Root promised to embody in a note his remarks on clause three. This he did in a confidential letter to Méndez Capote, which was released to the Cuban press upon the commission's return to Havana.[9]

That evening the Cuban commissioners dined at the White House with forty-seven leaders of the executive, legislative and judicial branches of the United States Government. The solicitude of the Americans deeply impressed the Cubans. Genuine friendliness and interest marked the affair. The Cubans emphasized to the convention upon their return their considerate reception in Washington.[10]

The next day, Friday the 26th, the commissioners attended a luncheon given for them by Root. They talked at length with General Miles, Platt and Spooner. After lunch, accompanied by Wood, they met with Root from 3:00 to 6:00 P.M. Méndez Capote opened the session by requesting the Secretary of War to discuss clause three and explain in detail how the United States could consider itself bound permanently by the Treaty of Paris and derive obligations of permanent character when it was twice stated therein that those obligations referred only to the period of military occupation. Root replied that the points raised were to be determined at the proper time according to circumstances by the two governments. He maintained the United States had declared in the Treaty of Paris that its relation to intervention in Cuba would always be that of preserving independence; this limited the United States in that she could not threaten Cuba's independence without violating the law and treaties adopted. Root granted that the obligations contracted by the United States in the Treaty of Paris referred to the period of intervention, but since the United States understood that these obligations must be fulfilled, it assumed responsibility for the creation of a new republic.[11]

At this point, the Secretary of War read a letter from Senator O. H. Platt and gave the commissioners a copy, saying both he and the President agreed with it. Apparently Platt had returned to the capital at the request of Wood

---

[9] *La Discusión*, May 20, 1901; Root to Roosevelt, June 4, 1901 cited in Jessup, *Root*, I, 323. Commission Report.

[10] Commission Report; *New York Times*, April 26, 1901, April 27, 1901. No statements about the nature of the discussions with Root were released to the press because the commissioners were subject to attack from groups in Cuba and unable to defend themselves while negotiating in the United States. *New York Times*, April 28, 1901.

[11] Commission Report.

and Root. Root informed him of the Cuban apprehensions about intervention and asked for Platt's own interpretation.

In reply, I will say that the Amendment was carefully worded with the purpose of avoiding any possible thought that its acceptance by the Constitutional Convention would result in the establishment of a protectorate or suzerainty, or in any way interfere with the independence or sovereignty of Cuba; and, speaking for myself, it seems impossible that such an interpretation can be given to the clause. I believe that the Amendment should be considered as a whole, and it must be evident, on reading it, that its well defined purpose is to secure and safeguard Cuban independence and establish immediately a definite understanding of the friendly disposition entertained by the United States for the Cuban people, and its express intention of aiding them, if necessary in the maintenance of that independence.

These are my ideas, and although, as you suggest, I cannot speak for Congress, my belief is that such a purpose was well understood by that body.[12]

Méndez Capote then inquired whether, according to Root's declaration, it was to be understood that intervention would have no reference to the Cuban government, which would enjoy absolute independence. "Precisely," replied the Secretary of War. Capote interpreted the Secretary to mean that intervention would be made possible only in the event of a foreign threat either against the Cuban government, or in combination of alliance with the Cubans, or in the absence of any government in Cuba. "Precisely," said Root.[13]

Méndez Capote pressed for additional explanation of intervention. He claimed the consent to intervene would be of no value should the United States lack sufficient force to realize its object, since in international questions, force was the *ultima ratio*. Root thought this only partially true. Force was perhaps the last argument, but it did not always animate international law, since, if the legitimacy of certain rights were not respected, nations like Switzerland, Belgium and the Netherlands would cease to exist. More powerful countries had to respect these rights in order to avoid appearing as enemies of mankind. A small state, entrenched behind universally recognized

[12] Commission Report. Platt to Root, April 26, 1901; Portell Vilá, *Historia de Cuba*, IV, 230, maintains this letter was intended to deceive the Cubans. On May 1, O. H. Platt replied to Joaquín Quílez' inquiry of April 20, assuring the Cuban that his amendment followed the Teller clause of the Joint Resolution: clause three of the Platt Amendment recognized Cuban independence, otherwise, no right of intervention would have to be granted, clause four did so indirectly and clauses one and two recognized Cuban independence because treaties can be made only by an independent country. Each clause, Platt affirmed, was based on the "idea, not only that Cuba was to be independent, but that the United States recognized the fact." The letter was made public in Cuba. Quoted in Martínez Ortiz, *Los primeros años*, I, 301-302.

[13] Commission Report.

rights, was a small state possessed of a force respected by all – the only force of the weak. The United States sought the sanction of legal title as well as force, so it might intervene against attacks on Cuban independence. Such a treaty would also help prevent intervention and make sure, if it did become necessary, that it would be uncontested.[14] When Méndez Capote again sought reassurance that Cuba's sovereignty would be recognized, Root pointed out that Cuba's ability to create treaties, tariffs, a flag, merchant marine, army, navy and a diplomatic corps, would demonstrate Cuba's sovereignty.

To this Root added that clauses one and two of the Platt Amendment, dealing with treaties and debts, were intended as purely constitutional limitations, similar to those placed on Congress by the United States Constitution. Of course Root overlooked the fact that the United States, unsatisfied by the Cubans' own provisions, had imposed these limitations. To Betancourt's request for the meaning of the clause on sanitation, Root said the issue would be settled as the governments might mutually agree. When Méndez Capote returned to intervention, Root declared that intervention was incompatible with the existence of a Cuban government and would take place only in the case of anarchy or foreign menace. "Clause three cannot signify *destruction* but *conservation* of the independence of Cuba." [15]

There was little discussion of clause four, recognition of the laws of the United States Government in Cuba, when Root explained it pertained only to the legal acts of the Military Government. Before the session closed, Méndez Capote asked for one more conference, but Root explained this would have to wait until Monday because the President had urgent business concerning his coming trip. After the session adjourned, the Cubans agreed among themselves that a further interview would be unnecessary. They met the President and Secretary of War on the 27th and stressed for the last time their reasons for desiring economic concessions. The Cubans received unofficial assurance from McKinley and Root of assistance in advance of treaty negotiations between the two countries. McKinley and Root were sympathetic to reciprocity with Cuba but knew any breach in the tariff wall would entail a vicious political fight. So ended the conferences of the Cuban commission with the United States Government representatives.[16]

The commission left Washington on the night of the 27th with the impression that McKinley was supported in his Cuban policy, not only by the branches of government in Washington but by the public as well: the Platt

[14] Commission Report.
[15] *Mención histórica*, 478.
[16] Commission Report; *Mención histórica*, 478. The Cubans made much of this "promise" of eventual trade concessions.

Amendment was American national policy. Before returning to Cuba, the commissioners traveled to New York, visited the Stock Exchange and met with members of the New York Chamber of Commerce, who implied they were willing to support Cuban economic interests.

While the commission may have reflected different views in private unofficial conversations with various men in Washington, they displayed a united front in discussions with Root and made no concession or offer which could bind the convention in its reply to the Platt Amendment. They reported that they were well-treated, that General Wood's demeanor was strictly correct and that he did all he could to make the Cuban stay pleasant and to help fulfill their mission.[17]

While the *New York Times* thought that, as a result of their visit, the commission would ask the convention to accept the Platt Amendment, Root believed the trip to have positive results. Some real misunderstandings about the scope and effect of the Platt Amendment had been dissipated.

I think they really suspected, and perhaps some of them believed, that under the provisions of the law was concealed a real purpose to make their independence merely nominal and really fictitious.

Another achievement of the talks was

to furnish those who really wanted to accept the amendment with the material which they much desired to meet the arguments of the irreconcilables, and I think some of them have gone back to Cuba with the intention of using that material.[18]

Also, an attitude of "kindliness" toward the United States arising from their treatment in Washington began to rekindle among the Cubans. Root concluded, "How the result will pan out of course no one can tell, but it is evident that the situation is much improved as the result of the visit." The *Times* pointed out that the visit had one other value – tariff talks. Blasting the "narrow, selfish, and detestable spirit of Dingleyism," the old, slave-power Democrats, and the beet sugar and tobacco people who would impoverish Cuba and cause annexation, the *Times* called for a reduction in tariff duties.[19]

Actually, the Cubans achieved only their secondary purpose of obtaining information and interpretations enabling them to formulate a reply to the Platt Amendment. Any hope of negotiation for new bases of agreement must

---

[17] Commission Report; *Mención histórica*, 481-482; Manuel Márquez Sterling, *El proceso histórico de la enmienda Platt* (La Habana, 1941), 188, who quoted Méndez Capote in 1926 as saying "Wood stabbed us in the back," in Washington and the commission was thus forced to accept the American interpretations. Márquez Sterling was the Cuban ambassador to the United States who signed the treaty abrogating the Platt Amendment in 1934.

[18] Root to Platt, May 9, 1901, quoted in Jessup, *Root*, I, 320-21.

[19] *New York Times*, April 28, 1901, May 4, 1901.

have been quickly destroyed when Root set the tone of the sessions as informal exchanges and by his opening remarks about the historical interest of the United States in Cuba. Beyond requesting economic concessions, the Cubans did not even try to obtain new bases for agreement.[20]

With the commission back in Cuba, preparing to report to the convention, Senator Platt began to elaborate his views of Cuban-American relations. These views were more than the opinion of a single senator, rather they represented administration thinking on the subject. Of particular importance was his correspondence with Edwin F. Atkins. Atkins, who had been interested in sugar plantations around Cienfuegos since the 1880's, wrote to Platt on June 3, 1901, regarding the change of currency in Cuba. He added the following opinion:

The property owners of the Island, as you are aware, are very much in fear of independence, as they understand independence would mean in the hands of the insurgent element, and those now holding office.

The property owners having as a rule few votes, have so far held aloof from political matters in the Island, their one great desire being that the United States troops should remain, and United States authorities should keep control. . . .

Of course the suggestion of a reciprocity treaty with the United States, through which special advantages would be given to Cuban products would go far to remove this feeling, but the business element fully realizes the difference between the good wishes of the Administration in this respect, and the chances of getting such a reduction of duties through Congress.[21]

Atkins finished by pointing out that no assurances had been given the Cuban property owners of American protection against "vicious legislation or administration" by the Cuban government. He said the owners feared the action of men then representing Cuban government, the former New York *Junta* and insurgent government, with whom the United States Government so far had all its official dealings and unofficial communications.

Aside from Atkins' opinion and his attitude, more significant was the reaction of men of property to the Platt Amendment. They feared rather than welcomed it, desiring tighter United States control. Exceptions to this, associations like the *"Círculo de Hacendados"* and *"Sociedad Económico de Amigos del País,"* pressed the convention to accept the Platt Amendment.[22] Wood probably encouraged them to do so, assuaging their fears about lack of American control. But the Atkins letter indicates that the

[20] Márquez Sterling, *Proceso histórico*, 220-21, says Méndez Capote argued successfully with Root and that the Cubans negotiated satisfactorily with Root by forcing him to explain United States policy.

[21] Platt papers, Atkins to Platt, June 3, 1901.

[22] CDDC 3051, April 20, 1901, Wood to Roosevelt; Martínez Ortiz, *Los primeros años*, I, 291.

McKinley administration steered the middle course, eschewing the pressures brought to bear by American property owners in Cuba.

Platt's reply reveals his belief that his amendment stretched the limit of the possible.

Affairs in Cuba, of course are far from satisfactory, but the United States government must have a policy with regard to Cuba, and that policy must be one which is the best possible under conditions as they exist. I think annexation is absolutely out of the question. In the first place that foolish Teller resolution stands not only in the way of that, but all other action which we might take if it had never been passed. I think I know enough of congressional sentiment to know that this is regarded as a pledge of the government against annexation. That being out of the way, what next? We cannot forever remain in military occupation. We have promised them an independent government, and when that is established, it seems to me that we must withdraw. That is what the amendment which is called by my name proposes. . . . Personally, I was in favor of very much more stringent measures and requiring much more as to our future relations, but is [sic] legislation you must consider the preponderance of popular sentiment. As you say, it is difficult enough to bring these Cuban delegates to the acceptance of the terms we propose. If we had proposed more stringent terms, we should not only have had that difficulty vastly increased, but we should have had a party in the United States and in Congress giving aid and comfort to the Cuban radicals. . . . It is easy to say that we ought to insist on more, it was impossible to pass through Congress any thing more drastic than we did. . . . I see nothing for it except to try the experiment of an independent republican government in Cuba, and while I see the dangers and possible disasters, I have more hope than some do that the experiment will be fairly successful. I think it depends very largely, however, on the attitude of people who have something to lose in Cuba. . . . We cannot make a treaty with Cuba while it is in our military occupation, so that it seems to me that the only solution is, annexation being impossible, to have an independent government and a reciprocity treaty with it which shall be mutually advantageous.[23]

The Platt Amendment was prepared with an estimate of what could be effective and pass Congress. Only withdrawal was permissible to the American people. Nothing in Platt's letter to Atkins indicated that the Senator wanted to annex Cuba or that he thought his amendment an equivalent to annexation. On the contrary, it prevented annexation. Platt's desire for more stringent measures meant he believed Cuba needed more support. He opposed the Teller Amendment because he wanted the administration free to meet unforeseen exigencies. His view on reciprocity also indicated he wanted to deal with an independent government, not a vassal in a *zollverein*. Clearly,

---

[23] Platt papers, Platt to Atkins, June 11, 1901. Based on this letter, Portell Vilá, *Historia de Cuba,* IV, 9, argues that Platt intended the amendment to be a substitute for annexation.

the Senator from Connecticut saw his amendment as a realistic device for underwriting Cuban independence.

Senator Platt explained his views publicly in three articles during the spring and summer of 1901. In an address given in April to the American Academy of Political and Social Science and printed in the *Annals* in July, Platt stressed the need for safeguards against future unrest.

Unless we provide now for continued independence and peace in the Island of Cuba there is no way in which they can be assured unless, in case the necessity arises, we declare war and enter upon the business of subjugating and annexing it. It must be seen by all who have the real welfare of our country at heart that our only true policy is to see that a republican government is now established under conditions which recognize our right to maintain its stability and prosperity. Cuba has menaced our peace quite too long, and having once undertaken to remedy an intolerable situation there it would be inexcusable folly to ignore the possibility and indeed the probability of future trouble, or to fail to guard against its recurrence.[24]

The problem as Platt saw it was providing liberty for Cuba, yet ensuring good government in a land so close to the United States. He resolved it by maintaining that the United States had the right of self protection through determination of what relations should be, but the system and details of government should be left to Cubans alone. America had no right to stop their desire for universal suffrage, for example,

The right to intervene for the abolition of a bad government, and the right to intervene for the maintenance of a good government in Cuba, rest upon the same foundation. It is as much our duty to exercise our power in the maintenance of an independent, stable and peaceful government there as it was to exercise it in the destruction of a monarchical, oppressive and inhuman one. Duty and self-interest coincide in this respect. The extension of the principles and institutions of free government, wherever possible and practicable, is no less our duty than the protection of our own citizens in all their rights and interests in a foreign country.[25]

Platt did not believe the Cuban situation promised much opportunity for free government. Liberty required a homogeneous people with high virtue and intelligence. But the Cuban heterogeneity, colonial background, poverty and illiteracy remained perplexing social problems. He did envision four factors that promised stability: guidance and aid of the United States, education of Cuban children, deference of the Negroes in public affairs, and the industrial and peaceful character of immigrants.[26]

[24] O. H. Platt, "Our Relation to the Peoples of Cuba and Porto Rico," *Annals*, XVIII (July 1901), 145-159; Platt papers, galley proofs of address given April 13, 1901.
[25] *Ibid.*
[26] Platt, "The Pacification of Cuba," *Independent*, LIII (June 27, 1901), 1468.

In another article, Platt supplied the rationale of the McKinley administration to the question of the duration of control, which centered on the word "pacification." [27] The Senator posed two solutions to the lingering Cuban question: annexation or independence. He dismissed annexation because Cubans could not be assimilated. It should be considered only in case of direct necessity. How then, he asked, could an independent republic be established which should subserve the interests of both the United States and Cuba? He said the Military Government had but one end in view: to afford the people of Cuba an opportunity to establish by themselves, and for themselves, an independent republic. "It was impossible for them to do it without our guidance." The Platt Amendment provided the means.

In no other way was it possible that future relations between the countries could be definitely agreed upon. That such agreement was necessary will not be questioned. Cuba was, and is today, a foreign power in the military occupation of the United States. . . . In other words, an agreement must now be had with the authorities framing the Constitution, thus binding the future Cuba; or the United States, waiting until the independence of Cuba shall have been recognized, must take whatever Cuba is then willing to give by treaty, be it much or little, or be contented with nothing at all.[28]

In disclosing one of the reasons for drafting the Platt Amendment, the Senator said the Cubans had timed their constitution, lacking any provision for future relations, to reach Congress just before it adjourned. Most delegates thought that upon receipt of the constitution, Congress would direct troops to withdraw, leaving all further stipulations to the Cubans; consequently they could ignore relations. Platt considered acceding to this to be fatal folly. In this emergency, Congress acted.

Platt mentioned a few of the problems being ignored by critics of the administration. Although the Cuban debt to Spain had been repudiated, there were still $ 600,000,000 in Spanish bonds outstanding and other bonds held in Germany and France. How could forcible assumption be prevented? How could Cubans be prevented from seizing Spanish property? Cubans expected help from America but would not agree in advance that America might assert that right. This type of independence the United States Government would not tolerate, because it would lead to loss of independence. After citing again the American defense requirement that no foreign power could be permitted to dominate or gain a foothold in the western hemisphere, Platt launched into his interpretation of the Teller Resolution and the critical word, "pacification."

[27] Platt, "A Solution of the Cuban Problem," *World's Work*, II (May, 1901), 729-735.
[28] *Ibid.*

The Teller Resolution did not stop the United States from saying anything about future relations. It was part of the declaration of war,

an assertion merely that we would not exercise the right of a conqueror and reduce the island to our possession; that our motives were disinterested, and that the war was a war for humanity, undertaken to put an end to abhorrent conditions near our shore, and not a war of conquest.... That we should assert in the same sentence our right and duty to put an end to abhorrent conditions in the island of Cuba, and also abandon our right to insist upon stability and peace thereafter, is inconceivable.[29]

Then Platt added his interpretation of pacification: "The securing of conditions in the island which would assure not only temporary but permanent peace under a stable government by the people." [30]

Platt advocated permanent pacification through a genuine republic.

It must be a real republic that will ensure our peace and quiet and safeguard our interests there. A mere paper republic, with a virtual dictator, or constantly recurring revolutions, would be nearly as disastrous to Cuba and dangerous to the United States as was the Spanish domination to which we put an end.[31]

For the next few years at least, Platt envisioned that his amendment would have to be in force. While he never discussed the time length intended, the implication was one of permanence. However Platt was a politician who devised his amendment to meet certain conditions and probably would have agreed that a removal of the conditions that instigated his amendment would in turn result in its removal.

Platt's reasoning showed continuity in administration policy. For the McKinley administration, withdrawal from Cuba as soon as the Spanish troops had departed, or as soon as the Cubans had framed a constitution, would have been a failure to perceive that the mutually distrustful social elements, illiteracy, irresponsibility and indebtedness would have caused recurring instability and the need to intervene again. Platt envisioned the right to intervene as a strong deterrent to the necessity of repeated intervention. With the development of this rationale, the President, the Secretary of War and the Senator, attempting to ease the burden of accepting the Platt Amendment, awaited the next act of the Cuban Convention.

---

[29] *Ibid.*
[30] *Ibid.*
[31] Platt, "The Pacification of Cuba," *Independent*, 1464-68.

CHAPTER X

ACCEPTANCE OF THE PLATT AMENDMENT,
MAY AND JUNE, 1901

The Cuban commissioners arrived back in Havana on May 5 and presented their report to the convention two days later. All five members of the commission, Méndez Capote, Tamayo, Portuondo, Betancourt and Llorente, had signed the report, indicating their agreement. After it was read to the convention, with Cisneros presiding, it was decided to provide copies for the delegates. The members of the convention discussed publishing the document in some form. So the afternoon ran its course, and the session adjourned without further action.[1]

The report of the commission and the private conversations between the members and their fellow delegates caused a revamping of attitudes and positions. The convention did not meet again until the 13th, and during the interval the delegates discussed and planned motions, weighed tactics and counted votes. As a sign of coming changes, Villuendas wrote an open letter, changing his position to acceptance of the Platt Amendment. He reasoned that the United States had changed since 1898; the whole nation, not just the Republicans, supported the Platt Amendment. It seemed to Villuendas that Cuba's alternatives were either annexation or a republic which accepted the amendment. Not wishing to oppose the inevitable, he chose the latter.[2]

When the convention met on May 13, Juan Gualberto Gómez immediately proposed passing the report on to the Commission on Relations. Sanguily objected, claiming it would be unrighteous and unlawful for the committee to receive the report before the house rendered its opinion. He contended that the delegation sent to Washington had violated its instructions by not obtaining new bases for transactions with the United States and he wanted to hear from the members of the commission. Villuendas believed that the report counselled acceptance of the Platt Amendment, since the commis-

---

[1] *Mención histórica,* 568-9; Portell Vilá, *Historia de Cuba,* IV, 245; on the 11th, *Diario de la Marina* printed the report. Wood arrived back in Havana on April 30.
[2] *New York Times,* May 8, 1901.

sioners had not negotiated for new accords. Portuondo surprised his colleagues by relating the conduct of the commission in Washington, affirming his faith in the sincerity of the declarations of the Secretary of War and the President of the United States, and observing that the opinion of the commissioned delegates was not influential in Washington. If what he had heard was sincere, Sanguily asked Portuondo, why had he in a recent newspaper continued to reject the Platt Amendment? Portuondo's reply is not revealed in the evidence.[3] Núñez asked why the commission had not tried to negotiate new bases. Diego Tamayo declared he had received the impression that the Platt Amendment guaranteed the independence and sovereignty of Cuba. Llorente explained clauses three and six as defined by Root, whom he believed sincere; the old Cuban considered the Platt law immutable and consequently decided that any attempt to negotiate new bases would have been useless and would have put the commission in a ridiculous situation. If they rejected the Platt law there would be no settlement; in such a case they had to choose between their personal passions and their duties as representatives of a public.[4]

All members present must have felt the drama of the moment, when Sanguily asked his famous question: "*¿Si se rechaza la Ley Platt que sucederá?*" – "If the Platt law is rejected, then what will happen?" Berriel seconded his query. In a hushed hall, Llorente answered that he could not predict the future but believed the occurrence would be disastrous for Cuba. Berriel asked his old friend if rejection of the Platt law would imperil the creation of the republic of Cuba. Llorente said he could not answer this particular question but did feel that rejection would prolong the military occupation. Quesada asked if the other commissioners agreed, and Diego Tamayo answered, "*– Yo opino como el Sr. Llorente.*" – "I am of the same opinion as Sr. Llorente." Alemán asked the commission for Root's answer to their demand for a written interpretation of the Platt Amendment. Llorente replied that Senator Platt understood it better than anyone else, and Root had delivered a letter to the commission from the Senator. After passing the report to the Commission on Relations, the session adjourned.[5]

The commission had returned from Washington convinced that the United States would not modify its stand. Their professions of belief in the sincerity of Secretary Root and President McKinley began to convince their colleagues in the convention. Also, the commissioners started to blunt the criticism of their associates by conveying Root's informal explanations of

[3] *Mención histórica*, 570-71.
[4] *Ibid.*
[5] *Ibid.*, 572.

how the Platt law aided *Cuba Libre*. Above all, Llorente's words, coming from such a respected man, produced a solemn and profound impression.[6] Villuendas' *volte face* had produced a majority of three to two for the Platt Amendment on the commission.[7] At this point the convention recessed so members could campaign for the coming municipal elections.

During the week's recess, the press carried stories of the preparations for calling a vote on the Platt Amendment. Juan Gualberto Gómez was quoted as interpreting Root's explanation to mean that the United States would alter the Platt law if the Cubans insisted. Gómez had absented himself from the Commission on Relations meetings and was given twenty-four hours to file a minority report. The commission majority was disposed to propose advising the Constitutional Convention to accept the Platt Amendment as a basis for future treaties with the United States,[8] but the convention was still reluctant to accept the Platt law verbatim.

The public knew of the convention deliberations. *Diario de la Marina* cited ten men as still opposed to the Platt law, but stated that they could be outvoted by the remainder.[9] *La Discusión* printed both an abbreviated report of a new eight-point program to be offered by Diego Tamayo, Quesada and Villuendas, and the minority report of J. G. Gómez and Silva, which rejected any acceptance of clauses three, six and seven.[10] The majority report accepted the sanitation and military acts clauses, added one on reciprocity and continued to hedge in the others with qualifying remarks. Again, the Cubans were trying to limit the Platt Amendment with verbiage which would be entirely unacceptable to Root.

General Wood, who had been using his prestige and persuasive powers for the acceptance of the Platt law among merchants and politicians, counselled unequivocable acceptance to the convention members. On the 17th he cabled Root that Méndez Capote had told him the convention would accept the Platt Amendment with added interpretations. Wood had clauses three and seven translated, saw nothing wrong with them and sent them to Root. Root cabled back on the same day, however, that the words might be construed differently, and the Platt wording would be best. But the new majority of the Committee on Relations, Diego Tamayo, Enrique Villuendas and

---

[6] Martínez Ortiz, *Los primeros años*, I, 300.

[7] *New York Times*, May 14, 1901.

[8] *New York Times*, May 16, 1901.

[9] *Diario de la Marina*, May 16, 1901; Juan Gualberto Gómez, Cisneros, Eudaldo Tamayo, Silva, Alemán, Monteagudo, Portuondo, Manduley, Ferrer and Lacret.

[10] *La Discusión*, May 20, 1901; *Diario de la Marina*, May 20, 1901; *Diario* of May 22 carried some proposals by Morúa.

Gonzalo de Quesada, had on May 16 submitted another report.[11] This differed slightly from the press reports.

The new majority report amounted to a qualified acceptance of the Platt Amendment with most of Root's explanations added. Instead of claiming the Platt Amendment violated the Treaty of Paris and the Joint Resolution, the majority for the first time tied the independence of Cuba to these documents. The report quoted the Platt and Root explanations, then proposed to the convention that the following ordinance be appended to the constitution.

The Republic of Cuba, in use of its sovereignty, convenes with the Republic of the United States of North America that the following prescriptions, interpreted according to the declarations made by the Secretary of War Mr. Root that are contained in the report of the Commission that went to Washington, should be substantially the bases of a treaty between both countries.

1. That the Government of Cuba will never celebrate with any foreign power or powers, any treaty or convention that can limit or tend to limit the independence of Cuba, nor in some manner authorize or permit, any foreign power or powers, to obtain by colonization or for military or naval purposes or of other manner establish in or control any portion of said Island.

2. That said Government will not assume or contract any public debt for the payment of whose interest and final amortization, if the ordinary revenues after the expenses of running the Government are inadequate.

3. That the Government of Cuba consents that the United States can exercise the right to intervene for the conservation of the independence of Cuba, the maintenance of a Government adequate for the protection of life, property and individual liberty and in order to fulfill the obligations with respect to Cuba that have been imposed upon the U.S. by the Treaty of Paris and that should now be assumed and fulfilled by the Government of Cuba; understanding that the right of intervention will only be exercised in order to impede the action of a foreign power against Cuba, or in case of great perturbations internal capable of producing a state of anarchy. The intervention will always be a formal act of the Government of the United States, never the action of an isolated authority. The intervention supposed neither a protectorate nor suzereinty, and will last only for the time necessary for the re-establishment of normality in the Republic of Cuba; not being by said right of intervention, synonymous with intermeddling or interference with the affairs of the Cuban Government, but a guarantee of its independence.

4. That all the acts realized by the United States in Cuba during the military occupation, will be ratified, having validity, and that all the rights legally acquired will be maintained and protected.

5. (Same wording as Platt law.)

6. That the Isle of Pines will be omitted from the limits of Cuba proposed by the Constitution leaving it for a future agreement by treaty the property of the

[11] Martínez Ortiz, *Los primeros años,* I, 291; Wood papers, Wood to Root, cable of May 17, 1901, 4:37 p.m., Root to Wood, at 4:45 p.m. same day: *Mención histórica,* 483-87.

same. Although the Isle of Pines is actually comprehended in the limits of Cuba and regulated by the same Government and administration, the future Government of Cuba and that of the United States will agree by special treaty the definitive property of said Isle of Pines.

7. That in order to place the United States in condition to maintain and defend the independence of Cuba as well as for its own defense, the Government of the Republic of Cuba will sell or lease to the United States the necessary lands for coaling or naval stations at certain points on the coast to be agreed upon with the President of the United States. It is understood that the naval or coaling stations do not give to the United States right to intervene in the affairs of the interior government of Cuba, but that they are established with the sole and only end of protecting the seas of America from foreign invasion against the Republic of Cuba and against the United States.

8. That for major security in the future, the Government of Cuba will insert the foregoing dispositions in a permanent treaty with the United States. The Government of the Republic of Cuba will promote at the same time, a treaty of commerce based on the reciprocity among the natural and manufactured products of both nations.

Although these eight points closely resembled the Platt Amendment, they did not satisfy Root, less because he did not wish to be bound by the Cuban phraseology than because he knew he was already bound by the wording of the Platt law, which was congressional statute. Wood knew the majority report's contents before the convention convened on the 20th of May. The majority of the Commission on Relations proceeded with its report, taking it to the floor for discussion and possible adoption.

The minority report, dated May 18, represented a change on the part of the radicals, Gómez and Silva.[12] They still maintained that the Platt Amendment violated the Joint Resolution and the Treaty of Paris; they asked how Cuba could be an independent country under clauses three and seven of the Platt Amendment. But they conceded, in view of the apparent sincerity of the Secretary of War, to recommend attaching the following stipulations to the Cuban Constitution.

1. The Government of the Republic of Cuba, in the use of its sovereignty, will celebrate, under the precepts of the constitution, treaties or conventions that promise opportunity with all foreign powers, without other limitation than that of not celebrating. . . . [the rest of clause one of the Platt law is printed.]

2. Reaffirmed the government of Cuba's adherence to three clauses in its proposed constitution regarding debts.

3. Put Cuba under the Monroe Doctrine for defense and omitted intervention.

4. Added the Joint Resolution and the Foraker Act to the acceptance of Military Government acts.

[12] *Mención histórica*, 488-492; *New York Times*, May 20, 1901. Wood papers, Wood to Root, May 17, 1901.

5. Cuba would adopt those resolutions of international and private hygiene which would lead to the extinction of importable diseases.

6. Although the Isle of Pines was Cuban territory, Cuba would define its condition in a treaty with the United States.

7. Gave the right to use Cuban bases or coaling stations to the United States in times of danger to the Cuban republic.

8. Reciprocity treaty.

9. Permanent treaty of peace, friendship and mercantile relations.

The convention reconvened on May 20 to consider the reports of the Commission on Relations. After they were read by the secretaries, the convention voted to table the reports for twenty-four hours and adjourned.[13] At this point, the conservatives and moderates, unable to muster their four-man majority, changed their tactics from rushing a vote on the Platt law to blocking the radicals. The radicals, however, were splitting. They had become estranged from J. G. Gómez whom they believed to be softening in his attitude toward the Platt law.[14]

The next day, the convention heard new proposals by Berriel and Morúa, together with a request by Núñez for reconsideration of his February 25th motion.[15] Sanguily asked for discussion of the commission's minority report before the majority report. At this point Juan Gualberto Gómez retired the minority report and substituted the proposal of March 26, which had been tabled by the convention because it rejected the Platt Amendment. Thus Gómez sought to reinstate himself with the radicals. Villuendas had withdrawn his signature from the proposal to give it minority status. Sanguily appealed to the minority group because of the gravity of the situation. They argued until 6:00 P.M., with Sanguily maintaining a bitter two-hour attack on the radicals, contending that the United States had been honest in planning a republic in Cuba and that concessions by the convention were needed to achieve it.[16]

As the delegates debated, Root cabled to Wood on May 21 that he wanted the exact text of the convention committee report and recommendations as soon as possible. McKinley had wired him from the Pacific Coast that he would regret it if the Platt Amendment were not accepted unchanged. The

[13] *Mención histórica*, 572-74; Cisneros was reported by the *New York Times* of May 21, 1901, to inform the convention that the commission did not report the "true" opinion in the United States, for he had received letters from New York counselling rejection of the Platt Law. Such advice hurt Cuba.

[14] *New York Times*, May 22, 1901.

[15] *Mención histórica*, 575-76, 493-95, 486-88. Both motions argued for acceptance of the Platt law rewritten by Cubans. Bravo Corresoso appeared at the May 20 and 21 sessions, his only appearance since February 27. This delegate stayed away from the convention and opposed the Platt law.

[16] *New York Times*, May 22, 1901.

next day Wood cabled back that the Commission on Relations recommended acceptance of the amendment verbatim, with explanatory remarks as an appendix to the constitution. He assured his chief that the phraseology would not limit the amendment and that he would send up the text on the 23rd, presumably after translation. On the 23rd, Wood again asserted that the explanatory remarks would not limit the scope of the Platt law; Root, unsuspecting, replied that this was good, although he was apprehensive about the construction, which might cause further uncertainty and prevent McKinley from ordering withdrawal. Differences lingered between the convention, the commission, Wood and Root.[17]

Given the fact that the wording of the Platt Amendment was law to guide future administrations, it is difficult to see how the Cubans' verbiage could have assisted succeeding governments or how they thought their proposals could have been acceptable. The moderates and conservatives, however, were trying to avoid a rupture in the convention and told Wood they had inserted the additions to mollify the radicals.[18]

On the 23rd, Juan Gualberto Gómez defended his proposal, which was attacked by Manuel Sanguily, who talked until almost 7:00 P.M. Nothing exists in the evidence about Sanguily's remarks, but it is probable that he stood in the breach, wielding his great oratorical talent to assure what he believed to be the only chance for the creation of the republic.[19] The only absentees from this session were Bravo Correoso, Gener and Ríus Rivera.

The same men gathered the next day, with emotions working to an even higher pitch. Zayas spoke against the minority report because it was contrary to the majority report and the commission report. Juan Gualberto Gómez intermittently stood off Llorente, Zayas and Núñez; the latter two also argued. The members agreed to sit in session until the vote was taken on the minority report. Finally they voted; the minority report of J. G. Gómez, once the majority report and the prevailing opinion of the convention, was defeated 19 to 9.[20] This signified a major turning point for the convention.

[17] Wood papers, Root to Wood, cable of May 21, Wood to Root, cable of May 22, Wood to Root, cable of May 23, Root to Wood, cable of May 23.

[18] *New York Times,* May 21, 1901, for a devastating attack on the Cuban "farrago of *ex parte* notations to the Platt law," and the "grotesque rendering" of Root's interpretation that raised more doubts about Cuba's political maturity.

[19] *Mención histórica,* 578.

[20] *Ibid.,* 579-80. The vote, for: Lacret, Cisneros, Portuondo, Fortún, J. G. Gómez, Silva, Alemán, Ferrer, E. Tamayo. Against: J. M. Gómez, Quesada, Morúa, Monteagudo, Quílez, Giberga, Llorente, Berriel, Betancourt, Fernández de Castro, Manduley, Robau, Rodríguez, Sanguily, D. Tamayo, Núñez, Zayas, Villuendas, Méndez Capote.

On May 25th, with twenty-one members present, Morúa, Berriel and Giberga withdrew their amendments, and the Commission on Relations requested the reading of a new proposal which replaced the majority report of May 16th. It was tabled for twenty-four hours.[21]

The new proposal represented the last major Cuban attempt to conciliate both the radicals and the United States. It amounted to an acceptance of the Platt Amendment which was hedged in by qualifications and long explanations.[22] The report again based Cuban sovereignty on the Joint Resolution and the Treaty of Paris, then cited the need to render an opinion on the Platt law. The report quoted Root's interpretation of the third clause dated April 3rd and stated that it considered official his manifestations of April 25 and 26, because the commissioners were on a mission equally official. Then the report quoted Root's letter of March 29 regarding the limits of intervention.

Considering the Platt Amendment, the Root clarifications and the foregoing declarations, the report stated that the sense and limit of the Platt Amendment were not incompatible with the independence and sovereignty of Cuba.

The Constitutional Convention, with the object and purpose of accepting said provisions substantially, resolves and declares that the constitution of the Republic of Cuba, voted by this Constitutional Convention, be considered with the addition thereto of the amendment to the appropriations bill hereinbefore recited, with the meaning and scope explained in the preceding paragraphs and statements made in the following explanations.

First: that the stipulations contained in clauses one and two of the Platt amendment are constitutional limitations internal, that do not restrict the faculty of the Government of the Republic of Cuba to celebrate freely treaties political or mercantile with any nation nor its faculties to contract loans and create debts, but not so much as would subject it to the clauses established in the Cuban Constitution and to those declared in the two mentioned clauses.

Second: That the intervention to which clause three refers does not imply in some manner intermeddling or interference in the affairs of the Cuban Government, and only will be exercised by formal action of the Government of the United States in order to conserve the independence and sovereignty of Cuba when it appears as if it is menaced by any foreign action or to reestablish according to the Constitution of the Republic of Cuba a government adequate to fulfill its internal and international limitations in case there existed a true state of anarchy.

Cisneros explained that he voted for it because it opposed the Platt law, Fernández de Castro voted against it because it limited Cuban sovereignty.

[21] *New York Times,* May 25, 1901; *Mención histórica,* 581.
[22] *Mención histórica,* 499-505.

Third: That the clause Four refers to the acts justly realized during the military occupation and to the rights legally acquired by them.

Fourth: That the fifth clause contracts of standards and plans of sanitation that may mutually be convened between the Government of the Republic of Cuba and of the United States.

Fifth: That although the Isle of Pines is comprehended in the limits of Cuba and ruled by the same government and administration, the future government of Cuba and the United States will determine by a special treaty the ownership of said Isle of Pines, without supposing a prejudice against the rights of Cuba over it.

Sixth: That in virtue of clause seven, the Government of the Republic of Cuba remains qualified to concert with the United States a treaty to make the concession of coaling or naval stations in terms to be agreed by both governments, to be established with the sole and only end of defending the seas of America in order to conserve the independence of Cuba in case of an aggression exterior as for the proper defense of the United States.

The Government of the Republic of Cuba will concert at the same time a treaty of commerce, based on reciprocity in which will be assured mutual and special preference for the natural and manufactured products of both countries in the respective markets without limiting the faculty for promoting or convening greater preferences in the future.

The May 16th edition actually came closer to accepting the Platt Amendment, using many of the same words, than did the new proposal, which represented an attempt to appease the radicals. The comparative brevity of the interpretations was intended to mollify the United States. Wood received a copy of the new proposal, translated it and sent it to Root at 12:31 A.M. on May 27th.[23]

That afternoon the convention met to deliberate the new proposal. Cisneros proposed that they did not have the faculty to modify the constitution they had adopted, as was intended by the proposal of the commission, because the Platt law and the Root interpretations introduced modifications to the constitution.[24] The moderates and conservatives quickly defeated the old Marquis' motion, 20 to 7. They explained their votes and then turned to the new proposal. The radicals, now on the defensive, opposed any extension of the session but were defeated. The rest of the time was used in discussing the proposal.[25]

The test came on the afternoon of the 28th. The *New York Times* correspondent talked with the *convencionales* after they recessed on the 27th, reporting that by unanimous agreement the convention had decided to take a final vote on the acceptance of the Platt Amendment on the 28th. The

---

[23] Wood papers, Wood to Root, cable of May 27, 1901.
[24] *Mención histórica,* 582.
[25] *Ibid.,* 582-83.

conservatives and moderates claimed they would win acceptance of the Platt law by a vote of seventeen to eleven.[26]

Eudaldo Tamayo, Portuondo, Berriel and Sanguily argued all afternoon about the majority report. At last Alemán requested extension of the session until the vote was taken on the new proposal, and it was agreed. Juan Gualberto Gómez created consternation when he received permission to have read the oath the members had taken when the convention first met.[27] He claimed this oath obligated them to renounce any pact with foreigners. Sanguily instantly leaped to his feet, threatening that if this reading of the oath implied that those voting for the Platt law were perjurors, he would leave the convention, and other delegates would too. Gómez explained that *"lo expuesto por el Sr. Sanguily no cruzó por su mente,"* – "that idea expressed by Sr. Sanguily had not crossed his mind." But he would not relent. Eudaldo Tamayo joined the fight by calling the pro-Platt men traitors, but this the convention forced him to retract. J. G. Gómez spoke for an hour, rehearsing the history of the Revolution. When he finished, Villuendas read the new proposal. It passed, 15 to 14, with Mendéz Capote's vote breaking the tie.[28]

The justification for the votes provides insight to the motivations of the delegates. Robau said that he respected and had even anticipated the result.

I voted against it because I always have been, am and will be a follower of the revolutionary principles all my life, and only because of them have I the high honor to come among you.[29]

Quílez pointed out that his vote was not a contradiction of his proposal two months earlier to accept the Platt law without modification. Sanguily explained that he voted for it because there was no alternative, although he feared its dilution would cause the United States to reject it. Llorente based his acceptance on Root's interpretation; Quesada also believed in Root and the official declarations. Cisneros, rumbling that the Platt law was unconstitutional, contradictory and against absolute independence, warned that they could not sit there and enslave Cubans for the future. José M. Gómez

[26] *New York Times,* May 28, 1901.

[27] See Page 102.

[28] *Mención histórica,* 585-87. Those in favor were José Miguel Gómez, Llorente, Morúa, Monteagudo, Quesada, Berriel, Rodríguez, Sanguily, Betancourt, Núñez, Diego Tamayo, Quílez, Giberga, Villuendas and Méndez Capote. Those voting "no" were Robau, Alemán, Lacret, Portuondo, Fortún, Juan Gualberto Gómez, Manduley, Silva, Fernández de Castro, Ferrer, Eudaldo Tamayo, Zayas, Gener and Cisneros; absent were Bravo and Ríus Rivera; Portell Vilá, *Historia de Cuba,* IV, 253, states that only Wood's official pressure forced 15 votes together; yet there was also a growing annexationist sentiment due to Cuban disgust with the paralysis of the convention; *New York Times,* May 29, 1901, which printed the Platt Amendment, omitted the Cuban additions and believed it accepted without changes.

[29] *Mención histórica,* 585.

said the majority opinion was the only way to save the republic, and he had voted for it because he was sent to the convention not on his record, but to resolve the large problems presented there. He feared the delegates were forgetting their duty, and the Cuban people were becoming impatient. Berriel based his vote on the preamble of his amendment. Villuendas read a letter dated Havana, May 22, from Bravo Correoso, who declared he could not concur in the session or take part in the vote because he maintained the view expressed in the vote of February 26th and opposed the Platt Amendment. With that, Méndez Capote adjourned the session.

At 8:28 P.M. the War Department received a cable from Wood, announcing that the Platt Amendment had just passed the convention by a 15 to 14 vote. Wood said this was not indicative of true sentiment: some had voted against it knowing that 15 votes were already committed. At 8:45 P.M., after he had deliberated over the contents of the proposals of the 27th but before he received word of its passage, Root sent Wood the following message:

I do not think that the passage of the proposed appendix to the constitution as transmitted to me by you would be such an acceptance of the Platt amendment as to authorize the President's withdrawing the army from Cuba under the provisions of the Platt amendment.

Just before midnight, Wood replied that the appendix to the constitution as approved and passed by the convention was in the form sent to Root on Sunday the 27th.[30] Wood's troubles regarding the amendment were not yet over.

After Root directed Wood to send him an exact copy of the text of the majority report, he requested Senator John Coit Spooner to return to Washington, to assist in determining whether the clauses the Cubans would attach were substantially the same as the Platt Amendment or whether they altered it. Root, concerned about their friends in the convention, said he hoped to help them by accepting the resolutions if he could, because they were "having a pretty hard fight." [31] On the 30th, Root, Spooner and Platt met with McKinley for one and one-half hours, finally deciding that the Cuban reply was inadequate.[32]

Root incorporated this decision in a long letter to Wood, dated May 31st, for transmission to the convention. He spent most of the afternoon of the 30th at the Arlington Hotel, drafting this reply. In keeping with his policy

[30] Wood papers, cables, Wood to Root at 8:28 P.M. on May 28, Root to Wood at 8:45 P.M. on May 28, Wood to Root at 11:33 P.M. on May 28.

[31] John Coit Spooner papers, Root to Spooner, May 21, 1901, Spooner to Root, telegram of May 28, 1901.

[32] *New York Times,* May 31, 1901.

of patient firmness, he politely rejected the Cuban acceptance of the Platt Amendment and explained in careful language, point by point, his reasons for doing so. Root began by acknowledging receipt of Wood's cable of the 28th, which advised that the Constitutional Convention had passed without change the proposed appendix to the constitution which Root had received on May 27th. When Root received Wood's telegram, on the 29th, he had already written his message expressing his doubt that the passage of the proposed appendix (majority report) would be an acceptance of the Platt Amendment which would authorize the President to withdraw the army. Root explained that he thought the convention had passed the resolution that same day, before Wood received his dispatch.[33] Actually, Root's message of the 28th was not received until four or five hours after the convention had voted. Wood then simply waited for an official letter of instructions. The Cubans had apparently pressed the question, feeling unsure of holding their votes, before waiting to hear from the Secretary of War.[34]

Analyzing the appendix eventually passed by the convention, Root considered its operative part inadequate.

Without regard to the substance of the provisions thus declared to be accepted, it seems doubtful whether this action answers to the requirements of the act of Congress referred to.

After quoting the Platt Amendment in full, Root went on to explain:

This seems to require that the Convention shall not merely declare its assent to the act of Congress, but that the Convention itself shall expressly enact the provisions called for by the act of Congress, so that they shall constitute not provisions of the act of Congress assented to by the Convention, but shall become the act of the Convention formally and solemnly ordained by that body, and forming a part of the constitution of Cuba, either by incorporation into the body of the constitution, or in the form of an ordinance appended thereto. The resolution adopted by the Convention should, therefore, properly be followed by formal and final action through which the Convention does the thing which it expresses a willingness to do in the resolution of acceptance.

Before such final action is taken, I wish to confirm and more fully express the views indicated by me on the 28th instant. To do this the more intelligently, let me recall the relation which the President bears to the so-called Platt amendment. That statute having been enacted by the law-making power of the United States, the President is bound to execute it, and to execute it as it is. He cannot change or modify, add to or subtract from it. The executive action called for by the statute is the withdrawal of the army from Cuba, and the statute authorizes that action when, and only when, a government shall have been established under a constitution which contains, either in the body thereof or in an ordinance an-

[33] Wood papers, Root to Wood, May 31, 1901.
[34] Wood papers, Wood to Root, June 9, 1901.

nexed thereto, certain definite provisions specified in the statute. He is not authorized to act at all under the statute until a Cuban government is established under a constitution. When that is done it will be his duty to examine the constitution and see whether there are enacted therein in substance the same provisions which are specified in the act of Congress. If he then finds those provisions in the constitution he will be authorized to withdraw the army; if he does not find them there he will not be authorized to withdraw the army.

It is quite clear that if a government should now be organized in Cuba under the constitution adopted by the present Convention, without further or other action by that Convention defining the relations between Cuba and the United States, the President would be unable to find either in the constitution or in the ordinance annexed thereto, the provisions specified in the act of Congress called the Platt amendment, for the reason that the explanations which follow the acceptance of the Platt amendment in the resolution of the Convention, so change the provisions as accepted that they are no longer the same either in form or substance.

Root compared each of the resolutions to the corresponding Platt clauses. Generally, he found that the Cubans tried to assume a discretion or control which the Platt law could not permit. The appendix would not aid Cuba, he argued, adding that he knew no such ideas were entertained by the commission which visited the United States, or for several weeks after they returned. Their original interpretations of clauses three and seven were, he thought, satisfactory.

In addition to an unequivocal rejection of the Cuban alteration of the Platt Amendment, the press noted that the men in McKinley's cabinet protested the convention's use of Root's April 25th and 26th discussions with the commission. Root had specifically termed these conversations confidential and unofficial, carefully refraining from trying to make an official interpretation of a congressional statute. The Cubans had abused his confidence in their attempt to pass the Platt Amendment through the convention. The *New York Times* said the patience of the administration was exhausted, and its policy of conciliation had vanished. Congressman Charles H. Grosvenor of Ohio was quoted as describing the cabinet stand as no surprise.

Who imagined that those fellows would be allowed to sit in Congress down there in Cuba and amend the laws of the United States? We have stood all the nonsense we are going to from them. The sooner they stop this foolishness and attend to business the better it will be for them. If Congress ever gets another shot at them, they won't get off so easily as they did before.

Senator O. H. Platt noted that the error lay in the Cuban view of the Platt Amendment as a treaty. It was a law which they could either accept or reject but could not change. A tone of coldness crept into the utterances of spokesmen for the American administration, indicating their thought that the Cubans' evident frivolity of mind made it useless to mince matters.[35]

Still, Root's letter indicated that he wished to explain rather than dictate, so the Cubans would want to accept the American terms. But his letter was delayed in transmission by registered mail, and in the interim, Havana buzzed with doubt. On June first Wood cabled Root that the official text of the appendix would be submitted to him on Monday, the third.[36] Wood tried to explain why he let the Cuban additions pass, knowing that a formal rejection was coming down from Washington. He recalled that on May 22nd he had cabled Root that the Platt law would be accepted verbatim, with explanatory remarks not limiting the amendment, on the assurance of Méndez Capote and Tamayo. The next day Wood had directed them to proceed, thinking Root encouraged it. On the 26th (actually the 27th), Wood sent up a translated copy of the appendix. The General maintained that the Commission on Relations later changed some of its provisions to accommodate certain radical members. This, however, was an excuse. The accommodating provisions were contained in the draft Wood saw. He received Root's cipher telegram of the 28th at 9:15 P.M., but the convention had already made its decision.

The afternoon papers caused great excitement by announcing that the United States would not accept the Cuban amendment. Worried, Tamayo and Méndez Capote felt responsible for having pledged passage of the Platt Amendment without modifying its scope. They told Wood that the amendment had been accepted literally and that the added explanations and declarations were to be considered upon framing the treaty. To Wood, these men appeared either insincere or ignorant of the consequences. He showed them Root's answer of the 28th and urged adoption of the exact wording of the Platt Amendment. Explanations could be added, if needed, but the law must not be changed. Wood reproached the two men with their use of Root's confidential conversations. It is likely that the Cubans used Root's phrases not in bad faith or in ignorance, but in desperation, to mollify the radicals and get the votes, relying on Root's words to justify their own distasteful action. It is surprising there was not more misunderstanding among Root, Wood and the convention about what constituted acceptance.[37]

Wood then asked Root for further instructions, after estimating that at least a year would be needed to turn over the government to the Cubans

---

[35] *New York Times,* June 1, June 10, 1901; Root to Roosevelt, June 4, 1901, as quoted in Jessup, *Root,* I, 323.

[36] Wood papers, Wood to Root, June 1, 1901.

[37] *Ibid.*

after passage of the Platt Amendment.[38] More crucial than Cuban inexperience at this juncture was the fact that they had fought two wars of rebellion and had seen an overpowering foreign nation demand an intervening hand in their affairs. Theirs was a difficult and tragic position.

In Havana, most onlookers believed the Cuban delegates would not reconsider. The *convencionales* themselves were surprised at the rejection and at the last minute had removed six interpretive clauses from the amendment and placed them at the end in the form of a resolution.[39] The delegates blamed the commission; the commission blamed Wood and Root. The delegates claimed the United States was not acting in good faith, for Washington had known the nature of the report to be submitted. They said the Commission on Relations, quoting Wood and Root, had assured them that this form was acceptable to the United States. The conservatives attempted to adjourn the convention for a month, so they might urge their municipalities to order them to vote for the Platt law.[40] In this uncertain period before Root's letter arrived, knowing that Washington would reject their appendix to the constitution, the Cuban delegates met once more.

On June 5th twenty-three delegates gathered and returned the new proposal to the committee on style. The delegates agreed to Giberga's suggestion that the new proposal be included in an answer to Wood's letter of March 2nd.[41] They adjourned again, not sure if or when they would meet next. If the awaited letter from Root contained an ultimatum, they believed they would reject it. The conservatives and moderates, doubtful of mustering fifteen votes again, complained that the United States had not supported them and claimed Wood had told them up to the last moment that the United States was satisfied with their progress in framing the appendix.[42] While Wood had cautioned the members to accept the Platt law, he had also encouraged them to think that explanations would be acceptable.[43]

On the sixth, Wood received Root's letter of May 31, the official rejection of the Cuban proposal of the 28th. After conferring with Méndez Capote, Wood seized the initiative in the negotiations by cabling Root that he wanted to make some changes in the letter. He and Méndez Capote believed that presenting the letter to the convention would open up endless discussion. The task was to bring about a vote on accepting or rejecting the Platt law as written. The vote would be close, but nothing was to be gained by further

[38] *Ibid.*
[39] *New York Times,* June 1, 1901.
[40] *Ibid.,* June 2, 1901.
[41] *Mención histórica,* 588.
[42] *New York Times,* June 6, 1901.
[43] Wood papers, Wood to Root, June 9, 1901.

discussion. Wood suggested deletion of Root's point by point discussion of the Cuban proposal, wishing to include only the words most central to the argument.[44] He feared the balance of the letter would put the commission on the defensive with the convention for having its proposed resolution transmitted to Washington prior to acceptance. It was vital to hold together the votes they had; the majority might turn against the amendment if the convention and commission clashed. Wood offered to send either the suggested portion of the letter or all of it to Méndez Capote, to tell members of it semiofficially or to send it all to the convention, as Root might direct.

The Secretary replied the next day, saying his letter of instructions had attempted to explain to the delegates what action the President would consider his duty should the convention fail to act further. The portion Wood had quoted was enough to convey this, and he was to give a copy of that portion to the chairman of the Commission on Relations. Root approved Wood's views on the matter and allowed him to show the letter to members of the convention. Root repeated that the true course for the convention was to enact the provisions of the Platt Amendment as they were.[45] As was usual with letters of this sort, the information became public within twenty-four hours.[46] Wood showed the entire letter to Méndez Capote but officially transmitted his shortened version.[47] It was introduced into the convention on June 11th, but was known five days earlier and dated June 8th.

On the 8th the newspapers reported that the fifteen delegates who had voted for the Platt Amendment were still in favor and would try to force the radicals to a vote. On Monday the 10th, they would meet to discuss this. Although the conservatives were threatening dissolution in an attempt to obtain more votes from the electorate, neither side really wished to dissolve the convention.[48] Pressure from the United States had not caused anything resembling a revolution; rather, it seemed to rouse the island against the convention.

As Wood waited for the Cuban Convention to take action upon Root's latest communication, he summarized the events of the past seven months in a tone of discouragement.[49] For Wood, the United States Government had given the convention every possible opportunity both to propose acceptable

[44] See above, 173-74; Wood papers, Wood to Root, cable of June 6, 1901; Portell Vilá, *Historia de Cuba,* IV, 257-58, calls Wood's ultimatum "unpardonable cruelty and affrontery."
[45] Wood papers, Root to Wood, cable of June 7, 1901, Wood to Root, June 8, 1901, Root to Wood, June 8, 1901.
[46] *New York Times,* June 8, 1901; *Diario de la Marina,* June 12, 1901.
[47] Wood papers, Wood to Root, June 9, 1901; *Mención histórica,* 510-514.
[48] *New York Times,* June 8, 1901.
[49] Wood papers, Wood to Root, June 9, 1901.

relations themselves and to accept the Platt law with as little humiliation as possible. The Cubans had responded with deception and dilatory tactics.

Wood considered that "we have done all that we can do." Any further discussion would be a mistake; it was time for an ultimatum. There was no excitement in the island whatever as to whether the convention "accepts the Platt Amendment or goes fishing." The majority of the people were not discussing or even paying attention to the situation. Wood did not predict the next vote of the convention, but added that a few radicals "may have sense enough to see that if they do not accept it their opportunities to spend the Island revenues will be indefinitely deferred and consequently will vote for its acceptance." [50]

This long letter of Wood's is significant not only for its summary but for what it reveals of his own feelings. Even his stout constitution showed the pressure of the situation. His unquenchable optimism diminished and he said things he ordinarily would not admit. The next month, after concluding the Platt Amendment and the Church property agreement, he was to fall deathly ill with typhoid fever. Whatever his state of mind, he was in no condition to commiserate with the Cubans, who felt they had deep grievances. It is a tribute to both sides that such feelings were submerged before greater considerations.

On the tenth, Wood advised his chief that

I have seen a number of the members of the Convention today and some of them feel that the fact the matter is now brought to them in the shape of an ultimatum will tend to bring about a full appreciation of the gravity of the situation so far as the formation of the Cuban government is concerned, and that this may influence them to accept the Amendment.[51]

When the session reconvened on June 11th, the delegates heard the Wood abbreviation of June 8th.[52] Cisneros and Eudaldo Tamayo resisted holding a secret session but were overruled. Morúa submitted another motion, in effect accepting the Platt Amendment with changed wording.[53] Cisneros moved that they return Wood's June 8th communication without comment. This was rejected. After further argument they agreed by a vote of 19 to 4 that it would not be necessary to revise the accord of May 28th. They were bypassing the May 28th proposal and letting it stand, because they had to make an outright acceptance or rejection of the Platt Amendment. At that

---

[50] *Ibid.*
[51] Root papers, Wood to Root, June 10, 1901.
[52] *Mención histórica,* 589-90, 510-14.
[53] *Ibid.,* 515-17.

point, Villuendas, Quesada and Diego Tamayo moved to amend Morúa's motion by adding this statement:

The Delegates that subscribe propose, as an amendment to the Morúa motion, that the Convention declare that it will insert in an ordinance attached to the Constitution of the Republic the clauses contained in the Platt Law.

The amendment was tabled and the session adjourned.[54]

It was rumored that the conservatives were not ready to vote and had requested adjournment until the 12th. They scheduled a meeting at 9:00 A.M. on that date to plan their strategy for the afternoon session. They still held 15 votes, and several radicals were said to have compromised by agreeing not to attend the session.[55]

The next day, Wednesday, June 12th, the delegates assembled as usual.[56] Villuendas announced that the amendment by Diego Tamayo, Quesada and himself had been removed from the table; he read a new one which was offered in its place as an amendment to the Morúa project.[57] (It is difficult to see how they could amend without striking out all of Morúa's motion.)

Whereas: the Congress of the United States in a provision of the law of appropriations of the army for the year fiscal that terminates on the 30th of June of 1902, authorized the President of that Republic, in fulfillment of the Joint Resolution of the same Congress, of the 20th of April of 1898, to leave the government and dominion of the Island of Cuba to its people as soon as they had established in said island a government under a constitution, in which, or in an appendix to it they defined the future relations between the United States and Cuba, as determined in that provision.

With a view of the diverse communications by the Military Governor of Cuba to the Constitutional Convention with respect to the establishment of the relations between Cuba and the United States and of the further antecedents relative to the affairs recorded by the secretary of the convention, they propose the following resolution:

The Constitutional Convention proceeding in conformity with the order of the Military Governor of the Island of the 25th of July of 1900, by which it was convoked, resolves to add and adds to the constitution of the Republic of Cuba, adopted on the 21st of February, ultimo, with the following appendix:

Then followed, without change, the text of the Platt Amendment. Without discussion, the vote was taken on the amendment which passed 16 to 11.[58]

[54] *Ibid.*, 518.
[55] *New York Times,* June 12, 1901.
[56] *Mención histórica,* 591-93.
[57] *Ibid.*, 519-22. The whole motion is in capitals.
[58] *Ibid.,* 591-93. The votes for accepting the Platt Amendment were: José Miguel Gómez, José de J. Monteagudo, Martin Morúa Delgado, Pedro Betancourt, Leopoldo Berriel, Pedro González Llorente, Gonzalo de Quesada, Diego Tamayo, Manuel Sanguily, Alejandro Rodríguez, Emilio Núñez, Eliseo Giberga, Joaquin Quílez, José N. Ferrer, Enrique Villuendas and Domingo Méndez Capote. Those delegates who

The scene lacked the drama and emotional intensity of the May 13th and May 29th sessions. There was neither jubilation nor indignation, but merely resignation: sadly they went through with the imposed action. Then they explained their votes. Giberga declared that he had voted for it in the same spirit that he had voted for the previous accords (those that had come close to accepting the Platt law). Ferrer, the only new addition to the fifteen votes of the 28th, said:

I understand that it has been resisted enough already and it can be resisted no more. I considered it useful, beneficial and necessary to oppose the Platt law, as long as there was hope that it would be modified or retired by the American Congress, and voted against the opinion of Srs. Tamayo, Villuendas and Quesada. Today I consider said opposition useless, dangerous and sterile, considering the way the Supreme Court has opened up to the imperialism in the United States of the North, and lacking furthermore the hope that the Congress of that nation would reconsider its resolution known as the Platt law. For this and because it is the only way to establish the republic of Cuba.

Sanguily said he understood that the terms of the Platt Amendment fulfilled the Joint Resolution and were favorable to both the Constitution of the Republic of Cuba and the Cuban personality, which by any other method would disappear completely. Any resistance against this American imposition would definitely be dismal for Cuban aspirations. Méndez Capote adhered to the explanation of Ferrer; J. M. Gómez and Monteagudo to that of Sanguily. Morúa explained that he had accepted the Platt Amendment only because it could constitute the Republic of Cuba, hoping that independence was compatible with the situation established by Congress. Núñez and Quesada said,

We accept the Platt amendment because it signifies the constitution of the Republic of Cuba and is the complement, as it says in the preamble to said amendment, of the Joint Resolution that guarantees the independence and sovereignty of Cuba.

Berriel voted for it because any other method would have prolonged American occupation of Cuba indefinitely, which would have meant continued domination that the Cubans could not resist, given the impression of the latest communication from the Military Governor.

Giberga proposed passing the resolution on to Wood without sending it to the committee on style. This was agreed. Méndez Capote said, although it was irregular, there would be no discussion of the Morúa proposal in view

voted against accepting the Platt Amendment were: José B. Alemán, Luis Fortún, Salvador Cisneros Betancourt, Manuel R. Silva, José Lacret Morlot, Rafael Portuondo, Fernández de Castro, Juan Gualberto Gómez, Eudaldo Tamayo, Rafael Manduley and Alfredo Zayas. Four radicals, opposed to the Platt Amendment, absented themselves: Bravo, Ríus Rivera, Gener and Robau.

of the amendment just passed.[59] They agreed to meet in sections to choose commission members for drawing up an electoral law. After a ten minute recess, they reconvened, nominating Betancourt, Silva, Zayas, Bravo Correoso and Alemán. Méndez Capote announced that they would be advised at their homes of the date and time of the next meeting and then raised the session.

Quesada brought the news to Wood. The General cabled Root in cipher at 7:40 P.M. on the 12th, trying to reach the Secretary of War at his Rhode Island Avenue residence in Washington. F. L. Squires, a clerk in the War Department sent it on to Clinton, New York; it finally reached Root in Buffalo on the 13th. Meanwhile Wood had sent another cable at 2:56 P.M. on the 13th:

Am informed this morning by Tamayo that Platt amendment was passed and accepted yesterday exactly as written, without any change or modification whatever. Vote sixteen in favor and eleven against.

In Buffalo, Root said, "It means the independence of Cuba, and all that is best and freest in Cuba will be backed by all that is best in the United States." On the afternoon of the 14th, Wood cabled Root that telegrams from around the island indicated favorable reactions to the straight acceptance of the Platt Amendment. The situation was excellent, and work on the electoral law would start at once.[60] In Washington there was no definite word on American withdrawal from Cuba, but estimates ranged from three months to a year to prepare for the transfer of control.

At a rally a few days later, Villuendas explained his vote, which had been misconstrued in the press as an unintentional mistake. He approached the thorny problem of the amendment by saying he believed it his duty to accept, in order to make Cuban nationality possible.

Who are those mistaken, Sres. Zayas [Eudaldo] Tamayo, Portuondo or I? The future will tell; today we can only make conjectures; but if tomorrow fallacy or deception pretend to submerge the nationality of Cuba, and the people protest with the old rebelliousness, I, who fought once with arms to triumph. . . would not be the last to answer the trumpet's call, and would serve Cuba again if honor demanded it. . . .

But this is not the case; if the Republic of Cuba develops, we will say that those who accepted the Platt Amendment saved our country for progress by work, civilization and love.[61]

---

[59] *Ibid.* Here occur deletions in the text.

[60] Root papers, Wood to Root, June 13, 1901; Wood papers, Wood to Root cables of June 12, June 13, Tamayo to Wood, June 14, 1901, Wood to Root, June 14, 1901; *New York Times,* June 13, 1901.

[61] Martínez Ortiz, *Los primeros años,* I, 309-10.

Villuendas sat down to great applause. He was a veteran, young and bright, and the darling of the Cuban public, symbolizing in a sense the hope of the Cubans for the future. There was no rooted or fundamental hostility to the Platt Amendment then, and most people wanted to – and believed they could – make the best of it.[62]

Rafael Martínez Ortiz remembered that everyone appreciated the problem they faced except the fanatics, agitators, sentimentalists and those of no culture. "[A]ll the world understood that there was no other way." [63] Martínez Ortiz believed Cuba owed a debt of gratitude to Generals José Miguel Gómez and José de Jesus Monteagudo, who had convinced powerful friends in Las Villas to agree to the Platt law. And Manuel Sanguily, with his eloquence, made an "invincible battering ram." The public did not until later appreciate the *convencionales,* who sacrificed their pride and popularity to an extraordinary love of country. Without them, no Cuban Republic would have been established in 1902, and the Cuban personality would have been lost forever. (As Sanguily put it, *"La personalidad nacional cubana se hubiera perdido para siempre."*) For Martínez Ortiz, the first necessity was existence; only after the necessary creation of Cuban nationality could they build to sustain independence. Neither a prolonged occupation nor a revolt would have been as beneficial as acceptance of the Platt Amendment.[64]

Did the Cuban policy prevail after all? The delegates were never ordered to pass the Platt law but were advised of the consequences if they did not. The Cubans, weak as their position was, had at last forced the United States to give them an ultimatum. On the other hand, while Root had not succeeded in inducing the Cubans to initiate the relations desired by the United States, he had led them a long way from their position of February 27th without starting war. Root's policy of patient firmness succeeded insofar as they did vote in duly constituted session to attach the Platt Amendment officially to their constitution. But they did not do so voluntarily and acquiesced only after a long period of persuasion and pressure. Had they initiated a draft proposal of their own embodying the United States desires, there would have been no six-month negotiation. This, however, was impossible for Cubans who wanted independence before agreeing to relations with the United States. Their other alternatives were passive resistance and open rebellion, but neither the nature of the occupation nor the enervation of the Cubans permitted these.

Perhaps the United States was unduly concerned about minority groups

[62] *Ibid.*
[63] *Ibid.,* 308.
[64] *Ibid.,* 316-319.

in Cuba and should have let internal Cuban matters take their course, much like the expulsion of the Loyalists during the American Revolution. But no American government was willing to tolerate further bloodshed and chaos in Cuba. To have abandoned Cuba to the Cubans would have necessitated another intervention. While the Platt Amendment wounded the Cuban spirit necessary for republic building, at the same time it guaranteed *Cuba Libre* and prevented no single sovereign act except self-destruction.

CHAPTER XI

THE TRANSFER OF CONTROL,
JULY, 1901 TO MAY 20, 1902

As soon as Cuba accepted the Platt Amendment, the Military Government began to prepare for the transfer of control. Plans proceeded for electing a president and congress before the end of 1901, with installation of the Cuban government scheduled for May 20, 1902. In Root's words, the government of Cuba was to be transferred as a "going concern," with money in the treasury, civil servants functioning at their posts, law and order prevailing – a trust fulfilled and transferred.

During those eleven months Root and Wood faced the major problems of terminating projects of the Military Government, finding a market for Cuban sugar and other products, gradually turning over administrative posts to Cubans, actually transferring control and holding elections. But matters were delayed by about a month when Wood contracted typhoid fever. For a time he transacted business as usual with a temperature of 104 degrees and higher; then he became worse and during July he nearly died. Taken home, he recuperated during August, cruising in New England waters. By September 7th he was back in Havana, ready for work.[1]

He returned to Havana to learn that President McKinley had been shot by an anarchist at Buffalo. When McKinley died, Wood went immediately to the funeral in Canton, Ohio, after assuring the Cubans that the policy of departure would be kept.[2]

The Cubans retained a special fondness for the new President, Theodore Roosevelt. They remembered his dashing charge up San Juan Hill and his ardent championing of their independence. Several months before he became President, Roosevelt showed that his attitude toward Latin America was not acquisitive:

[1] Wood papers, Wood to Root, July 1, 1901; Hagedorn, *Wood,* I, 367-368.
[2] Wood papers, Wood to Root, Sept. 19, 1901; Hagedorn, *Wood,* I, 369; CDDC 3912, Sept. 12, 1901.

I am perfectly clear that we do not want to expand over another people capable of self-government unless that people desires to go in with us – and not necessarily even then. As you know, I most earnestly feel that this should be our attitude toward the other American states. Barring the possible necessity of fortifying the Isthmian canal, or getting a naval station, I hope it will not become our duty to take a foot of soil south of us. . . . I believe the South American states can work out their own salvation for themselves. I do not believe that of the Philippines at this time.[3]

In continuing the McKinley policy, Roosevelt adamantly supported the Monroe Doctrine and pledged himself emotionally as well as politically to create a free Cuba.

Before the end of June, the name of Máximo Gómez for president was coupled with a variety of possible running mates. But the old General wanted no part of politics and threw his weight behind Tomás Estrada Palma. Wood hoped the country would unite behind Estrada Palma for President and Bartolomé Masó for vice-president. But the disgruntled radicals around Juan Gualberto Gómez flattered Masó into running for president on a coalition ticket with the Democratic Unionists, a conservative group opposed to almost everything the radicals stood for.[4]

Meanwhile, Máximo Gómez visited the United States at Wood's behest to persuade Estrada Palma to run for office. At a dinner staged in his honor at New York's Union League Club, Gómez declared with feeling that he had never realized how sincerely Americans cared for Cuba. He reminisced about every Cuban living and dying with the idea of *Cuba Libre* before him; when an old Cuban died, he said to his son, "You will live to see Cuba free." Estrada Palma, who was also present, and Gómez both predicted that Cuba's future was to be part of the United States. Reportedly as a result of this trip and discussion with Cubans in New York, Estrada Palma overcame his apprehensions at having been away from the scene for so long and agreed to accept nomination when asked.[5] Gómez returned to Havana to face charges from opposition newspapers of being an annexationist, which he indignantly denied: "Yes, but none of those that say it have smelt as much powder as I have. . . ." His policy was cooperation with the United States in order to build a viable Cuba.[6]

Around the island, political factions were forming. In Santa Clara, José

[3] Roosevelt papers, Roosevelt to Frederic René Coudert, July 3, 1901.

[4] *New York Times,* June 25, 1901; *Diario de la Marina,* June 25, 1901; *Havana Post,* June 30, 1900, June 25, 1901.

[5] *New York Times,* July 7, 1901; *Havana Post,* July 3, 1901. Gómez' interpreter was Alejandro González, Wood's personal secretary and an old friend of Gómez.

[6] *Havana Post,* July 16, 1901, July 21, 1901, July 24, 1901; Martínez Ortiz, *Los primeros años,* I, 353.

Miguel Gómez, Villuendas, Robau, Alemán, Orestes Ferrara and Carlos Mendieta organized the *Partido Republicano Federal*. In Oriente, the Republicans were controlled by Demetrio Castillo Duany's *Partido Republicano Castillista*; to a lesser extent by Rafael Manduley. Pedro Betancourt controlled the Republicans of Matanzas, while Méndez Capote and Ricardo Dolz headed the Havana *Partido Republicano*. Oriente *Nacionalistas* found leadership in Bravo Correoso, Emilio Bacardí and Francisco Sánchez Hechavarria. Gener, Diego Tamayo and Quintín Banderas led the Havana *Nacionalistas*. In Puerto Príncipe, *Nacionalistas* were organized by Manuel Silva and General Loynaz del Castillo. The *Partido Nacional* claimed Rodríguez Fuentes as its leader in Matanzas and Pino Guerra in Pinar del Río. The Democratic Unionists of Havana and Matanzas were led by Eusebio Hernández, Eliseo Giberga, Enrique Collazo, Rafael Montoro, Fidel Pierra and Fernández de Castro. Havana had a *Partido Popular Obrero* led by the Socialist Diego Vicente Tejera and also a *Partido Nacionalista* under Gaston Mora. Pinar del Río saw a second conservative party called *Unión Patriótica*, headed by Alfredo Posta.[7]

Groups in the campaign of 1901 were regional in character, not national, functioning in the provinces under the control of local bosses. Groupings were mixed, and positions changed. Among Democratic Unionists, Montoro and Giberga were former *autonomistas*, Collazo and Hernández, revolutionaries. Silva of Puerto Príncipe was a radical with a Nationalist label. Bravo Correoso, who could not even bring himself to vote on the Platt Amendment, later led a group pledged to support Estrada Palma and the amendment. Gener dropped his support of Estrada Palma and joined the *Masoistas*.[8]

When the Republican factions of Havana, Santa Clara and Matanzas came out in support of the Platt Amendment, Juan Gualberto Gómez bolted the party, quit the editorship of *Patria* (the party newspaper) and formed the *Republicano Independiente* party. He threw his influence behind Masó, carrying much of the Negro vote and the Democratic Unionists with him. *Nacionales* and *Republicanos* viewed this with alarm; on September 23rd they held a meeting to hear Estrada Palma's reply to basic questions about his views, carefully phrased by Ríus Rivera and Sanguily. Estrada Palma's letter satisfied most of the leaders present, and after debate they agreed to support him.[9] A party of six men began organizing the campaign to elect Estrada Palma, who was little known by the people.

Estrada Palma agreed to accept the nomination if Cubans would work to-

---

[7] Riera, *Cuba política*, 44-45; *Havana Post*, Aug. 6, 1901.
[8] Riera, *Cuba política*, 44-45.
[9] *Ibid.*, 46-47; Martínez Ortiz, *Los primeros años*, I, 354-55.

ward a reciprocity treaty, economize in government, pay off the army over a period of years, and seek a treaty with the United States for protection on the basis of the Platt Amendment, which he asserted was compatible with independence. At a meeting of delegates of all the parties in Cuba, Estrada Palma was nominated as the candidate of all Cubans.[10] Estrada Palma had been president of the Cuban republic in 1877, during the ten years war, and had been imprisoned in Spain. Earlier he had been a conspirator, subsecretary of War and a representative to the assembly at Guaimaro in 1868. In New York, after Martí's death, he became head of the Cuban Revolutionary party, raising funds and organizing support for the rebels fighting in Cuba. Estrada Palma was 78 years old, a small, courteous and tenacious man.[11]

Masó, a large property holder who had paid his debts before going into the field for *Cuba Libre,* had been president of the republic in 1898. He was an uncensorable pariot, not robust, but spirited and trustworthy. He had little administrative ability, however, and his powers had begun to wane.[12]

When Máximo Gómez, the most popular man in Cuba, endorsed Estrada Palma, the triumph of the *Estradistas* (most of whom were *Nacionalistas*) was anticipated. The *Estradistas,* who had pledged firmly to cooperate with the Platt Amendment, represented the "elements most significant of separatism and intellectualism in Cuba." [13] They were in direct contact with the people and aware of their sentiments. They organized sooner and better than the Masó Coalition, which gathered a disparate following of radicals, conservatives and Negroes that looked formidable only for a month or so in the fall.[14]

In addition to the Habaneran-Matanzan group of Democratic Unionists and Gualberto Gómez' Republican independents, the Masó coalition contained the Republican Liberals of Santa Clara under Alemán and Robau (who broke with José Miguel Gómez), the *Nacionalistas* of Puerto Príncipe, headed by Silva and Cisneros Betancourt, Castillo Duany's Santiago faction, Habana's *Partido Nacionalista* and *Partido Obrero,* and the *Partido Nacional* of Matanzas.[15]

[10] *Havana Post,* Sept. 24, 1901, Sept. 29, 1901; Martínez Ortiz, *Los primeros años,* I, 359-66.

[11] Riera, *Cuba política,* 49; Martínez Ortiz, *Los primeros años,* I, 346-50.

[12] Riera, *Cuba política,* 49-51; Martínez Ortiz, *Los primeros años,* I, 346-53; R. Pérez Landa, *Bartolomé Masó y Márquez* (La Habana, 1937), 312-16, disagrees, arguing Masó was more popular with the people.

[13] *Ibid.*

[14] *Ibid.,* cf. R. Guerra Sánchez, *et al., Historia de la nación Cubana,* VII, 131; and Robinson, *Cuba and the Intervention,* 180-82.

[15] Riera, *Cuba política,* 48, 50-51.

While the political groups were forming, the Constitutional Convention leisurely occupied the time from June to October in framing an electoral law.[16] In the debate on the electoral law, Sanguily remarked that "[a] very curious thing happened which is always happening here: we think that we agree with the Americans, but the Americans are hardly ever in accord with us." This brought laughter from his colleagues, and Sanguily added that even when they all had the same view and strove for the same thing, "it finally seems that they want something different, very different from what we want and from what we imagine." Sanguily pointed out the necessity of passing an electoral law the United States would approve, to avoid the indignity of being offended again and to activate the constitution. Juan Gualberto Gómez was glad that the world could see the Platt Amendment was not accepted spontaneously by the convention, but in an "act to which the Assembly had to submit in the belief that greater evils would be avoided." [17]

At the Constitutional Convention's last session, on September 6th, 1901, the electoral law was approved and leaves were granted to the delegates. The law was transmitted to the Military Governor, who suggested holding only two elections instead of the large number proposed. The Cuban plan would have disrupted ordinary community life by sending Cubans to the polls half a dozen times in a few months. Wood stated that the Military Government would administer the election and the transfer of government to the new officers, thereby blocking the attempt by the convention members to perpetuate themselves in office. Wood also suggested that the convention nominate five of its members to perform as a board of scrutiny.[18]

Méndez Capote recalled the delegates, who accepted the Wood modifications and recommended Méndez Capote, Villuendas, Diego Tamayo, Morúa and Zayas for the board of scrutiny. These men became Republicans and Nationalists during the campaign, and other parties had no membership on the board. This was to be a vital issue in the election. Wood accepted the nominations, thanked the convention for accepting the proposed modifications, said the electoral law would be published immediately, and adjourned the convention. He suggested that one member of the board of scrutiny take charge of the records and archives of the convention until final disposition of them could be made; since the board would take over the *Teatro Martí*, records could remain there. He designated Méndez Capote

[16] CDDC 3051, Lt. Carpenter to Scott, Aug. 10, 1901, Aug. 11, 1901; Edwards to Scott, Aug. 12, 1901.

[17] BIA Library, 205A5, VII, sessions 43-52, Aug. 14, 1901, Aug. 31, 1901.

[18] *Ibid.*, Sept. 6, 1901, session 52; Wood papers, Wood to Méndez Capote, Sept. 28, 1901; Wood to Root, Sept. 12, 1901, containing the first mention of May as the month of departure in 1902.

President of the Central Board of Scrutiny and activated it on October 3rd.[19]
On October 16th, Wood reported to Root:

The Convention died without a struggle. They did not even go through the formality of assembling but quietly packed their grips and started home. The delay we allowed them was a wise stroke as they went home thoroughly discredited and objects of interest to no one. There is an extremely strong sentiment for annexation coming up and it is openly talked where months ago it was only whispered.[20]

The electoral law was modified to stipulate but two elections: one in December for civil governors, provincial councilors, representatives and senatorial and presidential electors, and another in February, when the electors would meet to vote for the president, vice-president and senators. Wood maintained that he would need that much time beween elections to settle contested cases.[21]

As the various factions readied themselves for fall campaigning before the December vote, Wood began to bombard Washington with petitions, statistics and pleas for some economic concession to Cuban produce from the United States. He reiterated that the planters had trusted in the Military Government and had gone farther into debt; now they were harvesting a crop of sugar of nearly prewar size and could not sell it. Since one-half or more of the Cubans depended on the industry, poverty, idleness, disease and discontent – the old causes of war and American intervention – were sure to reappear. World sugar prices had declined at the turn of the century, and cane men felt the pressure of government-subsidized, cartel-managed German beet sugar. If Cuba's sugar and tobacco revenues could rise, Wood argued, she would buy from 140 to 160 million dollars in necessities and luxuries from the United States. He had done his utmost to aid producers: no export duties, no internal revenue on sugar and tobacco, low duties on imported machinery.[22]

In his desire to develop Cuban stability, Wood began to argue more forcefully for immediate reciprocity and eventual annexation.[23]

[19] Wood papers, Méndez Capote to Wood, Oct. 1, 1901; Wood to Méndez Capote, Oct. 3, 1901; CDDC 3051, Méndez Capote to Wood, Oct. 16, 1901, where Méndez Capote said their duties were done.

[20] Wood papers, Wood to Root, Oct. 16, 1901.

[21] Wood papers, Wood to Root, Nov. 4, 1901; DIA 1947-24, Wood to Edwards, Oct. 23, 1901. On the 23rd of October Wood mailed to Colonel Edwards of the Division of Insular Affairs the translations of the Cuban Constitution, the Platt appendix, the electoral law and the order publishing the electoral law with modifications. For the Cienfuegos affair, an example of mismanagement in municipal government and restraint by the Military Government, see CDDC 2698.

[22] Wood papers, Wood to Root, Oct. 17, 1901.

[23] Wood papers, Wood to Roosevelt, Oct. 28, 1901.

With the control which we have over Cuba, a control which will soon undoubtedly become possession, combined with the other sugar producing lands which we now own, we shall soon practically control the sugar trade of the world, or at least a very large portion of it. Cuba has never been more than partially developed and she has only one-eighth or one-tenth of the population which she can easily support. Her trade now, even under these conditions of depression, is eighty million dollars per year. With better markets and lower tariff duties it would be over one hundred millions now. Cuba is an island which within the next fifty years will have a population of probably eight or ten millions of people and a trade running into the hundreds of millions. . . . I believe Cuba to be a most desirable acquisition for the United States. She is easily worth any two of the Southern States, probably any three, with the exclusion of Texas, and of all the territories involved in the Spanish war the Island of Cuba is infinitely the most valuable. Were she remote from our shores her condition would perhaps be of little importance to us, but she is so near to us that, whether we like it or not, we have got to look after her. . . . We can, of course, strangle the Island commercially, but just why we should compel our own people to pay a high price for one of the necessities of life in order to protect a purely artificial industry, while we have at our doors the best sugar land on earth, whose products can be put into our markets at such a rate as to gradually reduce the present cost of sugar to the consumer and give us a trade which will be in the hundreds of millions is not quite apparent; especially, when it is probable that as soon as our home sugar producers realize our policy is to give Cuba a chance they will undoubtedly transfer their industries to Cuba and the Island will, under the impetus of new capital and energy, not only be developed, but gradually become Americanized, and we shall have in time one of the richest and most desirable possessions in the world. . . .

Wood's desire for reciprocity led him to distort the Platt Amendment.

There is, of course, little or no independence left Cuba under the Platt Amendment. The more sensible Cubans realize this and feel that the only consistent thing to do now is to seek annexation. This, however, will take some time. . . .

Regardless of what the General's desire for Cuba to be able to sell sugar led him to say, Washington ignored his pleas during the months control was being transferred in Cuba.

In the political campaign, Bartolomé Masó was still evasive, saying he would serve wherever called by his people.[24] He had been drafted as a vice presidential nominee on the Estrada Palma ticket by the Republicans and Nationalists but was also being courted by Juan Gualberto Gómez and the Democratic Unionists to head an anti-Platt Amendment coalition. He had earlier written to José Lacret Morlot, severely criticizing the amendment and the missive became public knowledge. On the 31st of October Masó issued a manifesto opposing the amendment. Perhaps his radical followers thought this would bring a tide of supporters to the coalition banner. By November 1,

[24] *Havana Post*, Oct. 15, 1901; *La Discusión*, Oct. 28, 1901, Oct. 29, 1901.

with the election set for December 31st, Masó had come out for total Cuban independence, convinced that the people wanted him for president.[25]

Observers predicted that Masó would garner a large Negro following, a fireater element, many of the veterans' organizations (it was thought he would pledge to repay them sooner than would Estrada Palma), about half of the island's *republicano* factions and all the Democratic Unionists. But in mid-November, Masó, bewildering observers on both sides, repudiated anti-American speeches made in his behalf, called the Americans Cuba's friends and pledged his support to the constitution and the Platt Amendment.[26] This statement shattered the coalition. Masó had not been anti-American in policy or action prior to the campaign, and this feeling, coupled with the realization that he was losing the election, led him to retire.

As the campaign continued, Salvador Cisneros Betancourt agreed to run for vice-president on the Masó coalition ticket. Both Manuel Sanguily and Diego Tamayo were often mentioned for Estrada Palma's running mate. But Sanguily had made too many enemies, and his temperament was not suited for the office. Although he was an active revolutionary, Tamayo still had opponents in several quarters because he had once been an autonomist, and many criticized his close cooperation with General Wood. Finally, Luis Estévez Romero was chosen.[27]

During November the *Masoistas* realized they were losing the election campaign. At the end of the month, during Wood's absence in Washington, the Democratic Unionists began a campaign to delay the election. On the 26th, they sent Secretary Root a telegram:

National Convention of Havana which has proclaimed General Masó candidate for President of future Republic of Cuba respectfully asks you to recommend the representatives of the intervening government the strictest impartiality in electoral contest now on.[28]

Root coldly rebuked the *Masoistas*:

The representatives of the intervening government in Cuba are already aware that their duty requires them not merely to be strictly impartial in the electoral contest in Cuba, but to refrain from interfering in any manner whatever with the free expression of the wishes of the Cuban people at the polls. They have not violated this rule in the past and will not in the future. They will have nothing

[25] *Havana Post,* Nov. 1, 1901; Portell Vilá, *Historia de Cuba,* IV, 267, 273; Martínez Ortiz, *Los primeros años,* I, 351-54; Pérez Landa, *Masó,* 313, 391-6.

[26] *Havana Post,* Nov. 2, 1901, Nov. 20, 1901.

[27] *Havana Post,* Nov. 2, 1901; Dec. 12, 1901; *La Discusión,* Dec. 2, 1901; The *Post* of Nov. 27 carried the news that D. Tamayo had sworn Estrada Palma to Cuban citizenship again by proxy.

[28] DIA 1327-32, E. Bonachea to Root, cable of Nov. 26, 1901.

to do with the electoral contest except to enforce the electoral law prescribed by the Constitutional Convention and promulgated by the Military Governor on the 14th of October last.[29]

This did not cool the heat of the Democratic Unionists. Eusebio Hernández cabled Root that interference was inevitable. Since Estrada Palma was said to have the support of the United States Government, the people, alarmed at the attempt to force a president upon them, asked for a fair election. A delegation was leaving for Washington to tell Root the facts.[30]

On December 14th, Fidel Pierra, a Cuban with strong conservative merchant ties, presented a memorandum to Root. In it he complained that the Central Board of Scrutiny members were all candidates for congress, and none represented Masó. The board had changed the election law by new orders, failed to fulfill portions of the law and sanctioned illegal acts. For example, no action was taken when the Havana *ayuntamiento* tardily published an incorrect list of the largest taxpayers, giving Masó voters little choice and forcing a hurried selection of senatorial electors. The memorandum recommended deferring the election to January 31, 1902, annulling the illegal acts and reorganizing the central and provincial boards of scrutiny.[31]

On the 16th, after considering the application for postponement, Root pointed out that the effect of granting it would be to prolong American occupation and postpone Cuban independence. He did not believe this should be done for any candidate without substantial reasons, which Pierra did not provide. The board had been established before any candidate was named, composed of the president and four members of the Constitutional Convention, picked by that body. Just because the coalition picked a man who had no adherent on the board was no ground for changing it or the election machinery.[32]

When General Wood learned of the situation upon returning to Havana, he advised Root that the Masó coalition had petitioned because they were facing defeat at the polls. The General, amused at Root's hitting Pierra "between wind and water," assured the Secretary that the allegations were groundless. All boards of scrutiny were legally elected, but due to the absence of *Masoistas* on them, he directed that board decisions be referred to the Masó officers for possible protest before publication. Furthermore, Wood had agreed to substitute two presidential electors, as requested by the

[29] DIA 1327-32, Root to Bonachea, Nov. 29, 1901.
[30] DIA 1327-33, Hernández to Root, Dec. 3, 1901, cable; DIA 1327-36, petition Hernández to Wood; *Havana Post,* Dec. 7, 1901.
[31] DIA 1327-35, Pierra to Root, Dec. 14, 1901.
[32] DIA 1327-35, Root to Pierra, Dec. 16, 1901.

Masoistas. Wood stated that the protested tax list had been prepared by Mayor Miguel Gener and the *Masoista* dominated Havana city council. The list was quickly modified by the *ayuntamiento* to include newly qualified voters and drop those no longer eligible, and registration was extended by five days. Pierra had no case and had misrepresented the facts.[33]

When neither Root nor Roosevelt gave them any satisfaction, the Masó party withdrew from the election. Pierra stated that his party held the majority of Cuban voters, but convinced their votes would be cast to no purpose, they did not wish to sanction by their participation an irregular and fraudulent election.[34] Of course, had they actually held a majority of the votes, the *Masoistas* could have won the election, Wood and scrutiny board notwithstanding. The fact was that the majority sided with Estrada Palma.[35] Many Cubans may also have felt it impossible to defeat a man tacitly favored by the Military Government. Actually, any election irregularity would have been caught by Congress.[36]

The election campaign proceeded relatively quietly, the major incident being the stoning of Máximo Gómez in Puerto Príncipe when he stumped the area for Estrada Palma. Salvador Cisneros Betancourt, who had great influence in that province, branded Estrada Palma and Gómez traitors who had advocated quitting during the war; he cried that they should be hung if they ever came to Puerto Príncipe. This was typical campaign bravado and contrary to the truth; Gómez had fought almost single-handed for Cuba, while Cisneros had wanted to join the United States. Nevertheless, a mob prevented Gómez from speaking in Puerto Príncipe, a sign full of foreboding for the future of Cuban politics.[37]

---

[33] DIA 1327-37, Edwards to Wood, n.d. cable; *Havana Post,* Dec. 17, 1901, Dec. 18, 1901, Dec. 19, 1901. Wood papers, Wood to Root, Dec. 18, Dec. 30, 1901, Jan. 8, 1902.

[34] DIA 1327-33, Pierra to Root, Dec. 23, 1901; DIA 1327-46, Pierra to Roosevelt, Dec. 21, 1901; DIA 1327-51, Pierra to Roosevelt, Dec. 27, 1901; *Havana Post,* Dec. 22, 24 and 25, 1901; *La Discusión,* Dec. 23, 1901. Both papers criticized the retirement of the *Masoistas* and disparaged Cuba's political future.

[35] Riera, *Cuba política,* 49; Martínez Ortiz, *Los primeros años,* 346; Robinson, *Cuba and the Intervention,* 180-3.

[36] DIA 1327-54, Wood to Edwards, Jan. 7, 1902; DIA 1327-54, Wood to O. H. Platt, Jan. 7, 1902; Wood papers, Wood to Root, Dec. 30, 1901, Wood to Root, Jan. 8, 1902; CDDC 57, E. Núñez to Wood, Jan. 22, 1902, Report on the Investigation of the *Ayuntamiento* of Havana; *Havana Post,* Jan. 9, 1902, Feb. 9, 1902; Martínez Ortiz, *Los primeros años,* I, 380-81; Portell Vilá, *Historia de Cuba,* IV, 274-76.

[37] *New York Times,* Dec. 27, 1901; *Havana Post,* Dec. 27, 1901, Dec. 28, 1901. Other examples of Cuban political behavior and respect for law were when a police officer tried to arrest a mulatto for an assault he observed himself, the crowd tried to prevent it and the suspect stabbed the policeman, who eventually took his man in. In Havana

During the election, the board of scrutiny dealt with many questions of procedure and appeal. While the board could not annul an election, it could exclude a voter if he were proven disqualified. In such towns as Palmira, Trinidad, Mariel and Pinar del Río, many complained that the "ins" controlled local elections. In Cruces, Cienfuegos, Isabela de Sagua, Havana, Abreus and Matanzas, citizens claimed that electoral boards exceeded their authority, held illegal meetings and failed to post voter lists. All cases were investigated by the board of scrutiny.[38]

The election of electors on December 31st proceeded without mishap, and on the 24th of February, the electors met to vote for president. Tomás Estrada Palma, unopposed, was elected, with Luis Estévez Romero as his vice-president. Ten senators, thirty-one representatives and the governors of Pinar del Río, Santa Clara and Matanzas were Republicans. Nationalist groupings elected eleven senators, twenty-eight representatives and the governors of Havana, Puerto Príncipe and Santiago de Cuba. The *Masoistas* captured the main offices in Puerto Príncipe. With the exception of that province, most of the men elected were for Estrada Palma. For his cabinet, Estrada Palma picked two Nationalists (Manuel Díaz, Public Works, and Diego Tamayo, Government), two Republicans (Secretary of State, Carlos de Zaldo and José García Montes, Treasurer) and two independents (Eduardo Yero Buduen and Emilio Terry, Education and Agriculture, respectively).[39]

Secretary Root sent Estrada Palma congratulations and Estrada Palma expressed his gratitude in reply, but announced in the Cuban press that he made no promises and would be dominated by no one: *"Nadie me dominará."* [40]

As early as January, Wood began to prepare for the transfer of control. He substituted bonded Cubans for American disbursing officers and established an island board of health. When he advised Root of his plans for convening congress, the Secretary called him to Washington for consultation

the *Nacionalistas* were found trying to siphon off five percent of the police force salaries for the political campaign.

[38] CDDC 4779, J. G. Gómez to Wood, Dec. 6, 1901; CDDC 4209, abstract of Records of Board of Scrutiny.

[39] DIA 1327-53, cable, Wood to Root, Jan. 1, 1902; DIA 1327-58, Wood to Corbin, Feb. 25, 1902; C.O. 45 of Feb. 19, 1902, and C.O. 67 of March 9, 1902 in DIA file 1327; Riera, *Cuba política,* 55-56; Martínez Ortiz, *Los primeros años,* I, 370-79. See Appendix D.

[40] DIA 1327-58, Root to Estrada Palma, Feb. 27, 1902; DIA 1327-59, Estrada Palma to Root, March 1, 1902; *Havana Post,* Feb. 25, 1902, March 26, 1902, April 22, 1902. In March and April of 1902, the *Post,* not an organ of the Military Government, printed more than 13 editorials pleading for balance and temperance in the coming government and praising the Military Government. Estrada Palma, "The Future of Cuba," *Independent,* LIV (April 3, 1902), 789-791.

and instructions for turning the government over to the Cubans by May 20th.[41] Before that time Wood was to appoint a caretaker for the records of the Military Government, run inventory and audit, convene congress to count the electoral vote for president and vice-president and publish the constitution with its appendix. The personnel and laws of the Military Government were to continue until replaced by the new Cuban officials. However, in order to avoid both sweeping governmental changes and giving Estrada Palma men he did not want, Root approved Wood's policy of substituting men of Estrada Palma's choice before the government changed hands. The records of the Military Government were to be open to the Cuban government until they could be moved to Washington without detriment to the Cuban administration. Wood was to remind the new government of its obligations under the Platt Amendment and leave the coastal defenses intact until Cubans could be trained for the job. Root arranged with the United States Postmaster General for postal procedures to remain in operation until the two nations signed a postal convention. President Roosevelt asked Congress for funds to establish a consulate in Cuba.[42]

On May 5th, Wood welcomed the Congress of Cuba:

Gentlemen:

I have the honor, in the name of the President of the United States of America, and as Military Governor of the Island of Cuba, to welcome you and most earnestly wish you every success in the great work upon which you are soon to enter.

You have been convened solely for the purpose expressed in paragraph 11 of Order No. 101, dated Havana, April 14, 1902, and no legislative power will be vested in the Congress until after the formal transfer of the government to the government elect, which transfer will take place at noon, May 20, 1902.

You are requested to notify me officially, at the earliest possible date, who have been elected President and Vice-President of Cuba, and Senators and Representatives, in order that I may so transmit this information to the President of the United States.

It is important that this action be taken without delay in order that the President may be officially informed as to the personnel of the government elect.

Upon the completion of this duty the Congress will adjourn to meet at noon, May 20, 1902.[43]

Wood fulfilled Leopoldo Cancio's long held wish by transferring the offices of Auditor, Treasurer, Department of Immigration and Quarantine to the Department of Finance as separate branches therein. The Light House Board

[41] Wood papers, Wood to Root, Jan. 27, 1902, Feb. 21, 1902, March 7, 1902, April 29, 1902; Root papers, Root to Wood, March 24, 1902.
[42] Root papers, Root to Postmaster General, April 1, 1902, H. C. Payne (Postmaster General), to Root, April 16, 1902; Fitzgibbon, *Cuba and the United States,* 89.
[43] Wood papers, Wood to Senators and Representatives Elect of the Cuban Congress, May 5, 1902; DIA 2229-23, C.O. 101 of April 14, 1902.

was transferred to the Department of Public Works from Headquarters Division. Wood also issued regulations regarding future immigration. While the Cuban Constitution generally encouraged immigration, Section VII, Civil Order 155 prohibited the immigration into Cuba of any Chinese persons except diplomatic officers of the Government of China. Chinese persons who had been living in Cuba before April 14, were allowed to remain. The records of the Military Government revealed no rules against Negro immigration.[44] Root directed Wood to promulgate the names of the senators and representatives as soon as their credentials were approved and to publish the constitution on the morning of May 20th in the *Gaceta*. Root also told Wood what he was to say at noon on May 20th.[45]

On the 22nd of April, Estrada Palma landed at Gibara, travelled to his old home at Bayamo and gradually to Havana, where he was welcomed on the 11th of May.

Wood requested and received Estrada Palma's assurance that the 884 artillery troops to be left on the island would receive friendly protection from the new Cuban government and that rights of extraterritoriality given among friendly powers to visiting troops under international law would be provided.[46] On the 15th, Méndez Capote informed Wood that the canvasses of Cuba's six provinces verified Estrada Palma as president and Estévez Romero as vice-president. Thereupon Wood published Civil Order 158 on May 16th, listing the members of congress, the president and vice-president, and declaring that on 20 May the United States Military Government would cease, and control would pass to the Cubans.[47] Each of these steps was planned by Root.

Wood attempted to accommodate Estrada Palma but shivered with apprehension when the president-elect requested deferral of the municipal elections by an act of congress, on the grounds that a change so soon after the inauguration would be undesirable. Wood explained that only the Cuban people could legally make the decision, yet he allowed Estrada Palma to do it. Estrada Palma also wanted Wood to withdraw Civil Order 99, guaranteeing the immunity of judges. When Wood replied that the purpose of the order was embodied in article 87 of the Cuban Constitution, Estrada Palma

[44] DIA 195-13, C.O. 133 of May 7, 1902; C.O. 155 of May 15, 1902; letter to the author from Jane F. Smith, Chief, Social & Economic Branch, National Archives, September 30, 1966.

[45] Root papers, Rood to Wood, May 3, 1902; C.O. 148 of May 13, 1902.

[46] DIA 1327-64, C.O. 158 of May 16, 1902; *Havana Post*, April 22, 1902; Wood papers, Wood to Roosevelt, May 10, 1902. Wood to Estrada Palma, May 14, 1902; Estrada Palma to Wood, May 16, 1902.

[47] Wood papers, Méndez Capote to Wood, May 15, 1902.

stated that he intended to suspend that particular article until he had made certain changes. Estrada Palma, unsure of his backing, wanted a basis of support to ensure his government, but his irregularities jolted Wood's waning confidence in the course of the new regime.[48] Nevertheless, Wood carried out his orders to transfer the government.

Wood's policy governing expenditures was to finish what projects he could, leave the money provided for those he could not, curtail wherever possible and turn over the treasury with money in it. The amount of $ 689,191.02, certified by Estrada Palma's agent, was turned over in cash.[49] Over the four-year period, the total revenue was $ 57,197,140.80 and the expenditure $ 55,405,031.28, an excess of receipts over disbursement of $ 1,792,109.52. Wood inherited $ 1,863,958.46 from Brooke and bequeathed to Estrada Palma $ 1,613,828.13, spending roughly $ 250,000 more than he received during his governorship.[50]

Estrada Palma retrenched, believing money in the treasury signified a stable government. In its first year the Estrada Palma administration spent more on Customs, Postal Service and Rural Guard than did Wood in his last year, but less on ports, finance, jails, justice, municipalities, quarantine service, state and government. The chief Cuban savings were in public works, charities, agriculture and elections. Comparing equivalent time periods, Estrada Palma saved $ 107,627.34 in expenditure, at the loss of projects and services greatly needed. Wood could have kept 10 million dollars in the treasury but chose instead to provide the necessary services, keep money in circulation and rebuild the island. Estrada Palma's diligent austerity curtailed the programs Wood had developed.[51]

When at last the 20th came, Wood was ready to turn the government over to the Cubans. On the 18th he had been honored by gifts, banquets and overtures of respect. On the 19th Cubans commemorated Martí and other fallen patriots in solemn rites with flags at half staff. But at midnight, Havana rocked with the noise of horns, rockets, firecrackers, bands and cheering crowds. Cuba's natal day dawned and clear, with the blue of the water and the bright paint of the houses reflecting the sun in dazzling shafts of light and

[48] Wood, *Civil Report,* 1902, I, 4, 9, 195; Wood papers, Wood to Root, Dec. 4, 1906.
[49] CDDC 1084, McCoy to Wood, May 24, 1902.
[50] Wood papers, Wood to Root, Dec. 10, 1901, Root to Wood, Dec. 14, 1901, Wood to Auditor of Cuba, June 10, 1902, Wood to Root, Nov. 18, 1902; Wood, *Civil Report,* 1902, I, 196; U.S., Congress, House, *Report of the Secretary of War,* IV, no. 2, 57th Cong., 2nd Sess., 1902-1903, appendix B; Fitzgibbon, *Cuba and the United States,* 64-65.
[51] Wood papers, Wood to Hanna, Jan. 7, 1904; Hanna's reply, n.d., n.p., with comparison of costs of operation between Estrada Palma's first year and Wood's for 1901. Matthew Hanna remained in Havana as the U.S. military attache.

color. The city was bedecked with arches and bunting. Shortly before mid-day, from two or three hundred thousand people gathered around the Palace in the Plaza de Armas, on the Malecon and the flat rooftops. Promptly at noon, General Wood and his staff stepped into the audience hall of the Governor's Palace, which was filled with Cuban and American dignitaries, representatives of foreign states, members of the press and guests. Dressed in the formal blue uniform of the United States Army, Wood read the message with his cultured, New England baritone voice, accompanied by the slow booming of a forty-five gun salute from Cabanas:

Under the direction of the President of the United States, I now transfer to you as the duly elected representatives of the people of Cuba the government and control of the island; to be held and exercised by you, under the provisions of the constitution of the Republic of Cuba heretofore adopted by the constitutional convention and this day promulgated; and I hereby declare the occupation of Cuba by the United States and the military government of the island to be ended.[52]

Estrada Palma, in formal dress, standing next to Wood, received the con-tratulations of President Roosevelt from the General and then read his reply:

As President of the Republic of Cuba, I hereby receive the Government of the Island of Cuba which you transfer to me in compliance with orders communi-cated to you by the President of the United States and take note that by this act the military occupation of Cuba ceases.

Upon accepting this transfer I declare that the Government of the Republic assumes, as provided for in the Constitution, each and every one of the obli-gations concerning Cuba imposed upon the United States by virtue of the treaty entered into on the 10th of December, 1898, between the United States and Her Majesty the Queen Regent of Spain.

The remainder of Estrada Palma's speech covered the agreements on sani-tation, the Isle of Pines under Cuban jurisdiction pending a treaty, and certifi-cation of the transfer of funds.[53]

On the roof of the palace, Lieutenants McCoy and Carpenter pulled down the Stars and Stripes as the 7th Cavalry band played "The Star Spangled Banner," and the regiment presented arms in the Plaza de Armas. Wood and Máximo Gómez bent on the Cuban colors and raised them to full staff, ac-companied by the strains of "La Bayamesa," the salute of troops and the booming of ships' cannon. When the Cubans saw their emblem rise over the once-hated Morro across the bay, ten minutes of cheering filled the air. Wood

[52] Wood, *Civil Report,* 1902, I, 212; Hagedorn, *Wood,* I, 390; Martínez Ortiz, *Los primeros años,* I, 424-25; Grover Flint, *Marching with Gómez,* 197n., tells of a Cuban legend that freedom would come in May when the white flower *Libertad* bloomed.

[53] Wood papers, Estrada Palma letter of May 20, 1902. (Spanish with English trans.)

left the palace at 12:25 for the wharf where he boarded a launch for the
U.S.S. *Brooklyn*. At 3:45 she sailed out of Havana harbor. It was a great
day for Cuba.[54]

When Wood submitted his report for 1902, he wrote in recapitulation:

The work called for and accomplished was the building up of a REPUBLIC, by
Anglo-Saxons, in a Latin country where approximately 70 per cent of the people
were illiterate; where they had lived always as a military colony; where general
elections, as we understand them, were unknown; in fact it was a work which
called for practically a rewriting of the administrative law of the land, including
the law of charities and hospitals, public works, sanitary law, school law, railway law, etc.; meeting and controlling the worst possible sanitary conditions;
putting the people to school; writing an electoral law and training the people
in the use of it; establishing an entirely new system of accounting and auditing;
the election and assembling of representatives of the people to draw up and
adopt a Constitution for the proposed new Republic; in short, the establishment,
in a little over three years, in a Latin Military colony, in one of the most unhealthy countries in the world, of a Republic modeled closely upon lines of our
great Republic, and the transfer to the Cuban people of the Republic so established, free from debt, healthy, orderly, well equipped, and with a good balance in
the treasury. All of this work was accomplished without serious friction. The
Island of Cuba was transferred to its people as promised, and was started on its
career in excellent condition and under favorable circumstances.[55]

Secretary Root, in his annual report for 1902, said the following in regard to
Cuba:

I venture to express the hope that this strong and well-deserved friendship of
Cuba may be permanent and never be alienated by our treatment of the smaller
and weaker power, and that the people of the United States may never lose their
deep interest in the welfare of the new Republic which they have called into
being with so much labor and sacrifice. I know of no chapter in American history
more satisfactory than that which will record the conduct of the military government of Cuba.[56]

Root kept track of what was done in Cuba and studied the subject as

carefully as any businessman ever studied his own business, or any lawyer ever
studied a case which he was to try.... I knew what was going on; and I feel
under a debt of the greatest gratitude to General Wood for what I think is one
of the most conscpicuous and meritorious pieces of work ever done by an
American.[57]

[54] Root papers, Wood to Root, May 20, 1902; Wood to Corbin, June 10, 1902;
Hagedorn, *Wood*, I, 389-92; U.S., Congress, Senate, "Inaugural of the President of
Cuba ..." doc. 363, 57th Cong., 1st Sess.
[55] Wood, *Civil Report*, 1902, I, 270 ff.
[56] U.S., Congress, House, *Reports of the War Department*, IV, no. 2, 57th Cong.,
1st Sess., 1902-1903, 8-9.
[57] Jessup, *Root*, I, 287.

Wood had appointed Frank Steinhart agent in charge of the records of the late Military Government of Cuba and repeatedly urged him to send them to Washington. He had nothing to hide but knew well enough that alterations by his enemies could prove harmful. He had arrived in Washington on the 28th, concluded the affairs of the Military Government, dictated his reports, put Steinhart and Colonel Scott in charge of publishing them, and sailed to Europe for the grand tour with his aides and family.[58]

During Wood's travels through Europe and after he reported for duty in the Philippines, he received doleful letters from Alejandro González and Steinhart, saying that Estrada Palma had aged, the government was doing nothing, Secretary of State Zaldo controlled affairs, the auditor's office was slowly being suffocated, and men of character like Varela, Diego Tamayo and Ernesto Fonts y Sterling were being forced out of public life. Wood inquired periodically of Cancio, Varona, Bacardí and others; their replies were discouraging. It is not within the purview of this study to cover the subsequent Cuban-American relations and the second intervention in 1906, but Root summarized the issue:

I felt very badly about the breakdown of the Government that we set up four and a half years ago with so much eclat; but it did break down and the only thing to do was to go in and set them up again and give them another chance. The great trouble was that they never really tried to put their own Constitution in force. The Congress never would pass the bills required by the Constitution to give anybody out of power a chance to get in by a fair election. Of course, a reasonably fair sort of an election is the necessary safety-valve. If that is closed, the boiler is bound to burst some time.

I hope you are well and that before very long we may see you and Mrs. Wood back again in the land where slanders and libels take the place of bolos.[59]

Wood answered that he too regretted the upset in Cuba but had feared it for

---

[58] Wood papers, Wood to Steinhart, June 23, 1902; Wood to Root, Oct. 17, 1902; J. D. Terrill to Wood, July 11, 1902; DIA file 2990; General Order #38, March 25, 1903, signed by the Secretary of War. Although Steinhart became U.S. Consul and later an influential millionaire in Cuba, the high point of life was working with Wood to build a republic.

[59] Wood papers, Root to Wood, Oct. 31, 1906; Steinhart to Wood, June 25, 1902, June 30, 1902; González to Wood, May 20, 1902, Aug. 24, 1903, Sept. 10, 1903, March 25, 1904, Aug. 31, 1904, Sept. 20, 1905; Wood, Diary, Feb. 8, 1909; Hanna to Wood, Aug. 9, 1903; McCoy to Wood, Oct. 18, 1906; Bacardí to Wood, March 3, 1907; Wood to Cancio, July 25, 1907; Cancio to Wood, Oct. 18, 1907; Wood to Varela, Feb. 3, 1904; J. de Armas to Wood, Sept. 26, 1905; Wood to Quesada and Varona, both of Jan. 29, 1907; Wood to González, Feb. 7, 1907; DIA 1561-34, A. A. Adee to Root, Aug. 22, 1902; See also Wood papers, Steinhart to J. G. Rockwood, Dec. 10, 1906, where he stressed need for peaceful change of office.

a long time.[60] He probably thought that events had justified his belief that the United States should have remained longer in Cuba.

Whatever the legacy in Cuba, the Spanish-American War brought capable leaders to the front ranks of the United States.[61] Congratulating Wood, Roosevelt epitomized the beliefs of that era:

For the last two years you have been one of the very few men who have had to do the great tasks of the world and who have done them well. . . . It has been a hard task, but I do not pity you a bit, for it seems to me that in this life the best possible thing is to have a great task well worth doing, and to do it well. You have written your name indelibly on the record which tells how this country met one of the crises of its history.[62]

[60] Wood papers, Wood to Root, Dec. 4, 1906.

[61] Wood papers, W. H. Moody to Wood, June 25, 1902, copy of speech he made at Detroit; Martínez Ortiz, *Los primeros años,* I, 428, 434, 436, a tribute to Wood, whom he called "essentially a reformer . . . a revolutionist in the better sense of the word, seeking in every possible way to elevate the moral level of Cuban society and prepare it for the real enjoyment and use of democratic institutions. . . . An indiscreet or hot-headed governor would have either humiliated the Cuban patriots or placed them in a position in which they could maintain their self-respect only by armed opposition. . . . Neither favor nor gift counted with him. . . . Friends and adversaries . . . joined . . . in this assertion; 'he was an honorable man.' "

[62] Wood papers, Roosevelt to Wood, March 27, 1901.

EPILOGUE: THE FIGHT OVER RECIPROCITY

The task of creating a prosperous Cuba had not been completed when the Military Government left the island. For an additional year and a half, President Roosevelt and Secretary Root fought to obtain a reciprocity agreement for Cuba. Their purpose was to ensure a market for Cuban sugar which would assist prosperity and stability; without reciprocity, the whole effort of the Military Government to rebuild Cuba would have been undermined. The fight over reciprocity arose not with Cubans, but with Democrats, high tariff men and beet sugar interests in the United States.[1]

After the death of McKinley in the fall of 1901, President Roosevelt continued the previous administration's policy of seeking reciprocal trade agreements with other nations. At the same time he proceeded to make reciprocity with Cuba into a moral issue. In his first annual message, Roosevelt said:

Our attitude in Cuba is a sufficient guaranty of our own good faith. We have not the slightest desire to secure any territory at the expense of any of our neighbors. We wish to work with them hand in hand, so that all of us may be uplifted together, and we rejoice over the good fortune of any of them, we gladly hail their material prosperity and political stability, and are concerned and alarmed if any of them fall into industrial or political chaos. We do not wish to see any Old World military power grow upon this continent, or to be compelled to become a military power ourselves.[2]

The President and others saw reciprocity as a debt the United States owed Cuba because of the loss of the Spanish market and the Platt restrictions on

[1] Accounts of the Cuban reciprocity issue are to be found in Fitzgibbon, *Cuba and the United States,* Ch. 8; Hagedorn, *Wood,* I, Ch. 17; J. L. Laughlin, and H. P. Willis, *Reciprocity* (New York, 1903); Healy, *U.S. in Cuba,* Ch. 16; U.S. Tariff Commission, *Effects of the Cuban Reciprocity Treaty* (Washington: GPO, 1929); Weigle, "The Sugar Interests & American Diplomacy, 1893-1903," unpublished Ph. D. thesis, Yale University, 1939, Chs. 8-10.

[2] U.S., Congress, House, *Annual Message of the President,* doc. 1, Dec. 3, 1901, 57th Cong., 1st session.

treaties. Completion of the work of the Military Government was a necessary act of humanity to avoid ruining the economy and inviting anarchy again. Roosevelt stressed America's obligation to fulfill its duty toward Cuba in the same unparalleled manner that it had prepared her for self-government and expelled Spain.[3]

Elihu Root, who had been preparing the ground for some reciprocity overture to the legislature since 1899, argued that this was not actually a tariff question, but one of "the effect of applying protectionist principles to this intermediate state which is entitled to a certain degree of protection from us. . . ." In his annual report for 1901, he alluded to the moral obligation but also pointed out Cuba's importance to American security.

Aside from the moral obligation to which we committed ourselves when we drove Spain out of Cuba, and aside from the ordinary considerations of commercial advantage involved in a reciprocity treaty, there are the weightiest reasons of American public policy pointing in the same direction; for the peace of Cuba is necessary to the peace of the United States; the health of Cuba is necessary to the health of the United States; the independence of Cuba is necessary to the safety of the United States. The same considerations which led to the war with Spain now require that a commercial arrangement be made under which Cuba can live. The condition of the sugar and tobacco industries in Cuba is already such that the earliest possible action by Congress upon this subject is desirable.[4]

By affording a market no one else could provide, the United States could supply the Cuban producer and society with enough income to provide for economic development.

Reciprocity might be defined as:

A term for an arrangement between two countries having a protective tariff against other countries, to admit each into the other's territories certain specified taxable articles of commerce duty-free, or at exceptionally light duties.[5]

Such arrangements were often called fair trade, as opposed to free trade and protection. The Dingley tariff of 1897 authorized the President to stipulate a twenty percent reciprocity with another country on certain items, but the power of interest groups who wanted to prevent such breaches in the tariff wall (which put rates at an average level of 57 percent *ad valorem*) was difficult to overcome. During his tenure as Military Governor, Wood repeated previous requests for tariff concessions for Cuba, but the United States delayed in making a reciprocity treaty because such agreements usually were negotiated between two independent states.

[3] DIA C705-230, Message from the President of the United States in regard to Reciprocity with Cuba, 57th Cong., 1st sess., S. doc. 405, June 13, 1902.
[4] *Report of the Secretary of War*, 1901-1902, 53.
[5] Laughlin and Willis, *Reciprocity*, 2.

Congress could have arranged reciprocity with Cuba prior to the establishment of an independent government in the island, but chose not to do so.
Frank D. Pavey, a lawyer with experience in Cuban affairs, and John Bassett
Moore, of Columbia University and the Department of State, argued that
Congress could pass a special tariff act because of Cuba's proximity and
need. No judicial or executive powers would be infringed upon; a reciprocity
agreement was precluded only by the policies of Congress itself. Both men
contended that the special nature of the foreign-nation-in-trust idea, cited in
the *Neely* v. *Henkel* decision by the Supreme Court, allowed mutual reduction with Cuba and was not prohibited by the most-favored-nation clause
of the Dingley tariff. Moore pointed out that reciprocity was not guaranteed
to all nations, was specific with some and not granted to others. Pavey believed that reciprocity could be framed in accordance with the Treaty of
Paris clause regarding protection of life and property.[6]

Obviously it was domestic politics, not law, that prevented a reciprocity
agreement with Cuba prior to the withdrawal of the Military Government.
Spotlighting congressional responsibility at this juncture were the contentions
of Secretary Root and Senator Platt. They strongly maintained that a trade
agreement could only be agreed upon between two sovereign nations, in accordance with the Dingley tariff law. It would look ridiculous for the State
Department to sign a treaty with the War Department, for no other body in
Cuba had authority. The Cuban Constitutional Convention of 1901 might
have been a likely body to deal with, but Root believed that he had so many
difficulties with the Cuban Convention and the American Congress regarding
political relations between the two countries, that he would not attempt to
consider economic relations at the same time. If relief were to be forth-
coming, Congress would have to provide it.

Something had to be done; the price of sugar was declining due to the
overproduction of bounty-fed European beet sugars. By 1900, when Cuban
sugar production began to return to prewar levels, sugar was bringing in less
than the two cents per pound it cost to produce and ready it for shipment.
General Wood knew that the European nations could not continue their
bounty system indefinitely and hoped to carry Cuba until prices rose.
Throughout 1901 he pressed Root for aid, and in early 1902 he stated:

The economic situation here has become serious. I am besieged from morning
to night with delegations from all over the island; and I fear that if we do not

[6] DIA C705-96, F. D. Pavey, "The Power and Authority of Congress to Pass a
Special Tariff Act for Cuba." Pavey was counsel for the Chamber of Commerce of the
Island of Cuba. DIA C705-98, J. B. Moore, "Opinion upon the Question Whether
Congress can pass a Special Tariff Act for Cuba."

get a reasonable reduction on sugar, we shall find it embarrassing to get out of here.[7]

Root had already decided that preparations to negotiate a reciprocity treaty could proceed without waiting for the establishment of a permanent Cuban government. To engage support for reciprocity, Root appointed F. B. Thurber, President of the American Export Association, as "Temporary Special Agent of the Military Government of Cuba," to collect data bearing upon Cuban-American commerce.[8] In Cuba, General Wood was paralleling Root's activities. He mounted a campaign, sending scores of petitions and telegrams to Root. In January of 1902, the General nominated a commission to go to Washington. It was headed by L. V. Placé and Luis de Abad, who spoke before the House Appropriations Committee and the Senate Committee on Cuban Relations.[9]

These Cuban commissioners created mixed feelings in Washington. Root thought the Cuban planters jeopardized chances for success by appearing ready to intrigue and accept temporary measures.[10] Senators and Congressmen asked the Cuban delegation and the War Department how much of the Cuban sugar crop had been bought in advance by the sugar trust of H. O. Havemeyer. Wood replied that Cubans were not selling because prices were too low. As of April 1902 only one-seventh of the Cuban crop had been exported.[11] Out of 850,181 tons of sugar produced that season, the trust bought some 50,000 tons, one-third of its usual tonnage from Cuba.[12] Since the world

[7] Wood papers, Wood to Root, Jan. 16, 1902. DIA C705-33, J. G. Gómez to L. V. Placé, Nov. 25, 1901. Cubans of all classes and beliefs proclaimed their plight and urged close economic ties.

[8] Wood papers, Root to Wood, March 6, 1901; Wood to Root, March 11, 1901; Root to Thurber, May 6, 1901, May 10, 1901.

[9] Root papers, Wood to Root, Feb. 2, 1901; DIA C705-192, Hearings on Reciprocity with Cuba, Committee on Ways and Means, 57th Cong., 1st Sess., Jan. 25, 1902 (Washington, GPO, 1902). Wood was called down by Root for sending pamphlets and letters to congressmen, Root papers, Root to Wood, Feb. 7, 1902.

[10] Wood papers, Root to Wood, Jan. 10, 1902, Wood to Root, Jan. 21, 1902.

[11] Dept. of Commerce and Labor, Bureau of Statistics. 1st series, 1903-04. *Monthly summary of Commerce and Finance of the United States* (Washington: GPO, 1903), 400.

[12] DIA C 390-63, Wood to Root, cable, March 6, 1902, *Cuban Sugar Sales*, 3-4, 12-13; Havemeyer refined about one-half of the sugar sold in the U.S. and bought about 65 percent of the foreign sugars bought by the U.S. He argued that reciprocity would aid Cuba more than the trust because he bought sugar from all over the world. He also maintained that he did not control the Cuban sugar crop, had no agents there and bought in Cuba from commission merchants. He offered to buy so much at a certain price on a certain day from commission merchants who made their profit on the difference between what the trust offered and what the Cuban might accept as a selling price. Havemeyer made no advances to planters. These were made by banks, other merchants. See also DIA C390-76, Wood to Edwards, April 3, 1902, cable, showing

price was set at Hamburg and not New York, the sugar trust did not control
the Cuban sugar crop.

While Americans consumed far more sugar than Cuba could produce, the
public resentment of the sugar trust was so great that it made the fight for
reciprocity harder to win. It seemed to many Americans that reciprocity
would aid the trust and not the Cuban. Cuban conditions were depressed,
but not as low as Wood and the Cuban planters proclaimed. The wealthiest
planters would have made a profit with or without reciprocity. The second
class of planters would have broken even without reciprocity and made a
profit with it. Those losing money without reciprocity would have broken
even with it. The fourth class of planters was composed of men who could
not be aided even by a 25 percent reduction in the United States tariff. Most
planters were in the third and fourth classes. Bankers would not loan money
to planters because prices were so low. Unemployment, debts and lack of
money were beginning to lead to serious social unrest.[13]

Two Americans who knew the country well argued that reciprocity would
prevent the need to annex Cuba. Edwin F. Atkins, in testifying before the
House Committee on Ways and Means, said, "If you want to bring about
annexation by the destruction of the Island of Cuba, I think it could be done
by refusing to give Cuba anything at all." General Tasker H. Bliss believed
that reciprocity would postpone annexation. Rejection of reciprocity would
force Cuba into union with the United States.[14] Arguing from different

further breakdown on disposition of Cuban sugar crop for 1902, where most of it
was being retained in the island to pay off debts or to wait for a price rise.

[13] DIA C390-90, Platt to Root, May 5, 1902, Wood to Root, May 8, 1902; DIA
C705-246, "United States Diplomatic and Consular Reports: Trade of Cuba for the
year 1901," Foreign Office, Great Britain, Oct. 1902, no. 2909, Annual Series, 40-42,
copy sent to Edwards by Steinhart; *Havana Post,* Jan. 15, 1902, typical of the many
articles appearing daily on the sugar crisis in the Cuban press; Wood papers, H. G.
Squires to John Hay, July 11, 1902, noting 123 mercantile failures as of June 30, and
that nearly 35 percent of the merchants were insolvent. The British consul thought
Cubans exaggerated their predicament; Squires did not. Wilson papers, Bliss to J. H.
Wilson, Feb. 28, 1902.

[14] U.S. House. "Hearings on Reciprocity," doc. 535, 57th Cong., 1st sess., Atkins,
19, 41. Wood and Atkins resented each other due to Wood's attempts to collect taxes
on Atkins' property near Cienfuegos. See also testimony of G. R. Fowler, a Cuban
Planter, 459-65; of Bliss, 378-96; Placé, 41-3; R. T. Oxnard, president of the American
Sugar Beet Assn., 164-177; W. R. Corwine, New York Merchants Assn., Evan Thomas,
C. P. Armstrong and Chas. Rubaden of the New York Produce Exchange, 99; J. H.
Post, Pres. of National Sugar Refining Co., 353; F. R. Hathaway of the Alma Sugar
Co., 244 ff.; technical testimony by Dr. H. W. Wiley, Chief of Bureau of Chemistry
of Dept. of Agriculture, 497-513, arguing that problem was chiefly overproduction,
not high American tariff. He thought free trade would aid the trust and ruin the U.S.
domestic sugar men. He advocated countervailing duties on German sugar. Germany
had 397 beet factories, United States, 44.

motives, both men sided with the administration's reciprocity effort to support Cuban independence.

As the administration forces prepared to fight for reciprocity, others began to fight against it. The government wanted an economic guarantee to promote political stability. American sugar magnates, few but influential, were reluctant to lose one of their sources of raw material. They pressured the United States Government to retain some control in the island. This group included Americans who owned sugar refineries in the United States, as well as Americans who owned centrals in Cuba. On the other hand, the raw sugar cane industry of Louisiana, in addition to the beet sugar interests of Michigan, Colorado and California, led by Henry T. Oxnard, waged a campaign against lowering the duties on raw sugar, which they argued would seriously damage their young industry.

On March 18, 1902, Sereno E. Payne, Chairman of the House Ways and Means Committee, introduced a reciprocal trade relations bill. In this succinct and moderate bill, Payne reasoned that the low price of sugar was due to the world price which was reduced because of overproduction. World consumption had been around ten million tons and in 1902, growers produced some eleven million tons. A crisis threatened Cuba at a time when the United States was supposed to release its ward into world affairs. Prices were at one and one-half cents a pound in early 1902 and it cost two cents to produce a pound of raw cane sugar. Yet Congress was bound to protect American revenues and a 20 percent tariff reduction meant a probable loss of seven to eight million dollars. But Payne thought the United States Government could stand this loss easily. Furthermore, a 20 percent reduction would not hurt United States beet and cane growers because the American public consumed more sugar than was produced within the country. The 20 percent proposed reduction would add 0.34 of a cent to the price of Cuban sugar and afford a margin of 0.15 of a cent on the present crop, thereby saving the Cuban planters from bankruptcy, and allowing them to obtain new credit. Payne assured the House that the planter would gain the benefit of reduction and not the sugar trust because the margin was so small and because the planters were not marketing their crops. He also pointed out that the United States could easily double its trade with Cuba. Dissenters on the Ways and Means Committee had wanted a bigger reduction.[15]

After bitter debate, the bill passed the House. It established a duty of one and one-third cents a pound on Cuban sugar (20 percent reduction), with the new duty to terminate on December 1, 1903, when it was considered that the

[15] U.S., Congress, House, Report 1276 pt. 1, Sereno Payne, March 31, 1902, 57th Cong., 1st Sess.

bounties on beet sugar would have been removed by the Brussels Convention. In the Senate, the sugar measure was delayed by the inquiry of the Cuba Relations Committee into the financial interests of the American Sugar Refining Company in Cuba. Although the trust held no monopoly of the Cuban sugar industry, the reciprocity bill's chances were hampered by the interest of the American refiners in the bill. The bill finally died in committee when it developed that General Wood had used insular funds to publicize the need for reciprocity. Wood was surprised at this reaction, for the American public seemed to forget that he was "representing the Cubans, and not the people of Nebraska or anywhere else." [16] Cubans were grateful for Wood's efforts on their behalf; but they did not obtain reciprocity during the spring of 1902.[17] Ironically, the delay played into the hands of the sugar trust. A huge crop was ready for market and as the price dropped lower, only the trust could benefit.[18] President Roosevelt had even submitted a special message to Congress on June 13, 1902, pleading for reciprocity, but July 1 saw Congress adjourn without action.

Since Cuba was now an independent nation, Roosevelt tried diplomatic channels. He found that the Cuban government had cooled toward the idea, mainly because the recent Brussels convention had reduced the bounty on European beet sugars and because Germany and Great Britain now sought reciprocity with Cuba. Those two powers suggested to the Cubans that their price and market problems were solved. The United States thereupon renewed its efforts, fearing the growth of foreign influence in Cuba. After several conferences, a treaty with Cuba was signed on December 11, presented to the Senate on December 17, and consented to on March 19, 1903.

[16] *New York Times,* June 13, 1902, as quoted in Hagedorn, *Wood,* I, 380n; DIA C705-228, *Washington Post,* June 12, 1902, Thurber testimony.

[17] Wood papers, Steinhart to Wood, June 18, 1902, statement of secretaries of insular government saying they were displeased at unjust attacks on Wood, and deemed the expenditure necessary and made in behalf of Cuba; Wood received literally hundreds of telegrams beseeching him to obtain a reduction in the U.S. tariff. E. J. Varona said that no problem was as urgent in Cuba and F. Gamba, president of the *"Centro General de Comerciantes e Industriales"* asked Wood to transmit a petition to the President, Wood papers, Varona to Wood, Oct. 3, 1901, Torralba to Wood, Sept. 9, 1901, Gamba to Wood, Oct. 3, 1901, E. J. Chapley to Wood, Oct. 9, 1901, Wood to Roosevelt, Oct. 7, 1901.

[18] Fitzgibbon, *Cuba and the United States,* 111, 209-213; Portell Vilá, *Historia de Cuba,* IV, 351, 372-76; U.S. House, Rept. 1276 pt. 1, March 31, 1902. Portell and Roig considered that reciprocity extended U.S. imperialistic control over Cuba, Martínez Ortiz deemed it generous. Still, men like Sanguily and Cisneros opposed reciprocity and tried to prevent Cuban land sales to foreigners. Free trade would have ruined Cuba at that point in her economic development. Platt papers. Platt to W. H. Putnam, Dec. 5, 1904 and others advising them not to invest in Cuba because the competition of Cubans, Englishmen and Germans was too keen.

However, the Senate stipulated that the House must also agree to the treaty. After the Cubans ratified the Senate version, Roosevelt called Congress into special session in November. The House ratified on the 19th and the Senate on December 16. The reasons for this change were the collapse of the beet sugar interests, which had sold out to Havemeyer, and the combined pressure of the President, the manufacturers and those who fought for reciprocity on moral grounds.[19]

The treaty left the free list undisturbed, admitted a number of Cuban products (including sugar and tobacco) to the United States at a twenty percent tariff reduction and various American products to Cuba at reductions from twenty to forty percent, enabling the United States to compete with European commerce. The treaty specified that no other foreign country's sugar was to be admitted at a lower rate than that provided by the Dingley Tariff. The treaty was to continue for five years, and from year to year thereafter, until abrogated by either government upon one year's notice.

After the reciprocity treaty went into effect, the differences between the Hamburg and New York prices decreased. Advantages accruing to Cuba were most noticeable during the first decade of its operation, as the sugar industry expanded along with American consumption (62.2 pounds per capita in 1900 compared with 119.2 pounds in 1928). More significant was the growth of Cuban sugar in the American market compared to the slower increase of sugar from other countries and noncontiguous United States territories. In 1900 Cuba furnished 17.6 percent of America's foreign sugar supply, noncontiguous territories 13.8 percent and other countries 68.7 percent. By 1925 Cuba supplied 59 percent of the total, noncontiguous territories 40 percent, and full duty sugar made up only .6 percent. In general terms, the United States bought about eighty percent of Cuba's exports and about forty percent of Cuba's imports came from the United States, amounting to 1.8 percent of America's foreign trade.[20]

Data produced in 1929 by a United States Tariff Commission study of the effects of the Cuban reciprocity treaty reveal a close correlation between the results and the intentions of the Roosevelt administration. The commission pointed out that reciprocity primarily aided the Cuban planter and made little difference to the United States export trade, which was aided more in Central and South America by efficiency and geography than by preferential treatment.[21]

[19] Healy, *United States in Cuba*, 200-206.
[20] Jenks, *Our Cuban Colony*, 136; *Monthly Summary of Commerce and Finance of the United States*, 1903-04, 400, 399, 401, 1152, 303, 364, 362; U.S. Tariff Commission, *Effects of the Cuban Reciprocity Treaty*, 1-2.
[21] Tariff Commission, *Effects of ... Reciprocity*, 7-10.

The reciprocity treaty caused no serious sacrifice of revenue to either government, but the United States Government suffered a direct loss which accrued to the Cuban sugar producer. American exporters enjoyed reductions in various categories of products up to forty percent, but because the dollar value of Cuban exports to the United States was about four times that of American exports to Cuba, United States concessions were the larger.[22]

Under reciprocity, America benefited less than Cuba. The Tariff Commission maintained:

Prior to reciprocity United States imports from Cuba were much greater in value than exports to Cuba, and after the treaty became effective the imports from Cuba grew more rapidly than exports to Cuba.

Americans liked Cuban sugar more than Cubans cared for American products. Where sugar sales depended on price, American goods depended on competition, prices, style, credit, stock supply. The treaty did not affect the tobacco trade, and development of minor export products, encouraged by the reciprocity treaty, actually dwindled in favor of quicker sugar profit. The tariff advantage did not directly increase Cuban sugar exports, but it operated to confer a price premium on sugar planters, as had been expected by the advocates of reciprocity. Furthermore, the treaty diverted very few Cuban exports from other destinations to the United States.[23]

The basic motives for reciprocity were strategic, not economic, and its intangible effects were indistinguishable from those of political relations between the United States and Cuba. The political relations established by 1902 gave confidence to capital, which began to enter Cuba after the reciprocity treaty. Still, one authority concluded that "The purpose of the reciprocity treaty was to prevent the close political ties which bound Cuba to the United States from being weakened by any other preferential arrangement." [24] It is in connection with the United States interest in Cuban political security that reciprocity may be seen in its true perspective.

Cuba was a good market, but not in a class by itself. Reciprocity made little difference to the American exporter, who developed trade with all nations of the western hemisphere because of the industrial pre-eminence and favorable location of the United States. The following table affords a comparative set of figures for the growth of American trade.[25]

[22] *Ibid.*, 7-8. It is a general tariff rule that a country does not suffer loss of revenue when goods are not imported under a general preferential rule, i.e., preferential rates of duty for countries from which there are no imports do not result in sacrifice of revenue. Each country could adjust in other categories.
[23] *Ibid.*, 9-11, 13.
[24] *Ibid.*, 12; Jenks, *Our Cuban Colony*, 136.
[25] Tariff Commission, *Effects ... of Reciprocity*, 15.

Percent of imports supplied by the United States:

	1900	1925
Cuba	44.2	65.6
Canada	50.9	66.9
Mexico	59.2	69.1
Costa Rica	41.1	67.3

The Tariff Commission concluded that the aim of the Roosevelt administration had been inauguration of the new Cuban government under economic conditions that would inspire confidence in the future. The solution hinged largely upon profitable sales of Cuban sugar in the United States.[26] In this way, until 1910 (when Cuban sugar began to dominate the world market), reciprocity made a difference.

The United States Government did not insist upon a customs union with Cuba. Had America wanted to make Cuba a vassal, economic union could have been arranged prior to withdrawing the Military Government. Reciprocity was forced, not upon the Cubans, but upon Congress and domestic sugar interests, after Cuba became independent. Some Cubans wanted free trade, others wanted a *zollverein,* but as a fledgling nation without a mature economy, reciprocity was in her best interest. That this maturing of her economy never took place was due partly to the corrupt Cuban politicians and partly to economic exploitation by Americans who cared nothing about the social malaise they helped cause after 1902. The Cuban-American concentration on the easy profits of sugar led to *latifundia,* or absentee ownership of large estates. As a result, Cuba failed to industrialize or diversify her economy. Thus Cubans were susceptible to market changes that alternately caused prosperity and poverty, but rarely stability. In the general economic dislocation that followed World War I, Cuban indebtedness rose, and with it Cuba developed a connection to the United States which was not broken until after World War II.[27] Nothing but self-restraint stood in the way of Americans plundering Cuba in the 20th century.

Yet Roosevelt, Root, Platt, Payne and Wood did not conceive reciprocity as a way to dominate Cuba; instead it was part of their program to stabilize the island. They realized that a large United States market for Cuban produce would exert control over Cuba, but their purpose was to support independence with prosperity.

[26] *Ibid.,* 385, 170-71.

[27] Fitzgibbon, *Cuba and the United States,* 227, ch. 9. The records disclose no attempt by the Military Government to force the Cubans to pay off the loans they obtained during the Revolution. The matter was renegotiated in 1904 and 1909, resulting in the Speyer loans.

Most Cubans were ambivalent in their judgments of the Military Government of Cuba. They trusted Root and Wood, appreciated the development of their island, but were wounded at not being trusted to do it by themselves. This legacy was probably unavoidable; certainly Cuban politicians and historians have made the most of it. Nevertheless, the men charged with responsibility believed conditions demanded their course of action, and available evidence supports their estimate of the Cuban situation. It is difficult to see how the job could have been done otherwise except at great expense and over a much longer period of time.

In Cuba Wood seemed to evolve a philosophy that he later phrased in this way: "Our policy is to develop individualism among these people and little by little, teach them to stand on their own feet independent of petty chieftains." [28] Of course, Wood was speaking directly about governing the Philippine Moro Province, but he did point out that American colonial rule differed from Great Britain's in that the American deposed the local ruler and his customs, to give the common native a part in government. Unseating colonial rulers may have been a way to assert greater United States control, but behind Wood's actions rested an attitude traceable in the American heritage. He expected people to manage their own affairs and refrain from hurting others. If they could not do this, they could learn. Self-determination had to come after illiteracy, oppression, poverty and disease were vanquished. This is what he did in Cuba, and the Military Government was the best means of accomplishing the reforms. In Cuba, Wood became a proponent of active government for the public good, an attitude notable throughout the rest of his career. Leonard Wood's success as a leader was due not merely to being an able and powerful proconsul. He was also a reformer with high ideals and integrity who wanted free men to develop themselves and their society.

The successful fight for reciprocity consummated the program of the McKinley and Roosevelt administrations to prepare Cuba for nationhood. Cuban cooperation and American supervision had prepared the necessary educational, judicial, governmental and economic means to perpetuate a republic. The fact that these institutions required time to mature appeared to be compensated for by the Platt guarantee of stability. Leonard Wood's government of Cuba served both *Cuba Libre* and the United States national interest by safeguarding independence with prosperity and strategic security.

[28] Wood papers, Wood to J. St. Loe Strachey, Jan. 6, 1903.

APPENDIX A

["Joint Resolution For the recognition of the independence of the people of Cuba, demanding that the Government of Spain relinquish its authority and government in the Island of Cuba, and to withdraw its land and naval forces from Cuba and Cuban waters, and directing the President of the United States to use the land and naval forces of the United States to carry these resolutions into effect." *Statutes-at-Large,* v. 30, 738-39.]

Whereas the abhorrent conditions which have existed for more than three years in the Island of Cuba, so near our own borders, have shocked the moral sense of the people of the United States, have been a disgrace to Christian civilization, culminating, as they have, in the destruction of a United States battleship, with two hundred and sixty-six of its officers and crew, while on a friendly visit in the harbor of Havana, and can not longer be endured, as has been set forth by the President of the United States in his message to Congress of April eleventh, eighteen hundred and ninety-eight, upon which the action of Congress was invited: Therefore,

Resolved by the Senate and House of Representatives of the United States of America in Congress assembled, First. That the people of the Island of Cuba are, and of right ought to be, free and independent.

Second. That it is the duty of the United States to demand, and the Government of the United States does hereby demand, that the Government of Spain at once relinquish its authority and government in the Island of Cuba and withdraw its land and naval forces from Cuba and Cuban waters.

Third. That the President of the United States be, and he hereby is, directed and empowered to use the entire land and naval forces of the United States, and to call into the actual service of the United States the militia of the several states, to such extent as may be necessary to carry these resolutions into effect.

Fourth. That the United States hereby disclaims any disposition or intention to exercise sovereignty, jurisdiction, or control over said Island except for the pacification thereof, and asserts its determination, when that is accomplished, to leave the government and control of the Island to its people.

Approved, April 20, 1898.

APPENDIX B

[Treaty of Peace. Concluded at Paris December 10, 1898; ratification advised by the Senate February 6, 1899; ratified by the President February 6, 1899; ratifications exchanged April 11, 1899; proclaimed April 11, 1899. William M. Malloy (ed.), *Treaties, Conventions, International Acts, Protocols and Agreements between the United States of America and Other Powers* (Washington, 1910), v. 2, 1690-95.]

Article I

Spain relinquishes all claim of sovereignty over and title to Cuba.

And as the island is, upon its evacuation by Spain, to be occupied by the United States, the United States will, so long as such occupation shall last, assume and discharge the obligations that may under international law result from the fact of its occupation, for the protection of life and property.

Article VII

The United States and Spain mutually relinquish all claims for indemnity, national and individual, of every kind, of either government, or of its citizens or subjects, against the other Government, that may have arisen since the beginning of the late insurrection in Cuba and prior to the exchange of ratifications of the present treaty, including all claims for indemnity for the cost of the war.

The United States will adjudicate and settle the claims of its citizens against Spain relinquished in this article.

Article VIII

.... Spain relinquishes in Cuba ... all the buildings, wharves, barracks, forts, structures, public highways and other immovable property which, in conformity with law, belong to the public domain. . . .

And it is hereby declared that the relinquishment . . . cannot in any respect impair the property or rights which by law belong to the peaceful possession of property of all kinds, of provinces, municipalities, public or private establishments, ecclesiastical or civic bodies. . . or of private individuals, of whatsoever nationality such individuals may be. . . .

Article IX

Spanish subjects, natives of the Peninsula, residing in the territory over which Spain by the present treaty relinquishes or cedes her sovereignty, may remain in such territory or may remove therefrom, retaining in either event all their rights of property, including the right to sell or dispose of such property or of its proceeds; and they shall also have the right to carry on their industry, commerce and professions, being subject in respect thereof to such laws as are applicable to other foreigners. In case they remain in the territory they may preserve their allegiance to the Crown of Spain by making, before a court of record, within a year from the date of the exchange of ratifications of this treaty, a declaration of their decision to preserve such allegiance; in default of which declaration they shall be held to have renounced it and to have adopted the nationality of the territory in which they reside.

The civil rights and political status of the native inhabitants of the territories hereby ceded to the United States shall be determined by the Congress.

Article X

The inhabitants of the territories over which Spain relinquishes or cedes her sovereignty shall be secured in the free exercise of their religion.

Article XI

The Spaniards residing in the territories over which Spain by this treaty cedes or relinquishes her sovereignty shall be subject in matters civil as well as criminal to the jurisdiction of the courts of the country wherein they reside, pursuant to the ordinary laws governing the same; and they shall have the right to appear before such courts, and to pursue the same course as citizens of the country to which the courts belong.

Article XVI

It is understood that any obligations assumed in this treaty by the United States with respect to Cuba are limited to the time of its occupancy thereof; but it will upon the termination of such occupancy, advise any Government established in the island to assume the same obligations.

APPENDIX C

DISBURSEMENTS OF THE MILITARY GOVERNMENT

State and government	$ 2,780,781.16
Justice and public instruction	11,108,187.46
Finance	990,586.71
Customs service	2,912,326.06
Postal service	1,625,762.03
Quarantine	694,024.81
Census	380,393.44
Auditor	312,758.42
Treasurer	581,700.10
Rural guard and administration	5,253,244.58
(much of this went for school supplies)	
Agriculture, industry and commerce	1,121,699.28
Public building, works, ports and harbors	5,833,607.90
Jucaro and San Fernando railroad	57,338.51
Barracks and quarters	2,525,483.78
Charities and hospitals	4,124,986.60
Sanitation	9,706,258.20
Municipalities	4,477, 177.52
(other than charities, hospitals and sanitation)	
Miscellaneous	918,714.72
Total	$ 55,405,031.28
Excess of receipts over disbursements	$ 1,792,100.52

[Wood, *Civil Report*, 1902, I, 196.]

VOTE ON THE PLATT AMENDMENT, PRESIDENTIAL ELECTION

Province	Name	for	against	Party	War	1902	Party	Govt.	Office
Pinar del Río	Juan Ríus Rivera	absent		N	gen	Palma	N	Gov. & Sec. Agric.	Port Collector
	Joaquín Quílez	X	N		auton	Masó	MC	Gov.	Gov.
	Gonzalo de Quesada	X	N		diplo	Palma	N	U	Senate
Habana	José Lacret Morlot		X	N	gen	Masó	MC	Dns	Senate
	Alejandro A. Rodríguez	X		N	gen	Palma	N	Gov. & rurales	U
	Miguel Gener	absent		N	sep	Masó	MC	Mayor & sct.	Dns
	Emilio Núñez	X		N	gen	Palma	N	Gov.	Governor
	Diego Tamayo	X		N	del	Palma	N	Sec. St. Gov.	Cabinet
	Alfredo Zayas		X	N	sep	Palma	N	city coun.	Senate
	Manuel Sanguily	X		RD	del, diplo	Palma	N	rector Inst.	Senate
	Leopoldo Berriel	X		RD	prof. law		I	law prof.	Senate
Matanzas	Domingo Méndez Capote	X		RD	govt.	Palma	R	Sec. St. & Gov.	Senate
	Pedro Betancourt	X		RD	gen	Palma	R	Gov.	Senate
	Eliseo Giberga	X		RD	auton	U	UD	Dns	Dns
	Luis Fortún		X	RD	sep	Palma	R	audiencia	Senate
Villas (Santa Clara)	José Miguel Gómez	X		RD	gen	Palma	RF	Gov.	Gov.
	Enrique Villuendas	X		RD	col	Palma	RF	dist. court fiscal	House
	José B. Alemán		X	RD	gen, sec. war	Masó	MC	U	Gov.
	José J. Monteagudo	X		RD	gen	Palma	RF	rurales	Senate

Pedro González Llorente	X	RD	sep	U		sct	Dns
Martín Morúa Delgado	X	RD	sep	Palma	R	U	Senate
José Luis Robau	absent	RD	gen	Masó	MC	Dns	Senate
Camagüey (Puerto Príncipe)							
Salvador Cisneros Betancourt	X	RD	pres	Masó	NL	Dns	Senate
Manuel R. Silva	X	RD	sec. interior	Masó	NL	Dns	Senate
Oriente (Santiago)							
Eudaldo Tamayo	X		sep	Palma	N	sct	Senate
Antonio Bravo Correoso	absent	CP	sep cabinet	Palma	N	Dns	Senate
Rafael Portuondo	X	CP	gen.	Palma	N	dist. fiscal	House
José Fernández de Castro	X	CP	sep	Masó	UD	U	Dns
Juan Gualberto Gómez	X	RI	sep	Masó	RI	Dns	Dns
Rafael Manduley	X	RD	col	Masó	RI	dist. court	Senate
José N. Ferrer	X	RD	col		N	U	Dns
	31	16	11				

N – Partido Naciónal Cubano
RD – Coalicion Republicano-Democrática
CP – Concentración Patriótica (aligned with N)
gen – general in army of liberation
col – colonel in army of liberation
auton – autonomist (hostile to rebels)
sep – separatist (name for rebels)
diplo – rebel diplomat
del – rebel delegate to assembly
gov – government of province
govt – held cabinet job in rebel govt
pres – president of rebel govt.

Palma – Estrada Palma
N   in column 8 – Partido Naciónal
UD ,,   ,,   ,,   – Union Democrática
R   ,,   ,,   ,,   – Partido Republicano
RI ,,   ,,   ,,   – Partido Republicano Independiente
MC ,,   ,,   – Masócoalition
RF ,,   ,,   – Republicano Federal
NL ,,   ,,   – Nacionales Liberales
Dns – Did not serve
U – Unknown
sct supreme court
[Riera *Cuba política*, 23–67, *Mención histórica*].

APPENDIX E

MAP OF CUBA

CUBA

HAVANA —— PROVINCES

⊙ PROVINCE CAPITALS

〰 RAILROAD

MILES
0   100   200

KILOMETERS
0   150   300

E. HOERAUF   WESTERN WASH. ST. COLL.

FLORIDA

MATANZAS

PINAR DEL RIO

HAVANA

SANTA CLARA

PUERTO PRINCIPE

SANTIAGO DE CUBA

C. SAN ANTONIO

Pinar del Río ⊙

BAHÍA HONDA

Guanajay
Mariel
Marianao
Havana
Guanabacoa
Bejucal
Güines
Batabanó

I. DE PINOS

PENÍN. DE ZAPATA

Matanzas
Cárdenas
Isabela
Cruces
Palmira
Cienfuegos
Santa Clara
Remedios
Yaguajay
Morón
Trinidad
Sancti Spíritus
Júcaro
Puerto Príncipe ⊙
Santa Cruz del Sur

PTO. DE NUEVITAS
Nuevitas
Manatí
Puerto Padre
Gibara
Holguín
Banes
BAHÍA DE NIPE
Mayarí
Alto Cedro
Baracoa
C. MAISÍ

Niquero
Manzanillo
Bayamo
Jiguaní
Baire
Santiago de Cuba
GUANTÁNAMO BAY

C. CRUZ

24° N.
22° N.
20° N.

84° W.   82° W.   80° W.   78° W.   76° W.   74° W.

United States
Mexico
Central America
CUBA
Haiti

APPENDIX F
PLATT AMENDMENT

Provided further, That in fulfillment of the declaration contained in the joint resolution approved April twentieth, eighteen hundred and ninety-eight, entitled, 'For the recognition of the independence of the people of Cuba, demanding that the Government of Spain relinquish its authority and government in the island of Cuba, and to withdraw its land and naval forces from Cuba and Cuban waters, and directing the President of the United States to use the land and naval forces of the United States to carry these resolutions into effect,' the President is thereby authorized to 'leave the government and control of the island of Cuba to its people' so soon as a government shall have been established in said island under a constitution which, either as a part thereof or in an ordinance appended thereto, shall define the future relations of the United States with Cuba, substantialy as follows:

I

That the government of Cuba shall never enter into any treaty or other compact with any foreign power or powers which will impair or tend to impair the independence of Cuba, nor in any manner authorize or permit any foreign power or powers to obtain by colonization or for military or naval purposes or otherwise, lodgment in or control over any portion of said island.

II

That said government shall not assume or contract any public debt, to pay the interest upon which, and to make reasonable sinking fund provision for the ultimate discharge of which, the ordinary revenues of the island, after defraying the current expenses of government shall be inadequate.

III

That the government of Cuba consents that the United States may exercise the right to intervene for the preservation of Cuban independence, the maintenance of a government adequate for the protection of life, property, and individual liberty, and for discharging the obligations with respect to Cuba imposed by the Treaty of Paris on the United States, now to be assumed and undertaken by the government of Cuba.

IV

That all acts of the United States in Cuba during its military occupation thereof are ratified and validated, and all lawful rights acquired thereunder shall be maintained and protected.

V

That the government of Cuba will execute, and as far as necessary extend, the plans already devised or other plans to be mutually agreed upon, for the sanitation of the cities of the island, to the end that a recurrence of epidemic and infectious diseases may be prevented, thereby assuring protection to the people and commerce of Cuba, as well as to the commerce of the southern ports of the United States and the people residing therein.

VI

That the Isle of Pines shall be omitted from the proposed constitutional boundaries of Cuba, the title thereto being left to future adjustment by treaty.

VII

That to enable the United States to maintain the independence of Cuba, and to protect the people thereof, as well as for its own defense, the government of Cuba will sell or lease to the United States lands necessary for coaling or naval stations at certain specified points, to be agreed upon with the President of the United States.

VIII

That by way of further assurance the government of Cuba will embody the foregoing provisions in a permanent treaty with the United States.

BIBLIOGRAPHY

Unpublished Manuscript Collections

William E. Chandler papers, Library of Congress.
Joseph Benson Foraker papers, Library of Congress.
Hermann Hagedorn papers, Library of Congress.
Frank R. McCoy papers, Library of Congress.
William McKinley papers, Library of Congress.
John Tyler Morgan papers, Library of Congress.
Orville H. Platt papers, Connecticut State Library.
Theodore Roosevelt papers, Library of Congress.
Elihu Root papers, Library of Congress.
John Coit Spooner papers, Library of Congress.
Henry M. Teller papers, Colorado State Historical Society.
James Harrison Wilson papers, Library of Congress.
Leonard Wood papers, Library of Congress.

Unpublished Theses

de Vol, Ethel May. "The Mind of the Senate Relative to Cuba, Feb. 15, 1898." Unpublished Master's thesis, University of California, 1934.
Vergara, Pedro. "The Attitude of the United States Toward Cuban Independence, 1895–1902." Unpublished Master's thesis, University of California, 1934.
Weigle, Richard Daniel. "The Sugar Interests and American Diplomacy in Hawaii and Cuba, 1893–1903." Unpublished Ph.D. thesis, Yale University, 1939.

Published Government Documents

Cuba

República de Cuba. Secretaria de Hacienda. Sección Estadística. *Industria azucarera y sus derivados.* La Habana, 1901–1903.
República de Cuba. Secretaria de Hacienda. Estadística General. *Comercio exterior,* La Habana, 1902–1903.

República de Cuba. Senado. *Memoria de los trabajos realizados durante las cuatro legislaturas y sesión extraordinaria del primer periodo congresional, 1902–1904*, (includes *Mención histórica*). La Habana, 1918.

Germany

Die Grosse Politik der Europäischen Kabinette. 1871–1914. Edited by J. Lepsius, A. Mendelssohn Bartholdy and F. Thimme. 40 Vols., Berlin, 1922–1927.
German Diplomatic Documents, 1871–1914. Edited by E. T. S. Dugdale. 4 Vols., London, 1929.
German Foreign Ministry Archives. Series I. Reels 108, 109, 119. Series III. Reels 4, 5 (microfilm).
Schwertfeger, B. *Die Diplomatischen Akten des Auswärtigen Amtes 1871–1914.* Berlin, 1924.

United States

Brooke, John R. *Civil Report*, 1899. (House Documents.)
Bureau of Insular Affairs. *The Establishment of Free Government in Cuba.* Washington, 1904.
Census of Cuba, 1899. Washington, 1900.
Congressional Record.
Department of Commerce and Labor. Bureau of Statistics. "Commercial Cuba." Washington, 1903.
Division of Insular Affairs. *Translation of the Law of Criminal Procedure for Cuba and Puerto Rico with Annotations, Explanatory Notes and Amendments made since The American Occupation.* Washington, 1901.
House Documents. Miscellaneous, 1898–1902.
House Reports. Miscellaneous, 1898–1902.
Magoon, Charles Edward. *Report on The Law of Civil Government in Territory Subject to Military Occupation by the Military Forces of the United States.* 2d ed. Washington, 1902.
Porter, R. P. *Report on The Commercial and Industrial Condition of Cuba.* Washington, 1898.
Root, Elihu. *Report of the Secretary of War*, 1899–1902. (House Documents.)
Rutter, Frank. *International Sugar Situation.* Washington, 1904.
Senate. *Cuban Sugar Sales.* Washington, 1902.
Senate Documents. Miscellaneous, 1898–1902.
Senate Reports. Miscellaneous, 1898–1902.
Tariff Commission. *Colonial Tariff Policies.* Washington, 1922.
Tariff Commission. *Effects of The Cuban Reciprocity Treaty.* Washington, 1929.
War Department. *Correspondence Relating to the War with Spain.* 2 Vols. Washington, 1902.
Wood, Leonard. *Civil Report*, 1900. 12 Vols. 1901. 15 Vols. 1902. 8 Vols.

Newspapers

Cuba

Diario de la Marina.
Havana Post.
La Discusión.

United States

New York Evening Post.
New York Times.
New York World.

England

London Times.

Unpublished Documents

United States

Bureau of Insular Affairs Library. "Record of Sessions of The Constitutional Convention of The Island of Cuba." 7 Vols.
National Archives. Diplomatic and Legal Branch. P. C. Jessup. "Memorandum on The Platt Amendment."
National Archives. Social and Economic Branch. Interior Division. Record Group 140. "Records of The Military Government of Cuba."
—. Record Group 350. "Records of The Bureau of Insular Affairs."

Books

Adams, Henry. *Education.* New York, 1931.
Ardura, Ernesto (ed.). *Brega de libertad.* La Habana, 1950.
Atkins, Edwin F. *Sixty Years in Cuba.* Cambridge, 1926.
Beale, Howard K. *Theodore Roosevelt and the Rise of America to World Power.* Baltimore, 1956.
Beals, Carleton. *The Crime of Cuba.* New York, 1934.
Benton, E. J. *The Law and Diplomacy of The Spanish American War.* New York, 1908.
Borrero Pérez, J. G. *La Cubanía aniquilada por la enmienda Platt.* Sancti Spiritus, 1958.
Bravo Correoso, Antonio. *Come se hizo la constitución de Cuba.* La Habana, 1928.
Bristow, Joseph L. *Fraud and Politics at the Turn of the Century.* New York, 1952.
Callahan, J. M. *Cuba and International Relations.* Baltimore, 1899.

Callcott, Wilfrid. *The Caribbean Policy of the United States.* Baltimore, 1942.
Campbell, Charles S. *Anglo-American Understanding, 1898–1903.* Baltimore, 1957.
Capote, Domingo Méndez. *Trabajos.* 3 vols. in 1, La Habana, 1929–30.
Casuso, Enrique. *Politica cubana y sistema Americano.* La Habana, 1901.
Chapman, Charles E. *History of the Cuban Republic.* New York, 1927.
Coolidge, Louis A. *An Old Fashioned Senator, Orville H. Platt.* New York, 1910.
Costa, Octavio. *Manuel Sanguily.* La Habana, 1950.
Crawford, W. R. *A Century of Latin American Thought.* rev. ed., Boston, 1961.
Cuba, Archivo Nacional. *Catálogo de los fondos existentes en el archivo nacional.* La Habana, 1957.
Dawes, Charles Gates. *A Journal of the McKinley Years.* Chicago, 1950.
Dennett, Tyler. *John Hay.* New York, 1933.
Dunn, Robert W. *American Foreign Investments.* New York, 1926.
Ellis, Elmer. *Henry Moore Teller, Defender of the West.* Caldwell, 1941.
Fitzgibbon, Russell H. *Cuba and the United States, 1900–1935.* Menasha, 1935.
Flint, Grover. *Marching with Gómez.* New York, 1898.
Foraker, Joseph Benson. *Notes on a Busy Life.* 2 vols. Cincinnati, 1916.
Ford, W. C. (ed.). *Letters of Henry Adams.* 2 vols. Boston, 1929.
Giberga, Eliseo. *Obras.* II. La Habana, 1930.
Gómez, Juan Gualberto. *Por Cuba libre.* La Habana, 1954.
González, J. *Martín Morúa Delgado: Impresiones sobre su última novela y su gestión en la constituyente de Cuba.* La Habana, 1902.
Grenville, J. A. S. and G. B. Young. *Politics, Strategy, and American Diplomacy.* New Haven, 1966.
Guerra Sánchez, Ramiro, *et al. Historia de la Nación Cubana.* 10 vols. La Habana, 1952.
Hagedorn, Hermann. *Leonard Wood.* 2 vols. New York, 1931.
Healy, David F. *The United States in Cuba, 1898–1902.* Madison, 1963.
Hellmann, Florence. *List of References on the Platt Amendment.* Washington, 1934.
Hernández Corujo, E. *Los fundamentos históricos y filosóficos de la constitución de 1901.* La Habana, 1953.
Hevia, Aurelio. *Colección de artículos y documentos.* La Habana, 1908.
Infiesta, Ramón. *Historia constitucional de Cuba.* La Habana, 1942.
—. *Máximo Gómez.* La Habana, 1937.
Jenks, L. H. *Our Cuban Colony.* New York, 1928.
Jessup, Philip C. *Elihu Root.* 2 vols. New York, 1938.
La Feber, Walter. *The New Empire.* Ithaca, 1963.
Langer, William L. *The Diplomacy of Imperialism.* rev. ed., New York, 1951.
Laughlin, J. Laurence and H. Parker Willis. *Reciprocity.* New York, 1903.
Leech, Margaret. *In the Days of McKinley.* New York, 1959.
Logan, J. A., Jr. *No Transfer: An American Security Principle.* New Haven, 1961.
López Hidalgo, Ambrosio Valentín. *Cuba y la enmienda Platt.* La Habana, 1921.
MacGaffey, Wyatt and C. R. Barnett. *Cuba.* New Haven, 1962.
Machado y Ortega, Luis. *La enmienda Platt.* La Habana, 1922.
Mañach, Jorge. *Marti: Apostle of Freedom.* New York, 1950.
Márquez Sterling, Manuel. *Proceso histórico de la enmienda Platt, 1897–1934.* La Habana, 1941.

Martínez Ortiz, Rafael. *Cuba: Los primeros años de la independencia.* 2 vols. Paris, 1929.
May, Ernest R. *Imperial Democracy.* New York, 1961.
Menocal y Cueto, H. *Origin y desarrollo del pensamiento Cubano.* 2 vols. La Habana, 1945.
Morgan, H. Wayne, ed., *Making Peace With Spain. The Diary of Whitelaw Reid, September–December, 1898.* Austin, 1965.
Morison, Elting E. (ed.). *The Letters of Theodore Roosevelt.* 8 vols. Cambridge, 1951.
—. *Turmoil and Tradition: the Life and Times of Henry Lewis Stimson.* Boston, 1960.
Munro, D. F. *The United States and the Caribbean Area.* New York, 1934.
Olcott, C. S. *Life of William McKinley.* 2 vols. Boston, 1918.
Ortiz, Fernández F. *Cuban Counterpoint.* New York, 1947.
Peraza Saraúsa, Fermín. "Indice del boletín" del archivo nacional. La Habana, 1944.
Pérez Landa, Rufino. *Bartolomé Masó y Márquez.* La Habana, 1937.
Perkins, Dexter. *A History of the Monroe Doctrine.* New York, 1955.
Portell Vilá, Herminio. *Historia de Cuba en sus relaciones con Los Estados Unidos y España,* 4 vols. La Habana, 1937–41.
Porter, Kirk (ed.). *National Party Platforms.* New York, 1924.
Porter, Robert P. *Industrial Cuba.* New York, 1899.
Pratt, Julius. *America's Colonial Experiment.* New York, 1950.
—. *Expansionists of 1898.* Baltimore, 1936.
Prinsen Geerligs, H. C. *The World's Cane Sugar Industry, Past Present.* Manchester, 1912.
Quesada, Gonzalo de. *Cuba.* La Habana, 1905.
Quesada y Miranda G. (ed.). *Epistolario.* 2 vols. in 1. La Habana, 1948, 1951.
Randolph, Carman F. *The Law and Policy of Annexation.* New York, 1901.
Riera, Mario. *Cuba política.* La Habana, 1955.
Robinson, Albert G. *Cuba and the Intervention.* New York, 1905.
Roig de Leuchsenring, Emilio. *La enmienda Platt.* 2 vols. La Habana, 1935.
—. *La lucha Cubana por la república, contra la anexión y la enmienda Platt, 1899–1902.* La Habana, 1952.
Root, Elihu. *The Military and Colonial Policy of the United States.* Ed. by Robert Bacon and James Brown Scott. Cambridge, 1916.
Sanguily, Manuel. *Discursos y conferencias.* 2 vols. La Habana, 1919.
Santovenía y Echaíde, Emeterio S. *Armonias y conflictas en torno a Cuba.* Mexico, D. F., 1956.
—. *Theodore Roosevelt y la soberania de Cuba.* La Habana, 1958.
Scott, Hugh L. *Memories of a Soldier.* New York, 1918.
Scott, James Brown. *The Recommendations of Habana Concerning International Organization.* New York, 1917.
Smith, Robert Freeman. *The United States and Cuba.* New York, 1960.
Stanwood, Edward. *History of the Presidency.* 2 vols. New York, 1926.
Trelles y Govín, Carlos M. *Biblioteca histórica Cubana.* 3 vols. Matanzas, 1922, 1927.

Trelles, Nicanor. *Constitución Cubana: Comentarios a las leyes fundamentales de los Estados Unidos y su adoptación a Cuba.* La Habana, 1900.

Vagts, Alfred. *Deutschland und die Vereinigten Staaten in der Weltpolitik.* 2 vols. in 1. New York, 1935.

Varona, Enrique José. *De la colonia a la república.* La Habana, 1919.

Vaughan, W. *The Life and Work of Sir William Van Horne.* New York, 1920.

Vivanco, José C. *Constitución de la república de Cuba, comentada.* La Habana, 1902.

Whitaker, A. P. *The Western Hemisphere Idea.* Ithaca, 1954.

Wilson, James Harrison. *Under the Old Flag.* 2 vols. New York, 1912.

Winkler, Max. *Investments of United States Capital in Latin America.* Boston, 1928.

Wright, Irene A. *Cuba.* New York, 1910.

Wright, Philip G. *The Cuban Situation and Our Treaty Relations.* Washington, 1931.

Articles

A Cuban. "A Plea for the Annexation of Cuba," *Forum*, XXX, October, 1900.

Atkins, Edwin. "Cuba's Imminent Bankrupty," *North American Review*, CLXXIII, December, 1901.

Bangs, John Kendrick. "The Future of Cuba," *Harper's Weekly*, XLV, March 30, 1901.

Berle, A. A., Jr. "The Cuban Crisis," *Foreign Affairs*, XXXIX, October, 1960.

Brownell, Atherton. "The Commercial Annexation of Cuba," *Appleton's Magazine*, VIII, October, 1906.

Bryce, James. "Some Reflections on the State of Cuba," *North American Review*, CLXXIV, April, 1902.

Capó Rodríguez, Pedro. "The Platt Amendment," *American Journal of International Law*, XVII, October, 1923.

Chapman, Charles R. "New Corollaries of the Monroe Doctrine, with Especial Reference to the Relations of the United States with Cuba," *University of California Chronicle*, XXX, April, 1931.

Clark, Victor S. "The Cuban Municipality," *Review of Reviews*, XXVI, August, 1902.

Cuba Review. (formerly *Cuba Bulletin and Review*) I–XVI, June 1903 to March 1918.

Cummins, Lejeune. "The Formulation of the Platt Amendment," *The Americas*, XXIII, April, 1967, 4.

Currier, C. W. "Why Cuba Should be Independent," *Forum*, XXX, October, 1900.

"Distrustful Cuba," *Nation*, LXXI, October 25, 1900.

Estrada Palma, Tomás. "The Future of Cuba," *Independent*, LIV, April 3, 1902.

Gay Calbó, Enrique. "Genesis de la enmienda Platt," *Cuba Contemporánea*. XLI, May, 1926.

Guerra Sánchez, Ramiro. "El General Leonardo Wood y la instruccion publica en Cuba," *Cuba Contemporánea*, XXXIII, July, 1920.

Guggenheim, Harry F. "Amending the Platt Amendment," *Foreign Affairs*, XII, April, 1934.

Harrington, Fred Harvey. "The Anti-Imperialist Movement in the United States, 1898–1900," *Mississippi Valley Historical Review*, XXII, September, 1935.

Hershey, Amos S. "Intervention and the Recognition of Cuban Independence," *Annals of the American Academy of Political and Social Science*, XI, May, 1898.

Hitchman, James H. "The Platt Amendment Revisited: A Bibliographical Survey," *The Americas*, XXIII, April, 1967, #4.

—. "The American Touch in Colonial Administration: Leonard Wood in Cuba, 1898–1902," *The Americas*, XXIV, April, 1968, #4.

—. "United States Control Over Cuban Sugar Production, 1898–1902" *Journal of Inter-American Studies and World Affairs*, XII, January, 1970, #1.

Holbo, Paul S. "Presidential Leadership in Foreign Affairs: The Turpie-Foraker Amendment," *American Historical Review*, LXXII, #4, July, 1967.

Hunter, J. M. "Investment as a factor in the Economic Development of Cuba, 1899–1935," *Inter-American Economic Affairs*, V, Winter, 1951, 82–100.

Kennan, George. "Cuban Character," *Outlook*, LXIII, December 23, 1899.

Lockmiller, David. "The Settlement of the Church Property Question in Cuba," *Hispanic American Historical Review*, XVII, November, 1937.

Mañach, Jorge. "Revolution in Cuba," *Foreign Affairs*, XII, October, 1933.

Marshall, E. F. "A Talk with General Wood," *Outlook*, LXVIII, July 20, 1901.

Nation, "Control of Cuba's Foreign Relations," LXXI, August 2, 1900.

Pavey, Frank D. "The Independence of Cuba," *North American Review*, CLXXII, March, 1901.

Platt, Orville H. "A Solution of the Cuban Problem," *World's Work*, II, May, 1901.

—. "Our Relations to the People of Cuba and Porto Rico," *Annals of the American Academy of Political and Social Science*, XVIII, July, 1901.

—. "The Pacification of Cuba," *Independent*, LIII, June 27, 1901.

Pomeroy, Earl S. "The American Colonial Office," *Mississippi Valley Historical Review*, XXX, March, 1944.

Rippy, J. F. "The Story of Investments in ... Cuba," *Inter-American Economic Affairs*, VI, 1952.

Robinson, Albert G. "Industrial and Commercial Conditions in Cuba," *Review of Reviews*, XXVI, August, 1902.

—. "Work of the Cuban Convention," *Forum*, XXXI, June, 1901.

Rodríguez, J. I. "Cuban Self Government," *Independent*, LII, December 13, 1900.

Runcie, James. "American Misgovernment of Cuba," *North American Review*, CLXX, February, 1900.

Sanguily, Manuel. "Sobre la genesis de la enmienda Platt," *Cuba Contemporánea*, XXX, October, 1922.

Sears, L. M. "French Opinion of the Spanish-American War," *Hispanic American Historical Review*, VII, February, 1927.

Shippee, Lester E. "Germany and the Spanish-American War," *American Historical Review*, XXX, July, 1925.

Spaulding, T. M. "Propaganda or Legend," *American Historical Review*, XXXIX, April, 1934.

"The Origin and Purpose of the Platt Amendment," *American Journal of International Law*, VIII, July, 1914.

Torriente y Peraza, Cosme de la. "The Platt Amendment," *Foreign Affairs*, VIII, April, 1930.

Vagts, Alfred. "Hopes and Fears of an American-German War, 1870–1915," *Political Science Quarterly*, LIV, December, 1939, and LV, March, 1940.

Wellman, Walter. "The Cuban Republic-Limited," *Review of Reviews*, XXII, December, 1900.

Whelpley, J. D. "Legal Reform in Cuba," *Independent*, LII, March 29, 1900.

—. "The Trade of Cuba," *Harper's Weekly*, XLV, May 25, 1901.

Willett and Gray. *Weekly Statistical Trade Journal*, XXX, March 8, 1906.

Willis, Henry Parker. "Reciprocity with Cuba," *Annals of the American Academy of Political and Social Science*, XXII, July, 1903.

Wood, Leonard. "The Existing Conditions and Needs in Cuba," *North American Review*, CLXVIII, May, 1899.

—. "The Military Government of Cuba," *Annals of the American Academy of Political and Social Science*, XXI, March, 1903.

—. "The Need for Reciprocity with Cuba," *Independent*, LIII, December 12, 1901.

INDEX

Abad, Luis de, 205
Abbott, Lawrence F., 23n, 87
Agramonte, Aristidos, 93
Agriculture, 21, 36, 60-61
Agriculture, Industry and Commerce (Dept.), 29, 35, 36
Aguinaldo, Emilio, 17
Alcaldes, 18, 32, 37-38, 57, 82-83
Aldrich, Nelson W., 72, 85, 116
Alemán, José B., 141, 163, 171, 181, 218
Alger, R. A., 11
Annexation, 1, 11, 107-108; Root's opposition to, 112; Platt on, 158, 160; Wood on, 190
Antilles, 19
Atkins, Edwin F., 157-158, 206
Audiencias, 46, 47, 49
Auditor of Military Government, 35
Autonomists, 3, 9, 29, 80-81, 98
Ayuntamiento, 18, 32, 37-38, 73

Bacardí, Emilio, 186, 200
Baker, Ray Stannard, 39
Banco Español, 33
Banco Nacional, 33
Banderas, Quintín, 8, 186
Batabanó, 120
Beneficencia, 31n
Berriel, Leopoldo, 102; commission proposal, 144-147; 163, 167, 169, 171-172, 180, 218
Betancourt, Pedro, 136, 146-147; in Washington, D.C., 149ff; 162, 181, 218
Bishop of Havana, 40
Bliss, Tasker, 45, 64-65, 206
Boxer Rebellion, 84, 88, 131
Bravo Correoso, Antonio, 102, 168, 172, 180n, 181, 186, 219
Bristow, J. L., 39

Brooke, John R., 7, 11-12, 17-18, 22-23, 39, 46, 51
Bülow, Bernhard von, 89
Burton, George H., 27, 38

Cambon, Paul, 122
Canada, 19
Canal, Isthmian, 11, 75, 88
Cancio, Leopoldo, 32-33, 73, 82, 195, 200
Carroll, James, 93
Casuso, Enrique, 97-98
Catholic Church, Church property agreement, 40-41; marriage law, 46
Census, population, post-revolution, 3; ordered by Root, 14; statistics on agriculture (1899), 61; pre-election, 79
Central America, 19
Cerro, 8, 9
Chandler, William E., 116-117
Cienfuegos, 81, 139, 157, 189n
Cisneros Betancourt, Salvador, 4-5; urges pre-convention troop removal, 95; 97, 103, 106, 108, 141-142, 145-146, 171, 178, 191, 193, 219
Civil Order 301, 92
Civil Order 455, 100
Cockrell, F. M., 139
Commission on Relations (Cuban Convention), Wood transmits McKinley's views, 115; Wood reveals Root's suggestions, 120; Tamayo presents executive terms, 121; selection of members, 137; 164, 169, 177
Communication system, severed, 3; cable and telephone, 26
Conant, E. L., 56
Congress, Cuba, structure of Senate and House; powers, proposed by Constitu-

Eliot, Charles W., 51, 52, 58
Elkins Act, 74
Employment, 60-61, 70, 189-190
England (see Great Britain)
Estévez y Romero, Luis, 29, 44, 191, 194
Estrada Palma, Tomás; 4, 7; responsive to U.S. proposal, 8; Guantánamo proposal, 91; supports executive clauses, 127-128; approves Constitution, 138; candidate for President, 185-187; 191, 193; elected, 194; inauguration, 195-198; 200
Evening Star (Washington, D.C.), 16

Factionalism, 3-9
Famine, 3
Farquhar, Percival, 69, 70
Fernández de Castro, José, 141, 219
Ferrer, José N., 141, 145, 180, 219
Finance Dept. (*Hacienda*), 29, 32, 33
Finlay, Carlos, 93
Fiscal (prosecutor), 43, 46
Foltz, F. S., 47
Fonts y Sterling, Ernesto, 200
Foraker Amendment (Act), 16, railroad construction, 69-70; Wood's opposition to, 73; relative to sanitation, 121
Foraker, Joseph Benson, 16, 72, 129
Forbes, Cameron, 56
Fortún, Luis, 218
Forum, proposals, annexation of Cuba by U.S., 107-108
Frye, Alexis E., role in education, 51, 52, 56, 58

García Montes, José, 194
García Vélez, Carlos, 45
Gener y Rincón, Miguel, 44, 46, 168, 180, 193, 218
Germany, trade with Cuba, 65-67, 90; as a threat in Caribbean, 88-90; 208
Geronimo, 21
Giberga, Eliseo, 97, 99, 102, 103, 124-126, 137, 140-143, 169, 176, 180, 218
Godkin, E. L., 87, 149n
Gómez, José Miguel, 145-146, 171-172, 180, 182, 218
Gómez, Juan Gualberto, 8, 93, 97, 102, 108-109, 136; Commission on Relations, 137; 138, 140; plan in response to Platt Amendment, 141; 144, 146, 162, 164-168; opposes Platt law, 171; Masó coalition, 185-186, 188, 190, 219
Gómez, Máximo, 4, 5, 7-9; organizer of

Nationalist party, 80; proposes delegate qualifications, 96; expresses confidence in American plan, 98; 105; fears concerning American withdrawal, 117; to Wood on continued need for occupation, 127; 128; supports Estrada Palma, 185, 187; 193, 198
González, Alejandro, 150, 200
Gorgas, William C., 93
Government, civil, Wood's view, 21; appointment of officials, 29; support of military, 31; provincial-municipal, 36; provision by Constitutional Convention, 104, 106
Great Britain, 65-67, 69-73, 74, 88, 90, 208
Griggs, John W., 6
Grosvenor, Charles H., 174
Guantánamo Bay, 90-91

Hacienda (Dept. of Finance), 29, 32, 35, 195
Hagedorn, Hermann, 22
Halle, Ernest von, 89
Hamburg, 206
Hanna, Mark, 16, 38; charges Wood with court interference, 40; on McKinley leadership, 122
Hanna, Matthew E., appointed Commissioner of Public Schools, 51; 52-53, 56-58, 197n
Harvey, George, 39
Havana City, 17, 26; sewage system controversy, 40; teachers' salaries, 52n; quality of government, 83; election of 1901, 193; natal day, 197; 220
Havana Jai-Alai Company, 40
Havana Province, 17, 36, 185-186, 194, 218, 220
Havana, University of, 50, 54-55
Havemeyer, H. O., 205, 209
Hay, John, 20, 88; origins of Platt Amendment, 113
Hay-Pauncefote Treaties, 11
Health, 26; yellow fever eradication, 93
Hepburn Act, 74
Hernández, Eusebio, 7, 97, 192
Hernández y Barreiro, Juan Batista, 29, 44
Higginson, H. L., 56-57
Hill, David, J. 149-150
Hoar, G. F., on Cuban education, 58; approves Platt Amendment, 128